echt 2

Teacher Handbook

Amy Bates

Anneli McLachlan
Mariela Affum
Marcus Waltl

OXFORD

OXFORD
UNIVERSITY PRESS

Great Clarendon Street, Oxford, OX2 6DP, United Kingdom

Oxford University Press is a department of the University of Oxford.
It furthers the University's objective of excellence in research,
scholarship, and education by publishing worldwide. Oxford is a
registered trade mark of Oxford University Press in the UK and in
certain other countries

© Oxford University Press 2021

The moral rights of the authors have been asserted

First published in 2021

All rights reserved. No part of this publication may be reproduced,
stored in a retrieval system, or transmitted, in any form or by any
means, without the prior permission in writing of Oxford University
Press, or as expressly permitted by law, by licence or under terms
agreed with the appropriate reprographics rights organization.
Enquiries concerning reproduction outside the scope of the above
should be sent to the Rights Department, Oxford University Press,
at the address above.

You must not circulate this work in any other form and you must
impose this same condition on any acquirer

British Library Cataloguing in Publication Data
Data available

978-0-19-849512-3

1 3 5 7 9 10 8 6 4 2

Paper used in the production of this book is a natural, recyclable
product made from wood grown in sustainable forests.
The manufacturing process conforms to the environmental
regulations of the country of origin.

Printed in Great Britain by CPI Group (UK) Ltd., Croydon CR0 4YY

Acknowledgements
Cover illustrations (top to bottom):
manfredxy/Shutterstock; Kiev.Victor/Shutterstock; Nikolai Tsvetkov/
Shutterstock; whitelook/Shutterstock.

Although we have made every effort to trace and contact all
copyright holders before publication this has not been possible in all
cases. If notified, the publisher will rectify any errors or omissions at
the earliest opportunity.

Links to third party websites are provided by Oxford in good faith
and for information only. Oxford disclaims any responsibility for
the materials contained in any third party website referenced in
this work.

Contents

Summary of units 4
Introduction 6
   Welcome to *Echt 2* 6
   Echt 2 components 6
      Student Book 6
      Teacher Handbook 7
      Audio CDs and audio files 7
      Grammar, Vocabulary and Translation Workbook. 7
      Kerboodle 8
      Video 8
   Teaching with *Echt* 8
      The National Curriculum from 2014 8
      Curriculum planning: Ofsted inspection framework 8
      Course progression 11
      Differentiation 12
      Strategy instruction 12
      Spontaneous speech 12
      Assessment 12
      GCSE-style activities 13

Teaching notes for *Echt 2*
Unit 1 In Urlaub 17
Unit 2 Mein Zuhause 41
Unit 3 Das Alltagsleben 63
Unit 4 Meine Klamotten 87
Unit 5 Virtuelle und reelle Welt 109
Unit 6 Willkommen in Berlin! 133
Sprungbrett 145
Workbook answers 153

Symbols used in this Teacher Handbook

📖 reading activity   〰 audio track

🎧 listening activity   GCSE GCSE-style activity

✏ writing activity   Differentiated activities at two levels:

💬 speaking activity   ⭐ reinforcement activity

🔄 translation activity   ➕ extension activity

Summary of units

	Vocabulary	Grammar and pronunciation	Strategies	Culture
Unit 1 **In Urlaub**	• Talking about holiday activities • Talking about a past holiday • Talking about how you travelled on holiday • Talking about the weather • Describing a past holiday and giving your opinion	• Using the infinitive • Using the perfect tense with *haben* • Using the perfect tense with *sein* • Using the imperfect tense • Using different personal pronouns and verb forms • Pronunciation: *u* and *ü*; *z*, *ei* and *ie*; long and short vowels	• Using conjunctions • Answering questions in German • Using sequencers • Listening for detail • Using intensifiers	• *Weihnachtsmärkte*
Unit 2 **Mein Zuhause**	• Talking about daily routines and household chores • Saying what there is in town and giving directions • Talking about where you live and where you lived before • Talking about your bedroom • Talking about your future home	• Using separable verbs in the present tense • Using *es gibt* with the accusative case • Using the present, perfect and imperfect tenses together • Using prepositions with the dative case • Using the future tense with *werden* • Pronunciation: *o* and *ö*	• Answering comprehension questions in English • Taking part in a role play • Varying your language • Using grammar you already know • Using three time frames	• *Moderne Möbel und das Bauhaus*
Unit 3 **Das Alltagsleben**	• Talking about daily routines • Talking about daily life in the German-speaking world • Making plans and excuses • Talking about healthy living • Comparing chores in different families	• Using reflexive verbs in the present tense • Using sequencers with reflexive and separable verbs • Using *wollen* + the infinitive • Revising *man soll* and *man muss* • Revising subordinate clauses with *weil* and *wenn* • Pronunciation: *ie*, *ei* and *au*; *sch*, *sp* and *st*	• Checking your written work for errors • Including cultural knowledge in your work • Reacting to the unpredictable • Writing without support • Recycling language	• *Deutscher Exportartikel: Fußballtrainer*

Summary of units

	Vocabulary	Grammar and pronunciation	Strategies	Culture
Unit 4 **Meine Klamotten**	• Saying what you are wearing and like to wear • Talking about your style • Talking about your shopping habits • Talking about shopping for clothes • Talking about special occasions	• Using verbs with the vowel change 'a' to 'ä' in the present tense • Using accusative adjective endings • Using possessive adjectives in the accusative case • Revising the future tense with *werden* • Revising the perfect tense with *haben* and *sein* • Pronunciation: *a* and *ä*; vowel changes in irregular verbs	• Translating into German • Revising *gern*, *lieber* and *am liebsten* • Improving your reading skills • Using *ich möchte* + the infinitive • Using three tenses together	• *Die Macht der Tracht*
Unit 5 **Virtuelle und reelle Welt**	• Talking about TV and film • Talking about different types of music • Talking about the internet and social media • Talking about technology today and in the past • Talking about volunteering projects	• Using subordinate clauses with *weil* and *da* • Using time–manner–place word order • Expressing opinions using *dass* • Recognising and using the imperfect tense • Revising the use of different tenses • Pronunciation: *r*; *z*, *ts* and *t*	• Inferring meaning • Learning the question words • Building more complex sentences • Narrating events in the past • Recognising and using compound nouns	• *Vom Jugendparlament zur Lindenstraße*
Unit 6 **Willkommen in Berlin!**	• Planning a trip to Berlin • Learning about life in Berlin	• Revising the future tense with *werden* • Using a range of tenses • Pronunciation: *z*, *w* and *zw*	• Carrying out online research • Dealing with unfamiliar vocabulary	• *Ost- und Westberlin*

5

Introduction

Welcome to *Echt 2*

Echt is a brand-new course for students aged 11–14, written to build the skills and knowledge they need to step up to the next level of study, while immersing them in German-speaking culture.

Echt inspires and prepares your students because:

- it immerses students in the German-speaking world with insights into culture and traditions
- it offers a flexible, two-level structure that can be taught over two or three years
- it provides logical grammar progression, vocabulary acquisition and language-learning strategies
- it includes reinforcement and extension pages in every unit of the Student Book, and individual activities in the Teacher Handbook
- it presents regular opportunities for assessment in the Student Book, Grammar, Vocabulary and Translation Workbook, and online via Kerboodle
- it has a full suite of accompanying resources, including a Grammar, Vocabulary and Translation Workbook, interactive grammar and vocabulary tests delivered via Kerboodle, editable schemes of work, and more.

Echt 2 components

Student Book

The content of the *Echt 1* and *Echt 2* Student Books can be taught over a two- or three-year Key Stage 3. Two- and three-year schemes of work can be found on Kerboodle.

The Student Book contains the following sections:

Units 1–5

Each unit consists of:

- *Los geht's!* – an introduction to the unit
- core lessons – the core content of the book; Units 1–5 have five core lessons
- *Kultur* – an aspect of culture from the German-speaking world
- *Sprachlabor* – grammar and pronunciation practice
- *Was kann ich schon?* – students test their reading, listening and writing, and use their marks to determine which activities they can move on to in the next section
- *Vorankommen!* – students are invited to reinforce or extend what they have learnt by working on bronze, silver or gold activities, depending on their score in the previous section
- *Vokabeln* – key vocabulary from the unit.

A summary of the content of each unit is given on pages 4–5 of this Handbook.

Unit 6

Unit 6 is designed to consolidate learning and explores the history and culture of Berlin.

It consists of:

- *Los geht's!* – an introduction to the unit
- core lessons – the core content of the book; Unit 6 has two core lessons
- *Kultur* – an aspect of culture from the German-speaking world
- *Sprachlabor* – grammar and pronunciation practice
- *Was kann ich schon?* – students test their reading, listening and writing.

Introduction

Sprungbrett

These pages at the end of the Student Book provide more targeted practice of skills required at GCSE-level study. The activity types alternate as follows:

- Units 1, 3 and 5: reading and writing activities
- Units 2 and 4: listening and speaking activities.

Grammatik

The key grammar points taught in all units are consolidated in a grammar reference section at the back of the Student Book.

Glossar

An alphabetised German–English glossary contains the key vocabulary in the Student Book for students' reference.

Teacher Handbook

Each unit contains:

- a unit overview table providing a summary of what is covered in the core lessons, including vocabulary, grammar, strategies and key language
- Planner boxes at the start of each lesson, including cross-references to other **Echt** components and suggestions for starters, plenaries and homework tasks
- teacher notes for all Student Book activities, including:
  ○ suggestions for reinforcement (look out for the ★ symbol) and extension (look out for the ➕ symbol), with ideas for how to adapt the Student Book activities to suit lower- and higher-attaining students
  ○ GCSE to signpost activities that are similar in style to those found in the GCSE exams
- answers for all Student Book activities
- transcripts for listening activities.

Answers for the Grammar, Vocabulary and Translation Workbook can also be found at the end of this Handbook.

Audio CDs and audio files

All audio content was recorded by native German speakers.

What's included in the audio CDs?

- Audio files for all Student Book activities.

What's included on Kerboodle?

- Audio files for all Student Book activities and *Vokabeln* pages. Audio files can be launched straight from 'hotspots' in the Kerboodle Book.
- Audio files for Kerboodle worksheets and assessments.

Grammar, Vocabulary and Translation Workbook

The Workbook follows the structure of the Student Book, so that students can further practise the grammar and vocabulary taught in each unit of the Student Book. The Workbook also provides regular translation practice. Cross-references to the relevant Workbook pages are included in the Student Book and vice versa.

Each unit contains:

- one vocabulary practice page for every core lesson of the Student Book
- one grammar practice page for each grammar point covered in the Student Book.

Every two units there are revision (*Wiederholung*) pages. These pages offer mixed practice of vocabulary and grammar from the previous two units, as well as translation activities. They also allow students to check their progress and provide opportunities for extension. The final page of the Workbook includes verb tables for reference.

The Workbook is designed for students to write in, so is ideal for homework and self-study. Rubrics are in English throughout so that students can work independently. Answers to all Workbook activities are provided at the back of this Handbook and on a separate answer card in the Workbook pack.

Introduction

Kerboodle

Echt Kerboodle consists of:

- *Echt* Kerboodle Books: a digital version of the Student Book, with digital tools and hotspots to launch audio tracks and video clips straight from the page, and a digital version of this Teacher Handbook
- *Echt* Resources and Assessment: a suite of additional teaching and learning materials including: self-marking grammar and vocabulary activities; extra reading, listening, writing, speaking and translation practice; videos exploring German culture with accompanying activities; and a range of paper-based and online assessments.

Video

Video series

The *Echt* video series is available on Kerboodle and provides:

- examples of key language in use, making the language relevant to students and translating language learning from theory into practice.
- an authentic view of life in a German-speaking country and an insight into German-speaking culture

Each video is set within the contexts of the corresponding unit. Activities focusing on each video episode are provided on Kerboodle.

A full transcript of each episode is provided on Kerboodle. A transcript is also available on screen when the video is played.

Phonics videos

Also provided on Kerboodle are phonics videos for further pronunciation support, which can be launched directly from the Kerboodle version of the Student Book.

Teaching with *Echt*

The National Curriculum from 2014

Echt has been carefully planned to ensure full coverage of the 2014 National Curriculum and Key Stage 3 Programme of Study for Modern Foreign Languages. In line with the higher profile given to the following key areas in the 2014 Curriculum, *Echt* offers:

- **grammar:** a wealth of features and resources to support students' needs, including: *Grammatik* boxes in the core lessons of the Student Book; further coverage of key grammar points in the *Sprachlabor* lessons; a *Grammatik* grammar-reference section at the back of the Student Book; a Grammar, Vocabulary and Translation Workbook covering all of the Student Book grammar points; grammar presentations and self-marking grammar activities on Kerboodle; and grammar quizzes that can be tracked in the Kerboodle Markbook

- **translation:** translation activities in the Student Book, Workbook and via suggestions in the Teacher Handbook (look for the ⟲ symbol), as well as on the reading and writing worksheets on Kerboodle and included as part of the Kerboodle assessment materials

- **authentic source materials and literary texts:** a range of inspiring authentic material of different types throughout the resources and particularly via the video series on Kerboodle.

Curriculum planning: Ofsted inspection framework

A new Ofsted inspection framework was introduced to schools in England and Wales in September 2019. The most notable change to the previous framework is that schools will be judged on the 'quality of education' – a judgement that is based around Ofsted's working definition of the 'curriculum'. Ofsted is clear that the new framework will credit schools that promote a rich and broad curriculum, with the main points of focus being the 'intent, implementation and impact' of the curriculum.

The table on the pages that follow highlights key questions relating to the new framework and how *Echt* addresses them.

Introduction

How *Echt* works with the new Ofsted inspection framework	
What is the curriculum offered by this course (including the knowledge, cultural capital and skills that will be gained)?	***Echt*** delivers a curriculum that supports students' acquisition of the grammar and vocabulary required for them to express themselves orally and in writing and in their understanding of aural and written texts. Throughout the course, insights into the culture and traditions of the Germanic world are shared. This curriculum aims to build students' confidence in German and interest in Germanic culture to encourage them to continue learning German post-KS3 and to prepare them for KS4-/GCSE-level study.
Why were these curriculum choices made?	Coverage choices regarding grammar, vocabulary and cultural knowledge were made in close consultation with active MFL teachers, and with reference to the 2014 National Curriculum, KS3 Programme of Study for MFL, MFL Pedagogy Review and 2016 GCSE specifications. The aim of the curriculum is that all students should reach the end of KS3 with a grammar and vocabulary toolkit at their disposal, enabling them to understand and express ideas that are meaningful to them.
How is the course sequenced (and why is it sequenced this way)?	***Echt*** has two stages: *Echt 1* and *Echt 2*. Each stage is arranged into six units – five main units and a shorter consolidation unit – to give students a specific context in which to develop their vocabulary, grammar and phonics knowledge. Language and strategies from previous units are built on and recycled, so that knowledge is deeply embedded. When planning the sequencing of topics, careful choices were made based on the following: • interests of students as they progress through KS3 • early introduction of ambitious phrases • early introduction and recycling of high-frequency vocabulary • logical ordering and recycling of grammar • time of year when a topic is most likely to be studied. Teacher reviewers and teacher focus groups advised on the ordering of this content.
How is progression built into the course?	The grammar, vocabulary and language strategy sequencing throughout the two stages of ***Echt*** allows students to: • build and develop their grammar and vocabulary toolkit as they go along, making particular use of: Student Book reference materials (*Vokabeln* pages and the *Grammatik* section); additional practice lessons (*Sprachlabor*); online material for grammar practice (worksheets and self-marking interactive activities); online material for vocabulary practice (vocabulary builders); grammar and vocabulary formative assessment quizzes for each unit, giving targeted feedback to identify any gaps • work at their own pace, extending knowledge and applying it in new contexts, using: *Vorankommen!* differentiation lessons; *Kultur* lessons; differentiated worksheets in speaking and writing and language-learning strategies • make steady progress with speaking, pronunciation and knowledge of sound-spelling links, with the help of: pronunciation boxes in the *Sprachlabor* lessons; phonics videos on Kerboodle; regular speaking activities in the Student Books and on Kerboodle, plus record-and-playback speaking activities • understand and use increasingly complex structures through: regular revisiting of phrase groupings and word families (see, for instance, the *Sprachmuster* feature boxes); stimulus texts and listening materials which increase in length and degree of complexity.

Introduction

How *Echt* works with the new Ofsted inspection framework	
How does the course help ensure students make progress?	There are diagnostic test pages (*Was kann ich schon?*) at the end of each main unit, leading on to differentiation and extension pages (*Vorankommen!*). They allow students to look back on the topics and language covered in the unit as a progress check, at a level that is right for them. Self-marking grammar and vocabulary quizzes on Kerboodle also provide a way for students to review the content of a unit. These offer targeted feedback, directing students back to problem areas for further study. Throughout the course, the authors have included regular repetition and recycling of vocabulary and structures to ensure that students embed this knowledge over time.
What assessments does the course offer and how do they help form part of the process of evaluating progress and identifying next steps?	Assessment is provided on Kerboodle. For each unit of the course, there are: • self-marking quizzes, testing vocabulary and grammar. Targeted feedback for each answer helps teachers and students to identify areas needing more work • 'Star' and 'Plus' end-of-unit assessments in reading, listening, speaking and writing on Kerboodle, making it possible to assign tests to your students based on their level of progress • a mark scheme that incorporates an assessment framework (see Assessment on page 12 of this Handbook for further information), so teachers can track where students are and what skills are needed to progress to the next level. Every two units there are: • GCSE-style assessment at two levels in speaking, reading, writing and listening. It covers a mix of topics and grammar points from the previous two units, ensuring students have embedded knowledge as they go along • a mark scheme that incorporates an assessment framework (see Assessment on page 12 of this Handbook for further information) and question styles are matched to those that students will encounter at GCSE. Teachers are supported in tracking progress at all stages of the course, with content on the Resources tab on Kerboodle – interactive activities, worksheets and presentations – available for revising and reinforcing problem areas in grammar knowledge, speaking, listening, reading and writing.
How does this course ensure students will know more?	As well as rigorous, logical grammar progression and regular recycling of grammar and vocabulary, **Echt** helps you embed language-learning strategies from the start that allow students to absorb, and engage with, a new language. There is an emphasis on Germanic culture throughout: the *Kultur* pages at the end of each unit help you develop students' cultural capital. There is also a video series set in Germany on Kerboodle.
How can/will this course be developed over time (includes adaptability)?	The Kerboodle package is regularly reviewed and updated based on ongoing research and feedback.

Introduction

How *Echt* works with the new Ofsted inspection framework	
How can resources in this course help teachers present subject matter clearly?	The Kerboodle digital book enables the teacher to present each Student Book lesson to the class, highlighting and enlarging images and texts where appropriate. Teachers can play audio directly to the class from the digital book page. Supplementary online resources (interactive activities, worksheets and presentations) can also be easily accessed from the book. Editable Microsoft PowerPoint presentations are provided for introducing and reinforcing key grammar points. The careful authoring and curation of listening and reading texts, plus the accompanying video series, allows students to engage with lively, natural communicative contexts which are pitched at their age level. Language is simplified and clarified to support learning while maintaining the ambitious aims of the course. The Teacher Handbook provides suggestions on how to get the most out of the Student Book activities, with tips for adapting activities for lower-/higher-attaining learners.
How can this course help reduce teacher workload (including how does it help teachers with their subject knowledge and knowledge of the course)?	*Echt* provides you with a toolkit of resources to help save time when planning, delivering lessons and assessing pupils' progress. The digital resources delivered via Kerboodle include a digital version of the Teacher Handbook, two- and three-year editable schemes of work, grammar presentations, GCSE-style assessments and a bank of worksheets and interactive activities linked to topics covered in the Student Books. There are also digital Student Books that can be used front-of-class with all of the audio for activities available at the click of a button.

Course progression

Echt is a two-part course, consisting of two Student Books of six units each. By offering two separate routes through the course, *Echt* caters for schools following a two-year or three-year Key Stage 3 approach:

Year	Term	Suggested two-year route	Suggested three-year route
1	Autumn	*Echt* 1 Units 1–2	*Echt* 1 Unit 1–Lesson 2.2
	Spring	*Echt* 1 Units 3–4	*Echt* 1 Lesson 2.3–Unit 3
	Summer	*Echt* 1 Units 5–6; Revision and Assessment	*Echt* 1 Unit 4; Revision and Assessment
2	Autumn	*Echt* 2 Units 1–2	*Echt* 1 Units 5–6
	Spring	*Echt* 2 Units 3–4	*Echt* 2 Unit 1–Lesson 2.2
	Summer	*Echt* 2 Units 5–6; Revision and Assessment	*Echt* 2 Lessons 2.3–2.5 Revision and Assessment
3	Autumn		*Echt* 2 Unit 3–Lesson 4.2
	Spring		*Echt* 2 Lesson 4.3–Unit 5
	Summer		*Echt* 2 Unit 6; Revision and Assessment

Introduction

Differentiation

Echt is designed to provide for learners of all abilities.

Key features include:

- go-further boxes (*Extra*) are included to help stretch more-able students

- ideas for reinforcement and extension activities can be found in the Teacher Handbook (look out for the ⭐ and ➕ symbols)

- each double-page lesson in the Student Book is supported by worksheets on Kerboodle

- the *Vorankommen!* lesson at the end of Units 1–5 in the Student Book provides differentiated material for lower- and higher-ability students

- assessment delivered via Kerboodle at *Star* (reinforcement) and *Plus* (extension) levels

- differentiated progress checks in the Workbook.

Strategy instruction

The *Strategie* boxes in the Student Book are designed to foster independent learning by teaching students how to manage their learning. We know from research that one of the reasons some students find language learning difficult or boring is because they don't know how to tackle the tasks. For example, they might not realise that a text is much less daunting if you begin by looking out for cognates or familiar words and skip what you don't know.

Care is taken to provide practice in using the strategies, so that students experience for themselves how they can make learning German easier, more effective and more fun.

Spontaneous speech

There are many opportunities throughout the course to encourage the development of spontaneous speech, both in and out of the classroom.

From the outset, students carry out simple conversations spontaneously, which helps to develop a good level of confidence and fluency. *Echt* sets out to greatly increase the use of the target language in lessons and meet Ofsted criteria in this area. Students listen regularly to young native speakers and communicate frequently in the target language.

They are taught how to ask questions and to respond to everyday requests. The video materials and other visual resources also inspire spontaneous speech.

Planned use of the target language over time using the speaking activities ensures that all groups of learners become confident speakers, with good intonation and pronunciation. Teaching that encourages 'exploitation' of core structures in the wealth of listening and reading material provided by *Echt* leads to fluent speakers who are also culturally aware.

Assessment

Regular opportunities for assessment and progress checking are included throughout the course, including the following:

- *Was kann ich schon?* activities at the end of every unit, leading on to differentiated tasks in Units 1–5

- unitised paper-based assessments in listening, speaking, reading and writing (incorporating translation) at two levels included on Kerboodle

- GCSE-style paper-based assessments in listening, speaking, reading and writing (incorporating translation) at two levels included on Kerboodle

- self-marking vocabulary and grammar quizzes that can be tracked in the Kerboodle Markbook

- self-marking end-of-unit quizzes that can be tracked in the Kerboodle Markbook

- record-and-playback speaking assessment for every unit on Kerboodle

- regular differentiated progress checks in the Workbook.

Assessment framework

The assessment framework provides a simple and common reporting language for all significant assessments to help schools improve students' progress and attainment.

The framework has been applied in *Echt* to the end-of-unit assessments and the GCSE-style assessments. At the end of each assessment, an overall mark is given, along with an assessment band and a GCSE grade band indicator.

The grade band indicators are approximate indicators and are designed to assist in the process of tracking and monitoring. They cannot and should not be used to replace teachers' professional judgment. Teachers should use their own discretion in applying them and should refer to their institution's assessment policy.

Here is how the framework has been applied to *Echt*:

'Star' assessment:

Overall assessment level (foundation)			
Marks out of 60	Marks out of 100	Assessment band	GCSE grade band indicator
1–29	1–45	Developing	1–2
30–48	46–74	Securing	3–4
49–60	75–100	Extending	5

'Plus' assessment:

Overall assessment level (higher)			
Marks out of 60	Marks out of 100	Assessment band	GCSE grade band indicator
1–29	1–45	Developing	1–3
30–48	46–74	Securing	4–6
49–60	75–100	Extending	7–9

GCSE-style activities

Student Book activities similar in style to those found in the 2016 GCSE specifications are marked in this Teacher Handbook with a GCSE symbol. The activities on the *Sprungbrett* pages are also designed to provide a bridge to GCSE. The GCSE-style speaking and writing activities can be marked using the suggested criteria below.

Marking speaking activities

For speaking activities that mirror GCSE-style activities, such as the photo card, general conversation or role play activities, the marking guidance below can be applied.

Photo card

The following applies to photo card activities that include three prepared questions and one unprepared question, but can be adapted for fewer questions:

Prepared questions	Award 1 point for each appropriate and unambiguous answer to the given three questions. Award ½ point if appropriate but ambiguous.
Unprepared question	Award 2 points for the unprepared question if they have understood and answered appropriately. Award 1 point if they gave an answer partially related (e.g. answered in wrong tense).
	0 for no rewardable material.

Total marks out of five.

Introduction

General conversation

General conversation activities can be marked out of 15, using the mark table below.
The marking criteria have been arranged in three broad themes, as follows:

- Communication (including content, pronunciation and intonation)
- Range and accuracy of language
- Interaction and fluency.

Within each mark band, there are three clear sub-themes; for example, 'Range and accuracy of language' references vocabulary, grammar and accuracy.

Points	Communication	Range and accuracy of language	Interaction and fluency
5	• Entirely relevant information, rich in detail, majority of answers extended. • Regular opinion and justification. • No loss of message through inaccuracy of pronunciation and intonation.	• Very wide range of familiar and unfamiliar vocabulary and expression with little repetition. • Very wide range of grammatical structures, including different time frames. • High level of accuracy in language used.	• Answers all questions, seeking clarification when necessary. • Examples of natural/ spontaneous interaction. • Confident delivery sustains good conversational flow.
4	• Entirely relevant information, good amount of detail, many answers extended. • Regular opinion, occasional justification. • Occasional loss of message through inaccuracy of pronunciation and intonation.	• Wide range of familiar (and occasionally unfamiliar) vocabulary and expression with little repetition. • Wide range of grammatical structures, including different time frames. • Language used generally accurate.	• Answers most questions, seeking clarification when necessary. • Some examples of natural/ spontaneous interaction. • Mostly confident delivery maintains good conversational flow overall.
3	• Mostly relevant information, some detail, some extended answers. • Regular simple opinion. • Some loss of message through inaccuracy of pronunciation and intonation.	• Range of familiar vocabulary and expression with limited repetition. • Range of grammatical structures, including different time frames. • Language used more accurate than inaccurate.	• Answers many questions, seeking clarification when necessary. • Limited spontaneity, reliant on pre-learnt structures. • Variable pace, sometimes confident, sometimes hesitant.
2	• Often irrelevant information, limited detail, short and simple answers. • Occasional simple opinion. • Regular loss of message through inaccuracy of pronunciation and intonation.	• Limited, familiar vocabulary with a high level of repetition. • Limited range of grammatical structures. • Limited level of accuracy in language used.	• Answers some questions, seeking clarification when necessary. • Very limited spontaneity, reliant on pre-learnt structures. • Slow and hesitant throughout.
1	• Mostly irrelevant information, very limited detail, short answers. • No opinion. • Frequent loss of message through inaccuracy of pronunciation and intonation.	• Very limited, familiar vocabulary with a high level of repetition. • Very limited range of grammatical structures. • Very limited level of accuracy in language used.	• Answers few questions, seeking clarification when necessary. • No spontaneity, reliant entirely on pre-learnt structures. • No natural flow of conversation.
0	No rewardable material.	No rewardable material.	No rewardable material.

Role play

The following applies to role play activities with five bullet points, but can be adapted for those with fewer:

Award 2 points for each clear and unambiguous response to a bullet point.
Award 1 point for each response in which meaning is partially communicated.

Divide the total by 2 to award a mark out of 5.

Marking writing activities

For writing activities that mirror GCSE-style activities, such as writing sentences describing a photo or longer writing tasks based on a bulleted list of prompts, the marking guidance below can be applied.

Photo description

The following applies to activities requiring four sentences, but can be adapted for fewer:

Award 1 point for each relevant and unambiguous answer to the given four questions.
Award ½ point for each relevant but ambiguous answer.
Add an extra point if there is at least one unambiguous example of opinion included.
0 for no rewardable material.

Total marks out of five.

Longer writing

Longer writing tasks can be marked out of 15, using the mark table below. The marking criteria have been arranged in three broad themes as follows:

- Content
- Range of language
- Accuracy.

Within each mark band, there are three clear sub-themes; for example, 'Range of language' references vocabulary and grammar.

Points	Content	Range of language	Accuracy
5	• Full coverage of bullet points. • Consistently goes beyond the minimum, introducing detail and interest. • Communication is clear and unambiguous.	• Very wide range of familiar and unfamiliar vocabulary and expression with little repetition. • Very wide range of grammatical structures, which add interest and variety. • Use of more than one time frame.	• High level of accuracy. • Some errors in more complex sentences. • Verbs, tense formations and time frames secure.
4	• Full coverage of bullet points. • Regularly goes beyond the minimum, introducing detail and interest. • Communication is mostly clear and unambiguous.	• Wide range of familiar (and occasionally unfamiliar) vocabulary and expression with little repetition. • Wide range of grammatical structures, which add interest and variety. • Use of more than one time frame.	• Mostly accurate. • Some errors in more complex sentences. • Verbs, tense formations and time frames mostly secure.

Introduction

Points	Content	Range of language	Accuracy
3	• Almost full coverage of bullet points. • Occasionally goes beyond the minimum, introducing detail and interest. • Communication is generally clear and unambiguous, with some lapses.	• Range of familiar vocabulary and expression with limited repetition. • Range of grammatical structures, which add interest and variety. • Use of one time frame.	• More accurate than inaccurate. • Some errors in more simple sentences. • Verbs, tense formations and time frames are sometimes unsuccessful.
2	• Partial coverage of bullet points. • Occasionally goes beyond the minimum, introducing detail and interest. • Communication is sometimes clear but often not.	• Limited, familiar vocabulary with a high level of repetition. • Limited range of grammatical structures. • Use of one time frame.	• Lower level of accuracy. • Higher incidence of error in simple structures. • Verbs, tense formations and time frames are often unsuccessful.
1	• Minimal coverage of bullet points. • Minimal response to bullets covered. • Communication is frequently unclear.	• Very limited, familiar vocabulary with a high level of repetition. • Very limited range of grammatical structures. • Use of one time frame.	• Low level of accuracy. • Frequency of error impeding communication. • Verbs, tense formations and time frames are mostly unsuccessful.
0	No rewardable material.	No rewardable material.	No rewardable material.

1 In Urlaub

Unit overview				
Page reference	**Vocabulary**	**Grammar**	**Strategy**	**Key language**
10–11 1.1 Ferienaktivitäten	Talking about holiday activities	Using the infinitive	Using conjunctions	Was kann man in den Bergen/am Meer/in der Stadt machen? Man kann…/(In den Bergen) kann man… schnorcheln, windsurfen, Kanu fahren, tauchen, zelten, klettern, eine Radtour machen, eine Bootsfahrt machen, Ausflüge machen, Sehenswürdigkeiten besichtigen, einen Stadtbummel machen, Wildwasser-Rafting machen Ich würde gern einmal nach … fahren.
12–13 1.2 Wo hast du deine Ferien verbracht?	Talking about a past holiday	Using the perfect tense with *haben*	Answering questions in German	Wo hast du deine Sommerferien verbracht? Ich habe meine Sommerferien in (Frankreich/Deutschland/Italien) verbracht. Was hast du dort gemacht? Ich habe eine Hop-On-Hop-Off Bustour gemacht/ eine Radtour gemacht/Tennis gespielt/ ein Konzert gesehen/ein Museum besucht/ Sehenswürdigkeiten besichtigt. Wie hat es dir gefallen? Wie war es? Es hat Spaß gemacht. Es war anstrengend/toll/cool/ prima/langweilig/entspannend.
14–15 1.3 #Wanderlust!	Talking about how you travelled on holiday	Using the perfect tense with *sein*	Using sequencers	Wie bist du gefahren? Ich bin mit dem Schiff/mit dem Auto/mit dem Fahrrad/mit dem Motorrad/mit dem Zug/mit dem Bus/mit dem Schneemobil gefahren. Ich bin mit dem Flugzeug geflogen. Ich bin quer durch (Frankreich/Italien/Spanien) gefahren. Ich bin von (Italien) nach (Frankreich) gefahren. zuerst, dann, danach
16–17 1.4 Wie war das Wetter?	Talking about the weather	Using the imperfect tense	Listening for detail	Wie war das Wetter gestern? Morgens/Mittags/Abends/Nachts war es wolkig/sonnig/stürmisch/neblig/windig/kalt/ heiß. Es gab Regen/Schnee. überall
18–19 1.5 Ich reise gern	Describing a past holiday and giving your opinion	Using different personal pronouns and verb forms	Using intensifiers	Wo hast du übernachtet? Ich habe in einem Tipi-Dorf/einer Jugendherberge/einer Ferienwohnung/einem Hotel übernachtet. echt/richtig/total bequem, ideal, wunderbar, wunderschön am ersten/folgenden/letzten Tag (Aktiv sein) ist für mir wichtig. (Österreich) hat mir (nicht) gut gefallen.

1 Los geht's!

Starter

- Students discuss and/or write down as many facts as they already know about festivals and celebrations in Germany or German-speaking countries. They will probably be most familiar with Christmas (for example, the Christmas markets and names of food such as *Lebkuchen*), but they may also have heard of *Oktoberfest* or *Karneval*. Depending on the ability of the class, you could invite students to share these facts with the group. To develop this task further, you could show some images of these festivals and celebrations.

Plenary

- Students test each other on key vocabulary from this lesson: holidays, countries and holiday elements. They could do this from German into English, or vice versa for a more challenging task.

1 Hier sind einige Feiertage (*holidays*) in Deutschland, in der Schweiz und in Österreich. Welche Feiertage sieht man auf den Fotos?

Students match the photos to the correct holiday, choosing from the list provided. Encourage them to look at the details in the photos and to read the list of holidays carefully. You may wish to remind students of the word *Tag* (this could be elicited through practice of days of the week).

Answers: **a** *Schweizer Nationalfeiertag;* **b** *Valentinstag;* **c** *Heilige Drei Könige*

2 Translate the holidays in activity 1 into English.

Students may not know the exact translation, but they can use the dates provided in activity 1 to help them. For example, *Silvester* takes place on 31st December, so it must be New Year's Eve.

Suggested translations:
Neujahrstag – New Year's Day; *Heilige Drei Könige* – Epiphany; *Valentinstag* – Valentine's Day; *Tag der Arbeit* – Labour Day; *Schweizer Nationalfeiertag* – Swiss National Day/Holiday; *Tag der Deutschen Einheit* – German Unity Day; *Weihnachten* – Christmas; *Silvester* – New Year's Eve

3 Was sind die Lieblingsreiseziele der Deutschen? Verbinde die Länder auf der Karte (1–7) mit den Ländernamen (a–g).

Students match the countries on the map to the correct German names.

Answers: **1** b; **2** a; **3** c; **4** d; **5** g; **6** f; **7** e

Sprachmuster

Students may remember the term 'compound nouns' from *Echt 1*. They may also be familiar with the idea of 'compounds' from science, recognising that it is something that has two or more different parts. These nouns also provide a good opportunity to practise 'ie'/'ei' sound combinations.

4 Look at the graphic about the elements of a perfect holiday for German people. Write the elements in their order of importance (1–9) in English.

The numbers represent the percentage of people surveyed who think the element is important. Explain to students that they need to start with the element which has the highest percentage and work down to the lowest percentage. You could recap the meaning of *Zeit* and *gut* here if additional support is needed.

Answers: **1** good weather 47%; **2** good food 32%; **3** time with loved ones 27%; **4** dream beach 23%; **5** lots of relaxation 19%; **6** a good hotel 17%; **7** immersion in local culture 16%; **8** sightseeing 15%; **9** time for myself 14%

Students can have some additional practice with numbers by writing out the percentages in full.

1 In Urlaub

Answers: **1** siebenundvierzig Prozent;
2 zweiunddreißig Prozent;
3 siebenundzwanzig Prozent;
4 dreiundzwanzig Prozent; **5** neunzehn Prozent; **6** siebzehn Prozent; **7** sechzehn Prozent; **8** fünfzehn Prozent; **9** vierzehn Prozent

5 **Look at the information about how German people like to travel to their holiday destinations. Complete the summary in English.**

Answers: **1** car; **2** train; **3** plane; **4** 7

➕ Students think about and note down vocabulary for methods of transport which could come under the *Sonstiges 3%* heading in the information; for example, *Schiff, Fahrrad*.

6 **Macht Dialoge.**

Using the model as support, students create a dialogue with their partner about what they find important on holiday. Encourage them to use the vocabulary from activity 4.

Sprachmuster

This is a useful opportunity to practise the pronunciation of this key vocabulary. Ask pupils if they can remember a national holiday with *Feiertag* in the title from activity 1 (*Schweizer Nationalfeiertag*).

19

1.1 Ferienaktivitäten

Objectives

- Vocabulary: Talking about holiday activities
- Grammar: Using the infinitive
- Strategy: Using conjunctions

Resources

- Student Book, pages 10–11
- CD 1, tracks 2–3
- Grammar, Vocabulary and Translation Workbook, pages 4–5
- Kerboodle, Unit 1

Key language

- *Was kann man in den Bergen/am Meer/in der Stadt machen? Man kann.../(In den Bergen) kann man...*
- *schnorcheln, windsurfen, Kanu fahren, tauchen, zelten, klettern, eine Radtour machen, eine Bootsfahrt machen, Ausflüge machen, Sehenswürdigkeiten besichtigen, einen Stadtbummel machen, Wildwasser-Rafting machen*
- *Ich würde gern einmal nach ... fahren.*

Homework and self-study

- Student Book, page 11, activity 7. Remind students not to use translation websites; all of the vocabulary and structures they need are in the Student Book.
- Grammar, Vocabulary and Translation Workbook, pages 4–5

Starter

- Students make a list or mind map of as many adjectives to describe activities as they can think of in German. This could be simple near-cognates such as *gut* or *interessant*, or more difficult words such as *langweilig*. They could just do this verbally rather than writing. You could return to this task as preparation for activity 4.

Plenary

- Students work in small groups. One student says a location (for example, *in der Stadt*) and the other students compete to see who can most quickly name a suitable activity (for example, *einen Stadtbummel machen*). For more of a challenge, they could include *man kann* in their answer. This could also be done as a written task using mini-whiteboards.

1 🎧 **Hör zu. Welche Ferienaktivitäten kann man am Meer (1), in der Stadt (2) und in den Bergen (3) machen? Schreib die richtigen Buchstaben (a–i) für die Reiseziele (1–3) auf.**

Students listen and write down the letters of the activities that people can do in each location.

Answers (letters in any order):
1 am Meer: a, b, g; **2 in der Stadt:** e, f, h, i
3 in den Bergen: d, c

〰️ **CD 1, track 2   Seite 10, Aktivität 1**

1 – Nun, was kann man am Meer machen? Mal sehen. Man kann schnorcheln.
   – Man kann auch tauchen.
   – Oder eine Bootsfahrt machen. Man kann eine Bootsfahrt machen.

2 – Und in der Stadt? Was kann man in der Stadt machen?
   – Man kann eine Radtour machen.
   – Oder Sehenswürdigkeiten besichtigen. Man kann auch einen Stadtbummel machen. Das macht Spaß.
   – Oder man kann Ausflüge machen.

3 – Und dann, in den Bergen, was kann man in den Bergen machen?
   – Man kann klettern.
   – Und man kann zelten. Das gefällt mir!

💡 **Tipp**

Practise the pronunciation of these key words before students use them in activity 2; pay particular attention to the pronunciation of the letter 'w'.

1 In Urlaub

2 💬 **Macht Dialoge mit den Reisezielen.**

Using the model as support, students create a dialogue with their partner about what people can do in different locations. Encourage them to use the additional vocabulary from the *Tipp* box. They could also write down their dialogue once they're finished, if you think this additional support will be needed for the upcoming writing task.

➕ Write the question *Was ist deine Meinung dazu?* on the board. Students should ask and answer it in their dialogue. You could also provide a sentence starter for the answer: *Ich finde das…*

⚙ Strategie

Before reading the information, ask students to recall what a conjunction is, and whether they can remember any conjunctions in German without looking at the box.

3 ✏ **Schreib einen Satz für jedes Reiseziel aus Aktivität 2.**

Using the example as support, students write sentences in German, detailing what people can do in each location. Remind them to use conjunctions and draw their attention to the 'verb-second' rule, which applies if they start their sentences with a location.

Example answer:
Am Meer kann man schnorcheln und auch tauchen oder eine Bootsfahrt machen.

4 🎧 [GCSE] **Listen to five young people talking about holiday activities (1–5). Copy and complete the table in English.**

Students note down for each speaker which activity they mention and their opinion of it. Before they start the task, brainstorm as a class some German adjectives which could appear; for example, *spannend, lustig, langweilig*. It would be useful to leave these on the board for reference during the task. (If this was done in the Starter activity, you could instead collate ideas at this point.)

Answers:

	Activity	Opinion
1	do a boat trip	(really) great
2	go on excursions	(really) boring
3	go sightseeing	cool
4	do white-water rafting	(really) exciting
5	camping	fun

🎵 **CD 1, track 3   Seite 11, Aktivität 4**

1 Was kann man am Meer machen? Ja, am Meer kann man eine Bootsfahrt machen. Das ist richtig toll.
2 Was kann man in der Stadt machen? Man kann Ausflüge machen. [yawns] Total langweilig.
3 Aber man kann auch Sehenswürdigkeiten besichtigen. Cool. Das gefällt mir.
4 Und was kann man in den Bergen machen? In den Bergen kann man Wildwasser-Rafting machen. Total spannend!
5 Man kann auch zelten. Das finde ich so lustig!

Aa Grammatik

Remind students of and/or elicit the meaning of *man kann*. Explain that it needs another verb ('I can swim', 'I can go', etc.) and that in German, there are two key rules to remember about this other verb: firstly, it must be an infinitive and, secondly, it must be positioned at the end of the sentence or clause.

5 💬 **Sagt eure Meinungen über Ferienaktivitäten.**

Using the example as support, students create dialogues asking for and giving opinions on holiday activities. You could model the task structure and pronunciation beforehand with a confident volunteer. Encourage students to use the vocabulary from activity 1 and the adjectives that were brainstormed in preparation for activity 4.

21

1 In Urlaub

6 📖 GCSE Read the posts about two holiday destinations. Complete the sentences in English.

> Answers: **a** white-water rafting; **b** snorkel; **c** dive with tropical fish; **d** go climbing, camping; **e** climbing paradise

7 🔄 GCSE Übersetz den Text ins Deutsche.

Students translate the text into German. Remind them that all of the vocabulary and phrases that they need are from this lesson.

> Suggested translation:
> Ich würde gern einmal nach Berlin fahren. Man kann eine Radtour machen und auch Sehenswürdigkeiten besichtigen. In Berlin kann man einen Stadtbummel machen. Echt toll!

⭐ Provide the first two or three words of each translated sentence (printed or just on the board).

1.2 Wo hast du deine Ferien verbracht?

1 In Urlaub

Objectives
- Vocabulary: Talking about a past holiday
- Grammar: Using the perfect tense with *haben*
- Strategy: Answering questions in German

Resources
- Student Book, pages 12–13
- CD 1, track 4
- Grammar, Vocabulary and Translation Workbook, pages 6–7
- Kerboodle, Unit 1

Key language
- *Wo hast du deine Sommerferien verbracht? Ich habe meine Sommerferien in (Frankreich/Deutschland/Italien) verbracht.*
- *Was hast du dort gemacht? Ich habe eine Hop-On-Hop-Off Bustour gemacht/eine Radtour gemacht/Tennis gespielt/ein Konzert gesehen/ein Museum besucht/Sehenswürdigkeiten besichtigt.*
- *Wie hat es dir gefallen? Wie war es? Es hat Spaß gemacht. Es war anstrengend/toll/cool/prima/langweilig/entspannend.*

Homework and self-study
- Student Book, page 13, activity 5
- Grammar, Vocabulary and Translation Workbook, pages 6–7

Starter
- To recap the perfect tense, provide students with a mini vocabulary test (printed or on the board) focusing on eight key verb forms from the lesson: *machen, gemacht, sehen, gesehen, besuchen, besucht, spielen, gespielt*. Use this task to give a brief recap of the perfect tense and its meaning.

Plenary
- Students play a memory game in pairs or small groups to practise the perfect tense. One student gives a perfect tense sentence (for example, *Ich habe ein Konzert gesehen*) and the next student repeats it and adds their own (for example, *Ich habe ein Konzert gesehen und ich habe eine Radtour gemacht*). This continues until someone forgets or makes a mistake and then the sentence starts again from the beginning.

---

1 🎧 **Hör zu. Drei Personen beantworten Fragen über die Sommerferien. Schreib vier Buchstaben (a–l) für jede Person (1–3) auf.**

Students listen to three people answering questions about their summer holidays and write down the four correct letters for each person. Tell them that each letter can only be used once and that there are two activities (from the *Was?* section) for each person.

Answers (letters in any order):
1 b, d, g, k; **2** c, e, i, j; **3** a, f, h, l

CD 1, track 4   Seite 12, Aktivität 1

1 – Wo hast du deine Sommerferien verbracht?
   – Ich habe meine Sommerferien in Deutschland verbracht.
   – Was hast du dort gemacht?
   – Ich habe eine Hop-On-Hop-Off Bustour gemacht und ich habe auch ein Konzert gesehen.
   – Wie hat es dir gefallen? Wie war es?
   – Es war toll!

2 – Wo hast du deine Sommerferien verbracht?
   – Ich habe meine Sommerferien in Italien verbracht.
   – Was hast du dort gemacht?
   – Ich habe eine Radtour gemacht und ich habe auch Sehenswürdigkeiten besichtigt.
   – Wie hat es dir gefallen? Wie war es?
   – Es hat Spaß gemacht.

3 – Wo hast du deine Sommerferien verbracht?
   – Ich habe meine Sommerferien in Frankreich verbracht.

23

1 In Urlaub

– Was hast du dort gemacht?
– Ich habe Tennis gespielt und ich habe auch ein Museum besucht.
– Wie hat es dir gefallen? Wie war es?
– Es war cool!

Aa Grammatik

Students met the perfect tense in *Echt 1*. You could use a questioning exercise to gauge what they can remember and/or recap key information; for example, the meaning of the terms 'auxiliary verb', 'past participle' and 'irregular', and word order rules. This could be done as a 'think, pair, share' task before asking individual students for feedback.

2 GCSE **Translate the sentences into English.**

Remind students not to translate the auxiliary verb in a literal way.

Suggested translations:
a *I visited sights/went sightseeing.*
b *I played tennis.*
c *He did a cycling tour.*
d *We did a hop-on-hop-off bus tour.*
e *I visited a museum.*
f *Where did you spend your summer holidays?*
g *They saw a concert.*

3 **Read Meszut's holiday review. Which activity (a–e) does he not mention?**

Answer: d

⊕ Students translate one or more sentences into English.

Suggested translations:
Last year I spent my summer holidays in France, in Mulhouse.
I went on a Segway tour and I visited sights.
We visited museums and we also ate well. On the last day we did a boat trip.
It was fun.

Sprachmuster

Remind students that the verb is the second <u>idea</u>, but not necessarily the second <u>word</u>. Use the example sentence in the *Sprachmuster* box to exemplify this.

Strategie

It would be useful to go over this information before students start activity 4. Translate the questions and answers in the box as a class, to further exemplify the use of inversion and correct pronouns.

4 **Macht drei Dialoge mit folgenden Informationen.**

Using the key language box as support, students create three dialogues in pairs, asking for and giving information about holidays based on the prompts. You could model the task structure and pronunciation beforehand with a confident volunteer. Assign roles, if necessary, to decide who will ask the questions and who will answer. Then remind students to swap roles when appropriate.

⊕ Students create and practise a dialogue, using their own ideas. This is freer practice as it isn't based on the prompts.

5 **Beschreib deine Ferien im letzten Sommer. Du kannst Meszuts Text aus Aktivität 3 als Beispiel benutzen.**

Using the text from activity 3 and the key language box from activity 4 as support, students describe in German their (real or imaginary) holiday last summer. Remind them to use conjunctions and to pay attention to the 'verb-second' rule.

★ Provide a more structured format for students to follow (in English or German); for example, in bullet point form: where, with whom, activities, etc.

1.3 #Wanderlust!

1 In Urlaub

Objectives
- Vocabulary: Talking about how you travelled on holiday
- Grammar: Using the perfect tense with *sein*
- Strategy: Using sequencers

Resources
- Student Book, pages 14–15
- CD 1, tracks 5–6
- Grammar, Vocabulary and Translation Workbook, pages 8–9
- Kerboodle, Unit 1

Key language
- *Wie bist du gefahren?*
- *Ich bin mit dem Schiff/mit dem Auto/mit dem Fahrrad/mit dem Motorrad/mit dem Zug/ mit dem Bus/mit dem Schneemobil gefahren. Ich bin mit dem Flugzeug geflogen. Ich bin quer durch (Frankreich/Italien/Spanien) gefahren. Ich bin von (Italien) nach (Frankreich) gefahren.*
- *zuerst, dann, danach*

Homework and self-study
- Student Book, page 15, activity 7
- Grammar, Vocabulary and Translation Workbook, pages 8–9

Starter
- Provide students with a list of eight to ten past participles. Most of them will be from Lesson 1.2 (for example, *besucht, gesehen*) and a few that will come up in this lesson (*gefahren, geflogen*). They write the infinitive forms of these past participles.

Plenary
- Students come up with short perfect tense sentences (for example, *Ich bin mit dem Bus gefahren*) and write the first letter of each word on a mini-whiteboard or on rough paper (for example, *I b m d B g*). They show this to their partner or group, who then write(s) down the sentence in full. This can be done with or without vocabulary sheets/support, depending on the ability of the group.

---

1 📖 **Was passt zusammen? Verbinde die Wörter (1–8) mit den Bildern (a–h).**

Students match the German methods of transport with the correct photo.

> Answers: **1** f; **2** h; **3** e; **4** g; **5** b; **6** c; **7** a; **8** d

➕ Students translate one or more of the phrases into English.

2 🎧 **Hör zu. Ist alles richtig?**

Students listen to the recording and check their answers from activity 1. Ensure that they correct any mistakes. After listening, they could do some whole-class, individual and/or paired reading aloud to practise pronunciation.

> 〰️ **CD 1, track 5   Seite 14, Aktivität 2**
>
> Wie bist du gefahren?
> 1 f – Ich bin mit dem Flugzeug geflogen.
> 2 h – Ich bin mit dem Schiff gefahren.
> 3 e – Ich bin mit dem Auto gefahren.
> 4 g – Ich bin mit dem Fahrrad gefahren.
> 5 b – Ich bin mit dem Motorrad gefahren.
> 6 c – Ich bin mit dem Zug gefahren.
> 7 a – Ich bin mit dem Bus gefahren.
> 8 d – Ich bin mit dem Schneemobil gefahren.

3 💬 **Zeichne ein Verkehrsmittel. (Draw a means of transport.) Dein Partner/Deine Partnerin muss raten (*has to guess*), was das ist.**

Students draw a method of transport. They then guess which method of transport their partner has drawn, using the example dialogue as support. You could model the task structure and pronunciation beforehand with a confident volunteer. Assign roles, if necessary, to decide

25

1 In Urlaub

who will ask the questions and who will answer. Then remind students to swap roles when appropriate.

Aa Grammatik

This is a good opportunity to gauge what students can remember and/or recap key information from Lesson 1.2; for example, the meaning of the terms 'auxiliary verb', 'past participle' and 'irregular', as well as word-order rules. This could be done as a 'think, pair, share' task before asking individual students for feedback.

4 ✎ **Schreib diese Sätze im Perfekt auf. Benutz das Verb ,fahren'.**

Students write sentences in the perfect tense, using the verb *fahren*, the pronouns and methods of transport provided.

> Answers:
> a Ich bin mit dem Fahrrad gefahren.
> b Er ist mit dem Zug gefahren.
> c Bist du mit dem Schiff gefahren?
> d Wir sind mit dem Bus gefahren.
> e Ich bin mit dem Auto gefahren.
> f Sie sind mit dem Flugzeug gefahren.

⭐ Tell students the number of words that are needed for each sentence. This can help them to remember *mit dem*, which can be challenging.

➕ Students translate into English the perfect tense sentences that they have written.

> Answers: **1** I went by bike. **2** He went by train. **3** Did you go by boat/ship? **4** We went by bus. **5** I went by car. **6** They went by plane.

5 📖 **Listen and read the blog posts. Are the statements true (T) or false (F)?**

Encourage students to refer to the glossary box to help them. As *quer* appears so frequently in the text, it would be useful to demonstrate the pronunciation before students listen to the recording. As a follow-up task, students could look up each person's route on a map.

> Answers: **a** T; **b** F; **c** F; **d** T; **e** F; **f** T

➕ Students correct the false sentences.

> Answers:
> b Ella went by train for the last stretch.
> c Markus travelled through Austria.
> e Roger first travelled by bike.

🎵 **CD 1, track 6   Seite 15, Aktivität 5**

See Student Book, page 15, for audio script.

🎁 Extra

Explain/elicit that if the subject of the verb changes (i.e. the pronoun *ich*), the auxiliary verb will also change (but the past participle will not).

⚙ Strategie

It would be useful to go over this information before students start the speaking and writing tasks. Exemplify and practise the pronunciation of these words.

6 💬 **Arbeitet in Gruppen von drei Personen. Ihr seid Ella, Markus und Roger. Verändert (Adapt) die Blogeinträge aus Aktivität 5. Beginnt die Sätze mit ,zuerst', ,dann' und ,danach'.**

Students choose a text from activity 5 and use the key information to form German sentences about the trip.

7 ✎ **Beschreib eine sehr lange Reise in deinem Leben.**

Students write a description of a long journey they have experienced. Encourage them to use the vocabulary from this lesson (including sequencers) and remind them that the information they give doesn't need to be true. As preparation, students could play a memory game in pairs or small groups, taking turns to add a new means of transport each time: Student A: *Ich bin zuerst mit dem (Zug gefahren)*. Student B: *Ich bin dann mit dem...* Student C: *Ich bin danach mit dem...*

⭐ Give students sentence starters to help them to structure their writing. If more support is needed, provide a writing frame with gaps for them to fill in with words of their choice; for example, *Ich bin nach ___ gefahren*.

1.4 Wie war das Wetter?

1 In Urlaub

Objectives
- Vocabulary: Talking about the weather
- Grammar: Using the imperfect tense
- Strategy: Listening for detail

Resources
- Student Book, pages 16–17
- CD 1, tracks 7–9
- Grammar, Vocabulary and Translation Workbook, pages 10–11
- Kerboodle, Unit 1

Key language
- *Wie war das Wetter gestern?*
- *Morgens/Mittags/Abends/Nachts war es wolkig/ sonnig/stürmisch/neblig/windig/kalt/heiß.*
  Es gab Regen/Schnee.
- *überall*

Homework and self-study
- Student Book, page 17, activity 7
- Grammar, Vocabulary and Translation Workbook, pages 10–11

Starter
- Provide a jumbled list of key time phrases linked to the general topic of holidays and the more specific topic of weather: *letztes Jahr, letzte Woche, vorgestern, gestern, heute, morgen* and *übermorgen*. Students sketch a rough timeline and arrange the words in the correct order.

Plenary
- To consolidate weather vocabulary and practise country names, provide students with a list of around five countries in German. They write a sentence for each country, describing how they think the weather was yesterday. It would be useful to give them countries which generally have a wide range of weather conditions in order to practise as much vocabulary as possible.

---

1 Wie war das Wetter gestern? Lies den Wetterbericht und füll die Lücken aus.

Students use the information and images provided to fill in the gaps in the text, describing what the weather was like yesterday. You may wish to remind students of the meanings of *es gab* and *es war*; they met these forms of the imperfect tense in *Echt 1*.

Answers: **1** windig; **2** Mittags; **3** stürmisch; **4** Schnee

2 Listen to these people talking about the weather. Which type of weather is <u>not</u> mentioned?

Before they start the activity, students could note down the German vocabulary that they would expect to hear for each of the possible answers. This will help them narrow down the options.

Answer: b

CD 1, track 7   Seite 16, Aktivität 2

– Wie war das Wetter in deinem Urlaub?
– Es war stürmisch und dann war es neblig.
– Ach nein, das ist aber schade.
– Nun, wie war das Wetter gestern in Deutschland?
– Morgens war es wolkig, aber nachmittags war es sonnig.
– Na gut!
– Wie war das Wetter vorgestern?
– Es gab Schnee. Ich bin Ski gefahren. Jippi!
– Sag mal, wie war das Wetter letzte Woche?
– Es war wolkig und es gab Regen.
– Ach nein!

27

1 In Urlaub

3 💬 **Spielt Tic-Tac-Toe. Wie war das Wetter gestern?**

Using the example provided and the key language box as support, students play noughts and crosses.

➕ Students create their own game grid, containing words rather than images. Filling the grid with English vocabulary is more challenging than German vocabulary, as they have to translate the phrases as well as listen to them.

🎭 Kultur

Ask students to work out from the context of the game what these phrases mean literally.

Answers: Three wins; Circle and cross

4 🔄 GCSE **Übersetz den Wetterbericht ins Deutsche.**

Students translate the weather report into German. Remind them of the 'verb-second' rule, and also that 'in the morning', 'in the afternoon', 'in the evening' and 'at night' are two or three words each in English, but just one word in German here (*morgens, nachmittags, abends, nachts*).

Suggested translation:
Morgens war es wolkig.
Nachmittags war es sonnig und windig.
Abends gab es Regen und nachts gab es Schnee.

Aa Grammatik

Remind students that the perfect tense and imperfect tense are different tenses and are not interchangeable. However, there's no need to go into too much detail at this stage. Keep an eye out for any misconceptions surrounding 'it was' and 'there was'.

⚙ Strategie

It would be useful to go over this information before students start activity 5.

5 🎧 **Listen to another weather report and complete the notes in English.**

As preparation, you could note down as a class the German vocabulary for each section in the notes, so students can listen out for these key terms. You may wish to pre-teach *Temperatur* and *Grad*.

Answers:		
Weather:	morning:	cloudy
	afternoon:	sunny
	evening:	(light) rain showers
	night:	stormy
Time:	sunrise:	6.59
	sunset:	19.12
Temperature:	high:	13°
	low:	5°

⭐ For additional support with numbers, which many students find particularly challenging, provide students with all four sets of numbers they need for the listening task (6.59; 19.12; 13; 5), so that their task is just to assign them to the correct heading.

➕ Students cover up the notes provided and complete the activity without this support, making notes on anything they can understand.

〰 CD 1, track 8   Seite 17, Aktivität 5

Morgens war es wolkig, aber am Nachmittag schien die Sonne. Alle Wolken waren weg. Keine Wolken mehr!

Abends gab es aber leichte Regenschauer.

Nachts war es stürmisch.

Sonnenaufgang war um 6:59 und Sonnenuntergang um 19:12.

Die Höchsttemperatur war 13 Grad und die Tiefsttemperatur: 5 Grad.

Bis bald!

6 📖 GCSE **Listen and read Azra's post. Complete the sentences in English.**

Encourage students to refer to the glossary box, but remind them that they do not need to understand every word of Azra's post.

*Answers: **a** Nils; **b** Croatia; **c** hot, sunny; **d** Greece;*
***e** sunny, rain; **f** foggy; **g** eat well; **h** stormy*

1 In Urlaub

CD 1, track 9 · Seite 17, Aktivität 6

See Student Book, page 17, for audio script.

7 ✏ **Schreib Caspars Fahrrad-Abenteuer auf. Verändere die unterstrichenen Sätze aus Aktivität 6.**

Students use the notes provided to create full sentences about Caspar's trip. Remind them to adapt the underlined sentences in the text in activity 6.

Suggested answer:
Hallo! Ich heiße Caspar und ich habe eine tolle Reise gemacht. Mein Fahrrad heißt Camille. Zuerst bin ich durch Italien gefahren. Das Wetter war windig und sonnig. Wie toll! Dann bin ich nach Frankreich gefahren. Es war oft sonnig aber auch stürmisch. Es war/Meine Reise war spannend!

➕ Students write their paragraph in the third person, rather than first person.

Suggested answer:
Er heißt Caspar und er hat eine tolle Reise gemacht. Sein Fahrrad heißt Camille. Zuerst ist er durch Italien gefahren. Das Wetter war windig und sonnig. Wie toll! Dann ist er nach Frankreich gefahren. Es war oft sonnig aber auch stürmisch. Es war/Seine Reise war spannend!

Aussprache: u and ü

This task requires teacher demonstration so that students have an excellent pronunciation model. Isolate the sounds first, then move on to using the example words that include the sounds. Depending on the ability of the class, you could also play some games; for example, partners saying alternate words in the sentence; whole-class repetition using different volumes or speeds; or trying to learn the sentence off by heart.

1.5 Ich reise gern

Objectives

- Vocabulary: Describing a past holiday and giving your opinion
- Grammar: Using different personal pronouns and verb forms
- Strategy: Using intensifiers

Resources

- Student Book, pages 18–19
- CD 1, track 10
- Grammar, Vocabulary and Translation Workbook, pages 12–13
- Kerboodle, Unit 1

Key language

- *Wo hast du übernachtet? Ich habe in einem Tipi-Dorf/einer Jugendherberge/einer Ferienwohnung/einem Hotel übernachtet.*
- *echt/richtig/total bequem, ideal, wunderbar, wunderschön*
- *am ersten/folgenden/letzten Tag*
- *(Aktiv sein) ist für mir wichtig. (Österreich) hat mir (nicht) gut gefallen.*

Homework and self-study

- Student Book, page 19, activity 7. Encourage students to use and adapt their work from activity 5; this isn't cheating!

- Grammar, Vocabulary and Translation Workbook, pages 12–13

Starter

- To revise previous learning which will be revisited in this lesson, ask students to list as many German words as they can for each of the following categories: past participles, conjunctions, sequencers and transport vocabulary. Students could brainstorm these as a class, or they could work individually and then compare their list with their partner and test each other. You could include as many categories as you wish, but these are the main areas covered in this lesson.

Plenary

- Read aloud some perfect tense sentences in the first person (using *haben*, *sein* or both, depending on the ability of the class). Students then turn them into the third person. They could respond verbally as a whole class, or on mini-whiteboards, or as a 'tell your partner the answer' task.

---

1 Read the posts on a holidays thread. Who stayed where? Match the places (1–4) to the people.

You may wish to pre-teach *übernachten* (and remind students of the 'ü' pronunciation they met in Lesson 1.4). The word *Nacht* may also give a clue to its meaning.

Answers: **1** @Christine222; **2** @Luxuslieber; **3** @Koalachen; **4** @Emma03

➕ Students also note down in English the opinions given for each accommodation type.

Answers: **1** ideal; **2** really great; **3** very comfortable; **4** brilliant

Strategie

Before reading through the information in the *Strategie* box, ask students to recall what an intensifier is and whether they can remember any in German. It may be useful to go over this box before starting activity 2.

2 Read the texts and find examples of the structures.

Before finding examples of the structures, you could exploit the text further by asking students to read (sections of) it aloud. They could do this alone, with a partner or as a whole-class task. Then explain to students that there are more examples of the structures in the texts than they need.

1 In Urlaub

Answers:

a (any three:) ich habe … verbracht, wir haben … übernachtet, ich habe/wir haben/(Niko) hat … gemacht, ich habe … besichtigt, ich habe … gesehen, das hat … gemacht, ich habe … gezeltet, (Österreich) hat (mir gut) gefallen

b wir sind … geflogen, ich bin … gefahren, ich bin … geklettert

c (Das Wetter) war, (Meine Ferien) waren

d man kann … besuchen, man kann … fahren

e (any four:) richtig, echt, sehr, ziemlich, ein bisschen

f (any three:) und, aber, auch, oder

g (any four:) am ersten Tag, am folgenden Tag, am letzten Tag, dann, danach

3 📖 **Read the texts in activity 2 again. Copy and complete the table in English.**

Remind students to read carefully to find the details they need.

Answers:

	Destination	Transport	Activities	Overall opinion
Feyi	Spain, Cadaqués	plane	hop-on-hop-off bus tour, visited sights, saw a play	Spain is wonderful and really cool; holiday was really great
Julius	Austria, mountains	bus	white-water rafting, climbing, cycling tour	liked Austria; will come back again soon

🎁 **Extra**

Tell students that they don't need to note every additional detail for every text; they should just fill in what they can.

Answers:

	Accommodation	Other things you can do	Weather
Feyi	hotel	visit the Dali house	sunny and hot
Julius	tent/camping	go canoeing, go on excursions	quite nice but a bit cold

4 ✏️ **Füll die Lücken aus. Du brauchst nicht alle Wörter zu benutzen.**

Students fill the gaps to create perfect tense sentences. They choose from the words provided. There are two distractors: *habe* and *geflogen*.

Answers: **1** haben; **2** verbracht; **3** sind; **4** gefahren; **5** haben; **6** übernachtet

⭐ Tell students which words are the distractors and therefore not needed.

➕ Students choose their own answers for the gaps and complete the task without looking at the words provided.

5 🔄 GCSE **Translate the text from activity 4 into English.**

Remind students that it isn't always appropriate to use the auxiliary verb *haben* (or 'have') in English (e.g. 'we have spent' as opposed to 'we spent').

Suggested translation:
We spent our summer holidays in Switzerland. We went/travelled by bus and we stayed in a guest house.

Aa Grammatik

Before going through the *Grammatik* box, ask students to recall as many pronouns as they can in both English and German. They may be able to label them as first, second or third person and/or as singular or plural. Use the information in the *Grammatik* box to elicit or explain to students that it's a good idea to use a range of pronouns, but that they need to remember to conjugate the verb correctly to match the pronoun.

31

1 In Urlaub

6 🎧 **Kuscheltiertour!** (*Cuddly toy tour!*) Hör zu und bring die Fotos (a–d) in die richtige Reihenfolge.

Students listen and put the images in the order in which they are mentioned in the recording. Pre-teach the word *Kuscheltier* to provide students with the context for the activity.

Answers: **1** b; **2** d; **3** a; **4** c

🎵 **CD 1, track 10   Seite 19, Aktivität 6**

1. Klaus ist mit dem Zug nach Wien gefahren.
2. Am ersten Tag hat er Sehenswürdigkeiten besichtigt.
3. Am folgenden Tag hat er ein Museum besucht.
4. Am letzten Tag hat er eine Segwaytour gemacht.

7 ✏️ Schreib deine eigene Kuscheltiertour. Benutz die ‚er/sie'-Form.

Using the prompts provided and the vocabulary from this lesson, students write about a cuddly toy 'on tour' in the third person. They should use all five sentence starters provided in the key language box.

1 Kultur

Resources
- Student Book, pages 20–21
- CD 1, tracks 11–12

1 📖 Was passt zusammen? Verbinde die Wörter (1–6) mit den Bildern (a–f).

Students match the items that can be bought at a Christmas market to the correct photos. They may be unfamiliar with some of these items, so check they know what the photos show by eliciting the English before they complete the matching task. You could then hold a class discussion about how these items differ from traditional Christmas items in the UK. These words can also provide useful pronunciation practice as they include some tricky sounds.

Answers: **1** c; **2** d; **3** a; **4** f; **5** b; **6** e

2 📖 [GCSE] Read the text about the Christmas market in Aachen and answer the questions in English.

This would be a good point to give students some background information about the tradition of Christmas markets in German-speaking countries. After they have completed the activity, ask students to read the information box next to activity 2. You could show some images of the *Printenmänner* biscuits and the models outside the market, and point out Aachen on a map of Germany.

Answers: **a** 1.5 million; **b** around 130; **c** presents/gifts and speciality food; **d** (really) romantic; **e** 20th November to 23rd December; **f** 11 a.m. to 9 p.m.

3 🎧 [GCSE] Hör zu. Wer sagt das: Sanya (S) oder Leo (L)?

Students listen and note down who says each of the statements listed. Encourage students to read through the statements carefully first as they are exactly the same as in the recording.

Answers: **a** S; **b** S; **c** L; **d** S; **e** L; **f** L

1 In Urlaub

🎵 CD 1, track 11   Seite 20, Aktivität 3

Sanya
- Was hast du letztes Wochenende gemacht?
- Ich bin zum Weihnachtsmarkt in Aachen gefahren.
- Was hast du gekauft?
- Ich habe ein paar Geschenke gekauft.
- Was hast du gegessen und getrunken?
- Ich habe heißen Kakao getrunken.
- Wie war es?
- Wunderbar.

Leo
- Was hast du letztes Wochenende gemacht?
- Letztes Wochenende habe ich mit meiner Familie den Aachener Weihnachtsmarkt besucht.
- Was hast du gekauft?
- Wir haben einen Nussknacker gekauft und wir sind auch Karussell gefahren.
- Was hast du gegessen und getrunken?
- Wir haben Stollen und Printenmänner gegessen.
- Wie war es?
- Mit Lichtern und Musik war das echt toll!

4 ✏️ GCSE Schreib eine SMS an deine Freundin.

Students write a text message in German, addressing the information in the bullet points. They should use and adapt key language from activity 3. Before the students begin writing their text message, you may wish to clarify how to translate the following parts of the first, second and third bullet points: You went <u>to the</u> Christmas market. = *zum*; You bought <u>some</u> presents. = *ein paar*; You drank <u>hot cocoa</u> and you ate <u>a potato pancake</u>. = *heißen Kakao, einen Kartoffelpuffer.*

Suggested answer:
Ich bin zum Weihnachtsmarkt gefahren. Ich habe ein paar Geschenke gekauft. Ich habe heißen Kakao getrunken und einen Kartoffelpuffer gegessen. Es war echt/richtig toll. Es hat Spaß gemacht.

⭐ Provide students with sentence starters for each bullet point, or a gap-fill style writing frame if more support is needed.

5 📖 Listen and read the poem. Then complete the English translation.

You could first play the recording without telling students what it's about, to see how much information they can understand. Then ask them to read the German text to check their understanding. Alternatively, ask students to look through the English translation and predict what the missing words will be. You may wish to pre-teach *wundersam* ('wondrous'). After they have completed the activity, ask students to read the information box above activity 5. You could explain a little more about this tradition (for example, that the gifts are left in boots and that Saint Nicholas rewards well-behaved children) and contrast this with the stories and traditions surrounding *Krampus*: the horned half-goat, half-demon figure who is said, during the Christmas period, to punish children who have misbehaved.

Suggested translations:
1 Christmas; 2 sack; 3 streets; 4 beautiful/lovely; 5 wondrous; 6 apples

⭐ Provide students with a selection of English words to choose from when completing the translation, including distractors if appropriate.

➕ Students try to improve the translation of the poem, or write their own new verse in German.

🎵 CD 1, track 12   Seite 21, Aktivität 5

See Student Book, page 21, for audio script.

6 💬 Lest das deutsche Gedicht laut. (*Read the German poem out loud.*)

This could also be done in pairs or small groups to practise listening skills: students pause at a point of their choice and the next student picks up.

Aussprache: *z*, *ei* and *ie*

This task requires teacher demonstration so that students have an excellent pronunciation model. Model the sounds first and then move on to using the example words that include the sounds. Depending on the ability of the class, you could also play some games; for example, partners saying alternate words, or whole-class repetition using different volumes or speeds.

33

1 Sprachlabor

Objectives

- The infinitive with *man kann*
- The perfect tense with *haben*
- The perfect tense with *sein*
- The perfect tense: *haben* and *sein*
- Pronunciation: long and short vowels

Resources

- Student Book, pages 22–23
- CD 1, tracks 13–14
- Grammar, Vocabulary and Translation Workbook, pages 4–13
- Kerboodle, Unit 1

Aa Grammatik

The infinitive with *man kann*

Before starting this section, explain or elicit the two main word-order rules with *man kann*:

- the infinitive goes to the end of the clause
- the verb is always the second idea, meaning that sometimes we have to say *kann man*.

1 Put the letters in the correct order to write the infinitives. Then translate the sentences into English.

Answers/Suggested translations:
a gehen – You can go shopping.
b besichtigen – You can visit the sights.
c machen – You can do/go on a cycling tour.
d klettern – You can rock climb/go rock climbing in Switzerland.
e schnorcheln – You can snorkel/go snorkelling at the seaside.
f zelten – You can go camping in the mountains.

2 Write *man kann* in the correct order in the blue gaps. Choose the correct infinitive for the green gaps.

Answers: *a* Man kann, machen; *b* Man kann, besichtigen; *c* kann man, laufen; *d* kann man, essen; *e* kann man, tauchen; *f* Man kann, zelten

Aa Grammatik

The perfect tense with *haben*

Before starting this section, explain or elicit how to form the perfect tense and the role of *haben* (as an auxiliary verb). You may wish to recap key terms such as 'auxiliary', 'past participle', 'prefix' and 'infinitive'.

3 Complete the sentences with the correct past participle form of the verb in brackets.

Answers: *a* verbracht; *b* besucht; *c* gegessen; *d* gesehen; *e* gespielt

4 Put the words in the correct order. Then translate the sentences into English.

Answers/Suggested translations:
a Ich habe meine Ferien in Italien verbracht. – I spent my holidays in Italy.
b Thomas hat den Eiffelturm gesehen. – Thomas saw the Eiffel Tower.
c Wir haben Basketball gespielt. – We played basketball.
d Was hast du gemacht? – What did you do?

5 Translate the sentences into German.

Suggested translations:
a Ich habe Volleyball gespielt.
b Wir haben meine Großmutter/Oma besucht.
c Jana hat Pommes gegessen.
d Am Wochenende haben meine Freunde/Freundinnen ein Konzert gesehen, aber ich habe ein Buch gelesen.

1 In Urlaub

Aa Grammatik

The perfect tense with *sein*

Before starting this section, explain or elicit how to form the perfect tense and the difference between *haben* and *sein* when used as auxiliaries. You may wish to recap key terms such as 'auxiliary', 'past participle', 'prefix' and 'infinitive', and remind students that *bleiben* is an exception to the 'verbs of movement' rule.

6 Choose the correct auxiliary verb (form of *sein*) to complete each sentence.

Answers: **a** bin; **b** Bist; **c** ist; **d** sind; **e** sind

7 Complete the sentences with the correct past participle from the list in the *Grammatik* box.

Answers: **a** gegangen; **b** gefahren; **c** gekommen; **d** gelaufen; **e** geflogen; **f** geblieben

Aa Grammatik

The perfect tense: *haben* and *sein*

Before starting this section, ask students to recall as much as they can about the perfect tense. You can then identify any misconceptions or gaps in their knowledge, ready for the following tasks on this grammar point.

8 Copy and complete the table with the past participles.

Answers:

Ich habe…	Ich bin…
gemacht	geblieben
gesehen	gegangen
besucht	gekommen
gegessen	geflogen
verbracht	gefahren
gekauft	

9 Complete the text with the correct auxiliary verbs or past participles.

Answers: **1** bin; **2** haben; **3** gespielt; **4** gemacht; **5** gegangen; **6** sind

⭐ Provide the answers as a multiple-choice list from which students can select, with distractors if appropriate.

Aussprache: long and short vowels

These tasks require lots of teacher demonstration to provide students with an excellent pronunciation model. You can also play the audio files to demonstrate correct pronunciation.

10 Listen and repeat the words from the table. Then practise with your partner.

Isolate the sounds first, then move on to using the words that include the sounds.

🎵 **CD 1, track 13   Seite 23, Aktivität 10**

See Student Book, page 23, for audio script.

11 Practise saying the sentences.

Depending on the ability of the class, you could play some games with this; for example, partners saying alternate words in each sentence, whole-class repetition using different volumes or speeds, or trying to learn the tongue twister-style sentences off by heart.

🎵 **CD 1, track 14   Seite 23, Aktivität 11**

See Student Book, page 23, for audio script.

35

1 In Urlaub

1 Was kann ich schon?

> **Resources**
> - Student Book, pages 24–25
> - CD 1, tracks 15–16
> - Kerboodle, Unit 1

Reading

1 Lies die Sätze. Richtig (R) oder falsch (F)?

Students decide if the statements are true or false.

> Answers: **a** F; **b** R; **c** R; **d** F; **e** R; **f** R; **g** F; **h** F; **i** R; **j** F

2 Read the holiday reviews and answer @Sonnenschein (S) or @Weltenbummler (W).

Remind students to read the texts right through to the end to ensure they pick up on the correct details for each question.

> Answers: **a** W; **b** S; **c** S; **d** W; **e** S; **f** W; **g** W; **h** W; **i** S; **j** S

Listening

3 GCSE Listen to Gino talking about his holiday. Choose the correct answer to complete each sentence.

Encourage students to develop good habits for multiple-choice questions by using their preparation time before starting the task to note down the relevant vocabulary. This will help them focus their attention while listening.

> Answers: **a** car; **b** France; **c** family; **d** two weeks; **e** by the sea; **f** football; **g** snorkelling; **h** hot; **i** a bit of French; **j** restaurant

CD 1, track 15   Seite 24, Aktivität 3

Letzten Sommer bin ich mit dem Auto nach Frankreich gefahren. Ich bin mit meinen Eltern und mit meiner Schwester gefahren. Wir haben zwei Wochen in einem Hotel am Meer verbracht. Ich habe mit meinem Vater am Strand Fußball gespielt und wir sind schnorcheln gegangen. Das Wetter war sehr gut. Es war sonnig und heiß. Ich habe auch ein bisschen Französisch gelernt! Jeden Abend sind wir ins Restaurant gegangen und manchmal habe ich in der Hoteldisko getanzt, wo ich nette Leute kennengelernt habe. Meine Ferien waren toll!

4 GCSE Listen to Daniel talking about St Moritz. Complete the sentences in English.

Point out to students that two details are needed for each of sentences c, d and f. Explain the importance of checking how much information is required for their answers.

> Answers: **a** in the (Swiss) mountains/in Switzerland; **b** winter holidays; **c** skiing and snowboarding (2 marks); **d** there's snow, but it's also sunny (2 marks); **e** go to the museum; **f** (any two:) hiking/mountain biking/camping; **g** the water is too cold

1 In Urlaub

CD 1, track 16 Seite 24, Aktivität 4

St. Moritz ist eine kleine Stadt in den Bergen in der Schweiz. St. Moritz ist super für die Winterferien. Hier kann man Ski fahren und snowboarden. Im Winter gibt es Schnee, aber es ist auch sonnig. Es ist wunderschön! Man kann auch in das Segantini Museum gehen. Dort gibt es Kunst zu sehen. Das Essen hier ist auch fantastisch, vor allem die Spezialitäten, wie zum Beispiel Raclette und Rösti.

Im Sommer kann man hier wandern oder mountainbiken und man kann auf dem Campingplatz zelten. Es gibt einen schönen See, aber das Wasser ist zu kalt zum Schwimmen.

Writing

5 Was kann man machen? Schreib einen Satz für jedes Bild. Benutz ,Man kann...'

Students write a sentence to describe each image. Remind them to use the phrase *Man kann...*

Answers:
a Man kann klettern.
b Man kann eine Bootsfahrt machen.
c Man kann Kanu fahren.
d Man kann zelten.
e Man kann Ausflüge/eine (Hop-On-Hop-Off) Bustour machen.

6 Beantworte die Fragen auf Deutsch.

Students answer the questions in German. Remind them of the word order rules regarding *Man kann...* (inversion; infinitive at the end of the clause).

7 [GCSE] Übersetz die Sätze ins Deutsche.

Students translate the sentences into German. Award one mark for a fully correct answer, or half a mark if there are minor mistakes.

Suggested translations:
a Ich bin mit dem Zug nach Wales gefahren.
b Ich habe eine Woche in Stuttgart verbracht.
c Zuerst habe ich Fußball gespielt.
d Es hat Spaß gemacht.
e Es war kalt und windig.

1 Vorankommen!

Resources

- Student Book, pages 26–27
- CD 1, tracks 17–19
- Kerboodle, Unit 1

Bronze

1 What can you do in these countries? Match the countries (1–6) to the correct sentences (a–f).

This task tests cultural knowledge as well as language skills.

Answers: **1** c; **2** e; **3** b; **4** a; **5** f; **6** d

2 [GCSE] Listen to Petra talking about her holiday. Which <u>two</u> details does she mention?

Remind students to read through the details listed before they listen to the recording.

Answer (any order): a, d

1 In Urlaub

〰️ CD 1, track 17   Seite 26, Aktivität 2

Ich bin letzten Winter mit meiner Familie in die Schweiz gefahren. Wir haben eine Woche in den Alpen verbracht. Es war sehr kalt aber sonnig. Ich bin jeden Tag Ski gefahren. Das hat viel Spaß gemacht. Abends habe ich gelesen und Fotos auf Instagram gepostet.

3 ✏️ **Write sentences in the perfect tense in German using the words.**

Students write the sentences based on the information provided. You may wish to remind students of the time–manner–place rule, or you could just instruct them to state the method of transport first. You could also remind them that all of these sentences will use the auxiliary verb *sein*.

> *Answers:*
> *a Ich bin mit dem Auto nach Schottland gefahren.*
> *b Ich bin mit dem Zug nach Frankreich gefahren.*
> *c Ich bin mit dem Flugzeug nach Deutschland geflogen.*
> *d Ich bin mit dem Boot/Schiff nach Spanien gefahren.*

Silber

4 📖 [GCSE] **Füll die Lücken aus. Du brauchst nicht alle Wörter zu benutzen.** Complete the sentences. You don't need to use all the words.

Students choose the correct word for each gap from those provided. Point out that there are two distractors.

> *Answers:* **1** *Sommer;* **2** *besucht;* **3** *drei;* **4** *war;*
> **5** *gemacht;* **6** *habe*

5 🎧 [GCSE] **Listen to Kai and Aysha talking about where they live. Who says these things: Kai (K), Aysha (A) or both (K+A)?**

> *Answers:* **a** K+A; **b** A; **c** K; **d** K; **e** A; **f** A; **g** K

〰️ CD 1, track 18   Seite 26, Aktivität 5

Kai

Ich wohne in Freiburg in Süddeutschland. Im Sommer ist es sehr heiß und sonnig.
Man kann hier viel Sport machen. Man kann mountainbiken und wandern. Im Winter kann man auch Ski fahren.
Man kann auch Ausflüge nach Frankreich oder in die Schweiz machen.

Aysha

Ich wohne in Berlin. Im Sommer ist es hier sonnig und im Winter ist es sehr kalt.
Man kann hier viele Museen besuchen und viele Sehenswürdigkeiten sehen, wie den Fernsehturm oder das Brandenburger Tor.
Man kann aber auch tolle Ausflüge machen. Es gibt viele Seen, wo man super schwimmen kann. Außerdem kann man in Berlin echt gut einkaufen.

6 ✏️ [GCSE] **Schreib einen Text (zirka 60 Wörter) über deine Ferien letzten Sommer. Du musst die Ideen unten erwähnen.** Write a short text (about 60 words) about your holidays last summer. You must mention the ideas below.

Students write approximately 60 words about their last summer holiday. Encourage them to use a variety of pronouns, conjunctions, sequencers, opinions and intensifiers. This will help consolidate all of the work they have done in Unit 1.

Gold

7 📖 [GCSE] **Lies den Blogeintrag und beantworte die Fragen auf Deutsch.**

Students read the blog entry and answer the questions. You may wish to explain that the information appears in the text in the same order as the questions, and that not all of the questions need to be answered in full sentences.

> *Answers:* **a** *letzten Dezember;* **b** *zwei Tage;* **c** *(sehr) kalt aber (ziemlich) sonnig;* **d** *den Kölner Dom;* **e** *Er hat Souvenirs (für seine Familie) gekauft und Würstchen und Pommes gegessen.* **f** *das Schokoladenmuseum;* **g** *Er hat viele Fotos (und Selfies) gemacht.* **h** *Sie haben Karten gespielt und Schokolade gegessen.*

1 In Urlaub

8 🎧 GCSE **Hör zu. Schreib die Tabelle ab und füll sie aus.**

Students copy and complete the table, noting down the information for each speaker. Ensure that they understand the questions in the table before starting, and remind them to answer in German.

Answers:

	1	2	3
Wohin?	Griechenland	Schweiz	Amerika
Wie lange?	eine Woche	zehn Tage	zwei Wochen
Wetter?	sonnig und heiß	geregnet	warm
Aktivität?	schnorcheln	wandern	Konzert
Meinung?	super	nicht so gut	total cool

CD 1, track 19   Seite 27, Aktivität 8

1 Thomas

Ich bin im Sommer mit meiner Familie für eine Woche nach Griechenland geflogen. Das Wetter war genau so, wie ich es liebe: sonnig und heiß. Ich bin im Meer schnorcheln gegangen. Meine Ferien waren super!

2 Kaya

Ich habe mit meinen Freunden in der Schweiz gezeltet. Wir haben zehn Tage am Lago Maggiore verbracht. Wir sind wandern gegangen. Leider waren die Ferien nicht so gut, weil es oft geregnet hat.

3 Sarina

Ich bin mit meiner Familie nach Amerika geflogen. Wir sind zwei Wochen dort geblieben. Es war warm, da es Mai war. Ich habe Taylor Swift in einem Konzert gesehen. Meiner Meinung nach war das total cool.

---

9 ✏️ **Schreib den Text in der Vergangenheitsform um.**

Students rewrite the German text in the past tense. They may wish to make notes in English in both tenses to help them with this challenging task.

Suggested answer:
Im Sommer bin ich nach Sylt gefahren. Ich bin zehn Tage dort geblieben. Ich bin wandern und schwimmen gegangen. An einem Tag habe ich eine Radtour gemacht. Es war wirklich toll.

10 ✏️ GCSE **Übersetz den Text ins Deutsche.**

Students translate the text into German.

Suggested translation:
Letzten Sommer bin ich mit dem Flugzeug nach Italien geflogen. Ich habe eine Woche in Rom verbracht. Es war ziemlich heiß. Ich habe Sehenswürdigkeiten besichtigt und danach bin ich schwimmen gegangen. Es hat viel Spaß gemacht.

11 ✏️ GCSE **Schreib einen Text (zirka 80 Wörter) über deine letzten Ferien.**

Students write approximately 80 words about a past holiday, guided by the bullet points: where they went, which transport they used, how long they were there for, the weather, three activities and their opinion. Remind them that the information and experience do not need to be true.

🎁 **Extra**

Before students declare their written work 'finished', remind them to check the *Extra* box and to use the suggestions to ensure their writing is the best it can possibly be.

2 Mein Zuhause

Unit overview				
Page reference	Vocabulary	Grammar	Strategy	Key language
32–33 2.1 Wie ist deine Alltagsroutine?	Talking about daily routines and household chores	Using separable verbs in the present tense	Answering comprehension questions in English	aufstehen, aufräumen, abtrocknen, abwaschen, vorbereiten, bügeln, Staub saugen, putzen, den Tisch decken, das Bett machen, zu Hause helfen, im Garten arbeiten das Schlafzimmer, das Bad/Badezimmer, die Toilette, das Esszimmer, die Küche, der Garten
34–35 2.2 Wie komme ich zu…?	Saying what there is in town and giving directions	Using *es gibt* with the accusative case	Taking part in a role play	Was gibt es in der Stadt? Es gibt…, Man kann dort… das Museum, das Café, das Restaurant, das Hotel, das Geschäft, der Flughafen, das Kino, der Park, die Kirche, die Moschee, die Synagoge, das Hochhaus, die Bushaltestelle, der Bahnhof, der Fluss, der Busbahnhof, die Imbissbude Wie komme ich am besten zum/zur…? Nehmen Sie die erste/zweite/dritte Straße links/rechts. Gehen Sie geradeaus/links dann rechts. Es ist auf der linken/rechten Seite. Fahren Sie mit dem Bus Nummer (36).
36–37 2.3 Bei uns	Talking about where you live and where you lived before	Using the present, perfect and imperfect tenses together	Varying your language	Wo wohnst du? Ich wohne/lebe/Wir wohnen/leben in einem/einer… das Doppelhaus, das Einfamilienhaus, das Reihenhaus, die Wohnung, der Wohnblock, das Hausboot, das Wohnmobil, das Schloss am See, am Stadtrand, auf dem Land, in den Bergen, an der Küste, in einem Dorf, in der Stadt im ersten/zweiten/dritten Stock Ich finde es/Das finde ich cool/attraktiv/schön/laut/toll/ruhig/grün/idyllisch/langweilig/interessant. Ich wohne/Wir wohnen (nicht) gern hier. Früher habe ich/haben wir … gewohnt. Ich fand es…/Das fand ich…, Es gibt/gab viel zu tun.
38–39 2.4 Mein Schlafzimmer	Talking about your bedroom	Using prepositions with the dative case	Using grammar you already know	In meinem Zimmer habe ich/gibt es… Hier haben wir… der Fernseher, der Computer, der Schreibtisch, der Schrank, der Kleiderschrank, das Bett, der Sessel, der Stuhl, der Teppich, die Kommode, Pompons (pl), die Lampe, die Lichterkette, Kerzen (pl), das Fenster, die Tür, der Boden neben, auf, über, vor, in, hinter Ich persönlich finde es (sehr/wirklich/echt/zu/gar nicht) chaotisch/ordentlich/perfekt/praktisch/hübsch/gemütlich/organisiert/bunt/bequem.

2 Mein Zuhause

Unit overview

Page reference	Vocabulary	Grammar	Strategy	Key language
40–41 2.5 Mein zukünftiges Zuhause	Talking about your future home	Using the future tense with *werden*	Using three time frames	*Ich werde in einem Reihenhaus/einem (großen) Einfamilienhaus/einem Doppelhaus/einer (modernen) Wohnung wohnen.* *Es wird (echt toll) sein./Das wird Spaß machen. Es wird (viele Zimmer) geben. Meine Wohnung/Mein Haus wird charmant/schön möbliert/perfekt/echt toll sein. Ich werde (viele Tiere) haben.* *Früher habe ich ... gewohnt. Heute wohne ich..., In der Zukunft werde ich ... wohnen. Es wird (Blumen) geben.*

2 Los geht's!

2 Mein Zuhause

> **Starter**
> - Students practise using the German alphabet by spelling aloud the words in activities 1 and 2 for their partner, who then guesses the word.

> **Plenary**
> - Ask students to summarise some new things they have learnt from the lesson, using a 3–2–1 activity: three key words, two interesting facts and one grammar point. They can share these with the class or with a partner.

1 Was ist das Lieblingsmöbelstück (*favourite piece of furniture*) Deutschlands? Jeden Tag verbringt der Durchschnittsdeutsche (*average German*) drei Stunden darauf. Rate mal! (*Guess!*)

Students decide which is Germany's favourite piece of furniture, on which they spend three hours every day.

> Answer: **b**

2 ,4ZKB' bedeutet ,Vier Zimmer, Küche, Bad'. Das ist der Code einer typischen Mietwohnung (*rented flat*). Welche Wohnung ist das?

Students match the description 4ZKB with the correct floor plan.

> Answer: **b**

➕ Students write codes for the other two floor plans. They could also write these out in full.

> Answers: **a** 3ZKB (drei Zimmer, Küche, Bad);
> **c** 2ZKB (zwei Zimmer, Küche, Bad)

Kultur

You could also give a literal translation of *Wohngemeinschaft*: 'living togetherness'.

3 Wer arbeitet wo? Füll die Lücken aus.

Students fill the gaps in the sentences with the correct German location for each job.

> Answers: **a** *Park*; **b** *Café*; **c** *Souvenirgeschäft*;
> **d** *Kirche*

Sprachmuster

You may wish to revise the terms 'stem', 'regular' and 'infinitive'.
Answer: Ich habe gearbeitet...

2.1 Wie ist deine Alltagsroutine?

Objectives
- Vocabulary: Talking about daily routines and household chores
- Grammar: Using separable verbs in the present tense
- Strategy: Answering comprehension questions in English

Resources
- Student Book, pages 32–33
- CD 1, tracks 20–21
- Grammar, Vocabulary and Translation Workbook, pages 14–15
- Kerboodle, Unit 2

Key language
- *aufstehen, aufräumen, abtrocknen, abwaschen, vorbereiten, bügeln, Staub saugen, putzen, den Tisch decken, das Bett machen, zu Hause helfen, im Garten arbeiten*
- *das Schlafzimmer, das Badezimmer, die Toilette, das Esszimmer, die Küche, der Garten*

Homework and self-study
- Student Book, page 33, activity 7
- Grammar, Vocabulary and Translation Workbook, pages 14–15

Starter
- Remind students that *Zimmer* means 'room'. Then provide them with gapped clues to form the German words for bedroom, dining room, living room, bathroom and children's room; for example, bathroom = _ _ _ _ zimmer (these words were introduced in *Los geht's!*).

Plenary
- Students practise speaking and listening with some dictation. They read aloud the text they created for activity 7 and their partner writes down what they say as accurately as possible, without looking at the written version. Remind them to write in German, not English. If they are completing this task at home, they can use or adapt phrases from activity 1.

---

1 🎧 Hör zu und lies.

For this activity, students are simply reading and listening to the information before answering questions in activity 2. Before moving on to the questions, you could exploit the text further by asking students to read (sections of) it aloud. They could do this alone, with a partner or as a whole-class task.

> 〰️ **CD 1, track 20   Seite 32, Aktivität 1**
>
> See Student Book, page 32, for audio script.

✱ Strategie

It would be useful to cover this information before students start activity 2. Point out the question words used in the comprehension questions (for example. 'Who...?', 'What...?'), which demonstrate what type of information is required.

2 📖 GCSE Read the cartoon about Milo's daily routine again and answer the questions in English.

> Answers: **a** because he works in a hotel; **b** Milo's colleague – he says she's hardworking but not at all nice; **c** the bedrooms; **d** washing up and drying up; **e** ironing; **f** His robot vacuum cleaner vacuums and his dishwasher washes up and dries up.

3 ✏️ Write three true/false questions about Milo's daily routine in English for your partner to answer.

Students can also mark each other's answers if time allows.

➕ Students also write some 'not in the text' questions.

2 Mein Zuhause

> 🎁 **Extra**
>
> Tell students that they need an umlaut in the third person singular form of the verb *abwaschen*: *ich wasche ab* but *er wäscht ab*. They will learn more about irregular verbs with vowel changes in Unit 4.

> **Aa Grammatik**
>
> Remind students that prefixes appear at the beginning of words. In German, these prefixes can move away from the verb. For more practice, use mini-whiteboards to give students some simple translations including separable verbs, gradually increasing the gap between the verb and prefix to demonstrate it always goes at the end of the clause.

4 🎧 **Listen to the people (1–5) answering the questions: *Wie ist deine Alltagsroutine? Wie hilfst du zu Hause?* Which activity do they not mention?**

Each speaker answers the questions ('What is your daily routine?', 'How do you help at home?') with two pieces of information. Students choose the activity which is not mentioned in the answer. Allow students time to note down the German vocabulary that they will need to listen out for before playing the recording.

> *Answers:* **1** *ironing;* **2** *cleaning;* **3** *washing up;* **4** *cleaning the toilet;* **5** *vacuuming*

> 〰️ **CD 1, track 21   Seite 33, Aktivität 4**
>
> 1 – Wie ist deine Alltagsroutine?
>   – Ich putze das Haus und ich arbeite im Garten.
>
> 2 – Wie ist deine Alltagsroutine?
>   – Morgens wasche ich ab und abends trockne ich ab.
>
> 3 – Wie ist deine Alltagsroutine? Wie hilfst du zu Hause?
>   – Ich decke den Tisch im Esszimmer und ich putze das Badezimmer.
>
> 4 – Wie ist deine Alltagsroutine?
>   – Ich sauge Staub und manchmal bügle ich.
>
> 5 – Wie hilfst du zu Hause? Wie ist deine Alltagsroutine?
>   – Ich arbeite im Garten. Ich decke auch den Tisch.

5 💬 **Macht eine Klassenumfrage: „Wie hilfst du zu Hause?"**

Students interview their classmates in German about household chores. You may wish to provide a pre-printed table for them to tick off when recording the survey results.

⭐ An alternative format would be to print out a list of five or six possible answers in full sentences (for example, *Ich wasche ab. Ich bügele.*), so students can tick those that their classmates mention.

➕ Students present their survey results to the class.

6 📖 GCSE **Wer sagt das: Aschenputtel (A) oder eine Aschenputtels Schwestern (S)?**

Students decide whether each sentence is something that Cinderella or one of her sisters would say. They need to use their knowledge of the fairy tale to help them. You may wish to pre-teach *kurz gesagt* ('to put it simply', 'in a nutshell').

> *Answers:* **a** A; **b** S; **c** S; **d** A; **e** S; **f** A; **g** S; **h** A

7 ✏️ **Beschreib deine Alltagsroutine.**

Using the sentence starters provided for support, students write about their own daily routine.

45

2.2 Wie komme ich zu…?

Objectives

- Vocabulary: Saying what there is in town and giving directions
- Grammar: Using *es gibt* with the accusative case
- Strategy: Taking part in a role play

Resources

- Student Book, pages 34–35
- CD 1, tracks 22–24
- Grammar, Vocabulary and Translation Workbook, pages 16–17
- Kerboodle, Unit 2

Key language

- Was gibt es in der Stadt? Es gibt…, Man kann dort…
- das Museum, das Café, das Restaurant, das Hotel, das Geschäft, der Flughafen, das Kino, der Park, die Kirche, die Moschee, die Synagoge, das Hochhaus, die Bushaltestelle, der Bahnhof, der Fluss, der Busbahnhof, die Imbissbude
- Wie komme ich am besten zum/zur…? Nehmen Sie die erste/zweite/dritte Straße links/rechts. Gehen Sie geradeaus/links dann rechts. Es ist auf der linken/rechten Seite. Fahren Sie mit dem Bus Nummer (36).

Homework and self-study

- Student Book, page 35, activity 5
- Grammar, Vocabulary and Translation Workbook, pages 16–17

Starter

- Students look at the words in activity 1 to see how many of them they know already or can work out by using their knowledge of (near-) cognates. They can also practise saying them aloud and could spell them for their partner for additional practice with the alphabet.

Plenary

- Students recall the key nouns from the lesson (those in activity 1) from memory with a partner. They take it in turns to say a word and can only use each word once. The aim is to recall all 14 words without repetition or pausing, so they can repeat this task until they manage this. To reflect on their learning, they could discuss afterwards which words were easiest to recall and why.

1 ✏ Schreib den richtigen Artikel ('der', 'die' oder 'das') für die Vokabeln auf.

Students write the correct definite article for each noun. You could give them some general rules to help; for example, nouns ending in -e are usually feminine and cognates are often neuter. They could also practise reading aloud the singular and plural forms. Ask students to check their answers in a dictionary or the *Glossar* at the back of the Student Book before listening to check their answers in activity 2.

> Answers: das Museum; das Café; das Restaurant; das Hotel; das Geschäft; der Flughafen; das Kino; der Park; die Kirche; die Moschee; die Synagoge; das Hochhaus; die Bushaltestelle; der Bahnhof

2 🎧 Hör zu. Ist alles richtig?

Students listen to the recording to check their answers from activity 1. Ensure that they correct any mistakes.

> 〰 **CD 1, track 22   Seite 34, Aktivität 2**
>
> das Museum – die Museen
> das Café – die Cafés
> das Restaurant – die Restaurants
> das Hotel – die Hotels
> das Geschäft – die Geschäfte
> der Flughafen – die Flughäfen
> das Kino – die Kinos
>
> der Park – die Parks
> die Kirche – die Kirchen
> die Moschee – die Moscheen
> die Synagoge – die Synagogen

46

2 Mein Zuhause

das Hochhaus – die Hochhäuser
die Bushaltestelle – die Bushaltestellen
der Bahnhof – die Bahnhöfe

3 🎧 **Listen to Nesrin talking about her city, Frankfurt. Which landmark in Frankfurt does she not mention?**

Before students list to the recording, you may wish to recap the meaning of *es gibt*. Encourage them also to note down the German for the six landmarks listed (a–f), so they know what to listen out for.

Answer: d

➕ An alternative and more challenging format would be to provide the transcript as a gap-fill task, with all of the nouns from the previous task removed, which students can then fill in when listening.

CD 1, track 23   Seite 34, Aktivität 3

Frankfurt gefällt mir gut.

Dort haben wir alles. Es gibt einen Bahnhof. Es gibt auch Kirchen, eine Moschee und eine Synagoge. Viele Hochhäuser gibt es. Es gibt Museen – das Naturmuseum ist echt toll! Es gibt viel zu tun – es gibt Kinos, Geschäfte und Cafés. Ich gehe nicht gern einkaufen, aber Kaffee trinke ich so gern.

Es gibt auch einen Park. Ich mag Sport und der Park ist mir sehr wichtig.

Ich freue mich auf deinen Besuch.

Grammatik

Recap the meaning of the accusative case and point out that the only change required is with masculine singular nouns.

4 📖 **Emilia besucht Nesrin. Was gibt es noch (*What else is there*) in Frankfurt? Lies Emilias Nachricht und wähl die richtige Antwort.**

Students read Emilia's message to Nesrin and choose the correct option to complete each sentence.

Answers: **a** *fliegt mit dem Flugzeug*; **b** *einen Flughafen*; **c** *der Main*; **d** *ein Café*

5 ✏️ **Was gibt es in deiner Stadt? Schreib einen Blogeintrag.**

Using the sentence starters provided for support, students write a blog entry describing their own town (or anywhere they are familiar with). Remind them that the information doesn't need to be true.

6 🎧 **Hör zu (1–5). Wohin gehen sie und wie kommt man am besten dorthin?** (*Where are they going and what's the best way there?*) **Schreib die richtigen Buchstaben (a–m) auf.**

For each conversation, students note down the letters of the location and the directions mentioned. Explain that they can only use each letter once.

Answers (letters can be in any order):
1 *b, h, k*; **2** *a, g*; **3** *e, i, j*; **4** *c, f, l*; **5** *d, m*

⭐ An alternative and visually simpler format would be to provide students with the locations and directions in a table form, so they can tick those that they hear, rather than having to listen and look for letters.

CD 1, track 24   Seite 35, Aktivität 6

1 – Wie komme ich am besten zur Bushaltestelle?
  – Gehen Sie geradeaus. Die Bushaltestelle ist auf der rechten Seite.
2 – Wie komme ich am besten zum Bahnhof?
  – Nehmen Sie die zweite Straße rechts.
3 – Wie komme ich am besten zum Busbahnhof?
  – Gehen Sie links, dann rechts. Der Busbahnhof ist auf der linken Seite.
4 – Wie komme ich am besten zum Café?
  – Nehmen Sie die erste Straße links. Das Café ist am Ende der Straße
5 – Wie komme ich am besten zum Fluss?
  – Fahren Sie mit dem Bus Nummer 36.

Sprachmuster

You could do some work on mini-whiteboards using the nouns from activity 1 for additional practice; for example, say a noun and ask students to write the correct form of the definite article with *zu*. This is also useful revision of vocabulary and articles.

47

2 Mein Zuhause

> ⚙ **Strategie**
>
> It would be useful to go over this before students start activity 7. You could add some notes to the board for each of these points when discussing them, so that students can refer back to them when preparing their role plays.

7 💬 GCSE **Macht Rollenspiele. Partner A beginnt. Dann tauscht die Rollen.**

Students conduct a role play, asking for and giving directions. Allow students some time individually to prepare and make notes. You could model the task structure and pronunciation beforehand with a confident volunteer.

You could also discuss with the class different ways of saying things if they get stuck in a role play. For example: if they can't remember the word for 'bus stop', they could ask for directions to the 'bus': *Wie komme ich am besten zum Bus?* Similarly, if they can't remember the phrase *Wie komme ich am besten…?*, they could ask a question using *Wo…?* instead: *Wo ist die Bushaltestelle?* Emphasise to students that using a foreign language is all about working with what they know and that the most important thing is to make themselves understood.

➕ Using the example as a model, students create their own role plays, asking and giving directions to some different places in a town. They could base it on their local area or you could provide a simplified map for them to work from.

2.3 Bei uns

2 Mein Zuhause

Objectives

- Vocabulary: Talking about where you live and where you lived before
- Grammar: Using the present, perfect and imperfect tenses together
- Strategy: Varying your language

Resources

- Student Book, pages 36–37
- CD 1, tracks 25–26
- Grammar, Vocabulary and Translation Workbook, pages 18–19
- Kerboodle, Unit 2

Key language

- *Wo wohnst du? Ich wohne/lebe/Wir wohnen/ leben in einem/einer…*
- *das Doppelhaus, das Einfamilienhaus, das Reihenhaus, die Wohnung, der Wohnblock, das Hausboot, das Wohnmobil, das Schloss*
- *am See, am Stadtrand, auf dem Land, in den Bergen, an der Küste, in einem Dorf, in der Stadt*
- *im ersten/zweiten/dritten Stock*
- *Ich finde es/Das finde ich cool/attraktiv/schön/ laut/toll/ruhig/grün/idyllisch/langweilig/ interessant.*
- *Ich wohne/Wir wohnen (nicht) gern hier. Früher habe ich/haben wir … gewohnt. Ich fand es…/ Das fand ich…, Es gibt/gab viel zu tun.*

Homework and self-study

- Student Book, page 37, activity 6
- Grammar, Vocabulary and Translation Workbook, pages 18–19

Starter

- It would be useful preparation for this lesson, particularly for the listening tasks (activities 1 and 2), to revise key adjectives such as *toll, laut, schön, grün, interessant, langweilig, cool, idyllisch* and *attraktiv*. Students could list them in two columns (positive and negative) or you could give students a simple vocabulary test.

Plenary

- Set up a 'trapdoor' speaking activity. This will need to be prepared in advance. Write a short paragraph including key vocabulary from this and previous lessons, with three different options for key words; for example, *Ich wohne in einem Doppelhaus/einem Einfamilienhaus/ einer Wohnung und ich finde das toll/langweilig/ idyllisch*. Students choose an option for each, then take turns to read the whole text aloud, trying to guess their partner's choices. If they choose correctly, they continue. If they are incorrect, they swap over and have to start again at the beginning next time.

---

1 🎧 **Hör zu. In welcher Art von Zuhause wohnen sie (1–6)? (*In what type of home do they live?*) Schreib die richtigen Buchstaben (a–f) auf.**

Students listen and write the correct letter to indicate each speaker's type of home. You may wish to remind students of the question *Wo wohnst du?* and the phrase *Ich wohne…* When discussing the answers to both activities 1 and 2, ensure that students know what terraced, detached and semi-detached houses are in English. The German words *Reihe* ('row'), *Einzel-* ('single') and *Doppel-* ('double') are useful to explain this.

Answers: **1** b; **2** f; **3** c; **4** a; **5** d; **6** e

CD 1, track 25   Seite 36, Aktivität 1

1 – Wo wohnst du?
  – Ich wohne auf einem Hausboot am See. Ich finde es toll!
2 – Wo wohnst du?
  – Ich wohne in einer Wohnung am Stadtrand. Ich wohne gern hier, weil es nicht zu laut ist.
3 – Wo wohnst du?
  – Ich wohne in einem Einfamilienhaus in den Bergen. Es gefällt mir dort, weil es so schön und grün ist.

49

2 Mein Zuhause

4 – Wo wohnst du?
– Ich wohne in einem Reihenhaus in der Stadt und ich finde es toll, denn es ist sehr interessant und gar nicht langweilig.

5 – Wo wohnst du?
– Ich wohne in einem Wohnmobil in einem Dorf. Das finde ich so cool, denn es ist total idyllisch!

6 – Wo wohnt ihr?
– Wir wohnen in einem Doppelhaus auf dem Land. Das Haus ist ganz schön, aber wir wohnen nicht gern hier, weil es so langweilig ist.

2 🎧 GCSE **Listen again. Where is each person's (1–6) home located, and what is their opinion of where they live? Make notes in English.**

You may wish to check understanding of the English 'idyllic' before students listen to the recording. You may also wish to remind students to pay attention to words such as *gar nicht* or *zu*, which affect the meaning.

> Answers: **1** on/by a lake – great; **2** on the outskirts of town – not too noisy; **3** in the mountains – beautiful, green; **4** in town/the city – great, interesting, not at all boring; **5** in a village – cool, (really) idyllic; **6** in the countryside – attractive (house) but (very) boring (area)

🎵 **CD 1, track 26   Seite 36, Aktivität 2**

See activity 1 for audio script.

Sprachmuster

It would be useful go through the *Sprachmuster* box before students start activity 3. You could elicit or remind students that they saw the same pattern in Lesson 2.2 with the word *zu*. You could do some work on mini-whiteboards if more practice would be useful; for example, you say a noun and ask students to write the correct form of the indefinite article with *in*. This could incorporate vocabulary from Lesson 2.2 for additional consolidation work.

3 💬 **Würfelspiel! Werft den Würfel zweimal. (*Dice game! Throw the die twice.*) Benutzt die Wörter aus Aktivität 1 (a–f).**

Students throw a die twice to give a random combination of a pronoun and a type of house. They then form a sentence to tell their partner. If dice are unavailable or unsuitable, write pairs of die scores on the board (for example, 1/6, 2/4, 3/5) and students can just work through these. It may be useful to model this task beforehand with a confident volunteer.

🎁 Extra

Students who include this information could ask their partner to translate it into English, so both of them are practising this additional vocabulary.

Grammatik

It would be useful to cover this before students start activity 4. Draw a timeline on the board to demonstrate that the perfect and imperfect are both in the past and compare them with the present tense *Ich wohne…* The perfect tense is used for a completed event ('I lived in Berlin') and the imperfect tense is generally used in a more descriptive way ('it was great'). If appropriate for the ability of the class, you could explain that the imperfect tense also means 'used to' and that they will learn more about this in Unit 5.

4 📖 GCSE **Read the blog posts. Copy and complete the table in English.**

Remind students to read the texts carefully to find the details they need to complete the table.

2 Mein Zuhause

Answers:

Name	Lives (type of house and place)	Opinion	Used to live (type of house and place)	Opinion
Omar	castle in Austria	romantic	detached house on the outskirts of town	lots to do, liked it
Lily	(second-floor) flat in town/ the city	interesting, lots to do, cool	semi-detached house in the countryside	beautiful, lots of animals, but too quiet
Zacharie	houseboat on Lake Constance	perfect, idyllic	detached house in the mountains	interesting, mountains were beautiful

5 **GCSE** Translate the underlined sentences in the blog posts into English.

> Suggested translations:
> Previously, I lived in a detached house on the outskirts of town.
> I really like living here because it's interesting.
> I found it really lovely and there were lots of animals.
> I find it perfect because it's really idyllic.

⭐ Provide students with the number of words in each translated sentence and/or the first letter of each English word.

Strategie

Before allowing students to look at the examples in the *Strategie* box, collate some ideas as a class for each bullet point. See if any of the ideas they come up with match those in the box. Can they then think of any more to add to your class mind map?

6 Herzlichen Glückwunsch! Du hast in der Lotterie gewonnen! Beschreib dein neues Haus und dein früheres Haus.

Students imagine that they have won the lottery and describe in German their new house and their old house. You could provide the sentence starter *Ich habe €… in der Lotterie gewonnen!* As an additional task, if time permits, they could present their work to their partner or to the class.

2.4 Mein Schlafzimmer

Objectives

- Vocabulary: Talking about your bedroom
- Grammar: Using prepositions with the dative case
- Strategy: Using grammar you already know

Resources

- Student Book, pages 38–39
- CD 1, track 27
- Grammar, Vocabulary and Translation Workbook, pages 20–21
- Kerboodle, Unit 2

Key language

- *In meinem Zimmer habe ich/gibt es... Hier haben wir...*
- *der Fernseher, der Computer, der Schreibtisch, der Schrank, der Kleiderschrank, das Bett, der Sessel, der Stuhl, der Teppich, die Kommode, Pompons (pl), die Lampe, die Lichterkette, Kerzen (pl), das Fenster, die Tür, der Boden*
- *neben, auf, über, vor, in, hinter*
- *Ich persönlich finde es (sehr/wirklich/echt/zu/gar nicht) chaotisch/ordentlich/perfekt/praktisch/ hübsch/gemütlich/organisiert/bunt/bequem.*

Homework and self-study

- Student Book, page 39, activity 6. Students write their presentation about their bedroom.
- Grammar, Vocabulary and Translation Workbook, pages 20–21

Starter

- To prepare for the grammar focus in this lesson, students make a list or mind map about articles, gender, and prepositions (you could also include cases, depending on how much detail you have gone into previously). They could give explanations, examples in English and/or German, or anything else they can remember. It would be useful to do this in pairs.

Plenary

- Students describe a location of two or more items to their partner using prepositions; for example, *Der Computer ist auf dem Schreibtisch.* Their partner draws a rough sketch (either on mini-whiteboards or as rough work in books) to represent this description.

---

1 **Was passt zusammen? Verbinde die Sätze (1–8) mit den Möbeln (*furniture*) (a–h).**

Students match the numbered descriptions of items in Grete's room to the lettered items in the picture.

Answers: **1** d; **2** g; **3** b; **4** a; **5** e; **6** h; **7** f; **8** c

2 **Hör zu. Bring die Texte aus Aktivität 1 (1–8) in die richtige Reihenfolge.**

Students listen to the recording and note down the order in which the texts from activity 1 are mentioned.

Answer: 3, 6, 4, 5, 7, 1, 2, 8

CD 1, track 27   Seite 38, Aktivität 2

Hey Leute! Ich bin Grete. Herzlich Willkommen in meinem Schlafzimmer! Ich habe ein paar Ideen, wie man sein Zimmer schön machen kann!

Wir haben Pompons auf dem Fernseher! Sie sind so hübsch!

Hier ist mein Schreibtisch mit meinem Computer. Natürlich gibt's auch einen Stuhl.

Hier gibt es den Kleiderschrank, und über dem Kleiderschrank hängt eine Lichterkette.

Vor dem Kleiderschrank habe ich meinen Sessel. Der Sessel ist wirklich bequem!

Hier ist mein Bett. Ich liebe mein Bett!

Neben der Tür ist meine Kommode und auf der Kommode steht eine coole Lampe mit Federn.

Der Teppich hinter dem Schreibtisch ist ganz bunt. Das gefällt mir.

Was noch? Ich habe Kerzen gekauft und die Pompons habe ich auf dem Flohmarkt gefunden.

Ich mag mein Zimmer so sehr. Vorher war es langweilig, aber jetzt finde ich es total gemütlich! Bis bald!

2 Mein Zuhause

3 💬 „Wie findest du...?" Macht <u>sechs</u> Dialoge.

Using the key language box as support, students ask for and give opinions about Grete's furniture. They should do this at least six times. Ensure that they understand the meaning of the adjectives before they start and practise pronunciation, if necessary.

➕ Students use conjunctions to list two or three things at once, rather than just one; for example, *Ich persönlich finde den Computer sehr praktisch und ich finde den Sessel echt gemütlich.*

🅰 Grammatik

Remind students that they have already seen this pattern with *in* and *zu* in Lessons 2.2 and 2.3. Avoid mentioning the accusative case at this stage as this may confuse students.

Sprachmuster

Remind students that *in + dem* and *zu + dem* can be contracted to *im* and *zu*, but explain that the other prepositions listed in the *Grammatik* box on this page do <u>not</u> form contractions.

4 🔄 GCSE Übersetz die Sätze ins Deutsche.

A common misconception is that all of the articles in the sentence change. You could model an example to explain or elicit that it is just the article <u>after</u> the preposition which changes.

> *Answers:*
> **a** *Das Bett ist neben der Tür.*
> **b** *Der Sessel ist vor dem Bett.*
> **c** *Die Pompons sind über dem Bett.*
> **d** *Der Computer ist auf dem Schreibtisch.*
> **e** *Die Kommode ist neben dem Kleiderschrank im Schlafzimmer.*

5 📖 Füll die Lücken mit den richtigen Wörtern aus.

Students fill each gap with the correct word, choosing from those listed.

> *Answers:* **1** *der;* **2** *Bett;* **3** *Schreibtisch;* **4** *Computer;*
> **5** *dem;* **6** *Kommode;* **7** *dem;* **8** *Teppich*

➕ Students choose their own word for each gap without looking at the options listed.

6 💬 Beschreib dein Schlafzimmer.

Using the sentence starters for support, students put together a short presentation about their bedroom. They could present this to their classmates and/or partner. As an additional task, they could write it up.

⚙ Strategie

Encourage students to refer to the *Strategie* box while planning their presentations for activity 6. Challenge them to include as many of the ideas as possible in the description of their room.

2.5 Mein zukünftiges Zuhause

Objectives

- Vocabulary: Talking about your future home
- Grammar: Using the future tense with *werden*
- Strategy: Using three time frames

Resources

- Student Book, pages 40–41
- CD 1, tracks 28–29
- Grammar, Vocabulary and Translation Workbook, pages 22–23
- Kerboodle, Unit 2

Key language

- *Ich werde in einem Reihenhaus/einem (großen) Einfamilienhaus/einem Doppelhaus/ einer (modernen) Wohnung wohnen.*
- *Es wird (echt toll) sein./Das wird Spaß machen. Es wird (viele Zimmer) geben. Meine Wohnung/ Mein Haus wird charmant/schön möbliert/ perfekt/echt toll sein. Ich werde (viele Tiere) haben.*
- *Früher habe ich … gewohnt. Heute wohne ich…, In der Zukunft werde ich … wohnen. Es wird (Blumen) geben.*

Homework and self-study

- Student Book, page 41, activity 7
- Grammar, Vocabulary and Translation Workbook, pages 22–23

Starter

- To revise previous vocabulary which will be useful in this lesson, students list the alphabet from A to Z. They then try to come up with a German word for each letter (without looking in their books, if possible), choosing from the topic areas of: household chores; places in a town; house types; rooms in a house; bedroom items; and local area.

Plenary

- Provide students with three locations or house types; for example, *ein Doppelhaus, Österreich* and *auf dem Land*. They write three sentences in the future tense using each word; for example, *Ich werde nicht in einem Doppelhaus wohnen, weil…*

---

1 📖 **Hör zu und lies. Wer wird hier wohnen? Schreib den richtigen Namen.**

Students listen and read the texts. They choose the correct person for each type of house depicted.

Answers: **a** Sascha; **b** Achim; **c** Adnan; **d** Rolf

〰️ **CD 1, track 28   Seite 40, Aktivität 1**

See Student Book, page 40, for audio script.

2 🎧 GCSE **Listen to the people (1–4) talking about where they will live in the future. Copy and complete the table in English.**

Students note down the information in English for each speaker. You may wish to go over the *Grammatik* box before starting this task, or simply tell students for now that *werde* and *wird* both mean 'will'. You may also wish to pre-teach key words such as *Küste* and *Balkon*, or simply remind students to listen out for near-cognates.

Answers:

	Where will they live?	What will it be like?	What will they have?
1	campervan on the coast	small but perfect	three cats
2	block of flats in town/the city	charming	a balcony
3	detached house in the countryside	beautifully furnished	a garden
4	castle in the mountains	really great	100 rooms

〰️ **CD 1, track 29   Seite 40, Aktivität 2**

1 Ich werde in einem Wohnmobil an der Küste wohnen. Es wird klein aber perfekt sein. Ich werde drei Katzen haben.

2 In der Zukunft werde ich in einem Wohnblock in der Stadt wohnen. Meine Wohnung wird charmant sein. Ich werde einen Balkon haben

2 Mein Zuhause

3 Ich werde in einem Einfamilienhaus auf dem Land wohnen. Mein Haus wird schön möbliert sein und ich werde einen Garten haben.

4 In der Zukunft werde ich in einem Schloss in den Bergen wohnen. Es wird echt toll sein. Ich werde hundert Zimmer haben.

Aa Grammatik

A common misconception is that 'going to' (for talking about the future) involves *gehen zu*. Explain that English has two forms of the future ('will' and 'going to'), but German just uses one verb to express both of these: a form of *werden*. Remind students that *ich will* ('I want') is a false friend.

3 💬 „Wo wirst du in der Zukunft wohnen?" Macht Dialoge.

Using the key language box as support, students work in pairs to discuss their future plans. You could model the task with a confident volunteer beforehand and remind students that what they say doesn't need to be true; they are just practising language.

🎁 Extra

Encourage students to use conjunctions to add any additional details. They can incorporate vocabulary from many previous topics, such as colours, family and friends, and countries.

4 📖 Was passt zusammen? Verbinde die Hashtags (1–4) mit den Tweets (a–d).

Students read the tweets and choose a suitable hashtag for each.

Answers: **1** b; **2** c; **3** d; **4** a

5 📖 Read the tweets again. Copy and complete the table with the correct tenses in German.

Students complete the table with the perfect and future tense forms of *wohnen* and *leben*. This is a useful opportunity to discuss the difference between the two verbs: *wohnen* is more closely linked to location and accommodation, whereas *leben* refers to general existence. Both would be translated as 'to live' in English.

Answers:

Infinitive	Perfect (past)	Present	Future
wohnen	ich habe gewohnt	ich wohne	ich werde wohnen
leben	ich habe gelebt	ich lebe	ich werde leben

6 🔄 GCSE Translate the underlined sentences in the tweets into English.

Suggested translations:
Previously, I lived on a small houseboat on/by a lake.
In the future, I will have a big garden.
Now I live in a terraced house and in the future, I will live in a castle on the coast.

⭐ Provide students with the number of words in each translated sentence and/or the first letter of each English word.

⚙ Strategie

You could demonstrate further examples with some simple verbs such as *machen* and *spielen*. Students should gain a sense of accomplishment if they can apply their newly acquired knowledge to these additional verbs.

7 ✏ GCSE Beschreib dein Traumhaus der Zukunft. Schreib einen Beitrag (*contribution*) zu einem Forum.

Students write a paragraph about where they live, have lived and will live, guided by the bullet points. Remind students that the information does not need to be true.

⭐ Provide students with sentence starters for each bullet point.

⚠ Achtung!

Students can use this box to check their written work for accuracy once they have completed activity 7.

2 Kultur

> **Resources**
> - Student Book, pages 42–43
> - CD 1, tracks 30–32

1 🎧 **Hör zu. Verbinde die Beschreibungen (1–3) mit den Bildern (a–c).**

Students listen and choose the image of the correct Bauhaus object to match each description. You may wish to explain that Bauhaus was the name of both a German art movement and an art school which was founded in 1919. Remind students that they don't need to understand everything, but should listen out for key words; for example, colours, or near-cognates such as *Material*, *Glas* and *Metall*. Refer them to the glossary box for help too.

> Answers: **1** c; **2** b; **3** a

CD 1, track 30   Seite 42, Aktivität 1

1. Nun, dieses Objekt aus Wolle hat gelbe, rote und weiße geometrische Formen: Dreieck, Quadrat und Kreis. Ich finde es toll. Geometrisch, attraktiv und modern. Es gefällt mir. Ich mag die Form, das Material und die Farben.
2. Dieses Objekt ist zu modern. Es ist funktional, aus Metall und Glas – das wirkt kalt. Ich finde diesen modernen Stil sehr uninteressant. Gar nicht attraktiv. Ich mag die Form und das Material gar nicht.
3. Dieses Objekt! Es ist so schön. Es gefällt mir. Stahlrohr! Was ist das für eine coole Idee! Und braun! Aus Leder. Total perfekt für mein Schlafzimmer. Ich mag die Form, das Material und die Farben.

2 🎧 **Hör noch einmal zu. Sind die Meinungen (1–3) positiv (P) oder negativ (N)?**

Students listen again and note down whether each opinion is positive or negative.

> Answers: **1** P; **2** N; **3** P

CD 1, track 31   Seite 42, Aktivität 2

See activity 1 for audio script.

3 💬 **Macht Dialoge.**

Using the key language box and example as support, students ask for and give opinions about the Bauhaus objects from activity 1. Before they start, ensure that they understand the meaning of the adjectives and practise pronunciation, if necessary.

> 💡 **Tipp**
>
> Encourage students to use conjunctions such as *und* and *aber* to develop their answers.

4 🎧 **Hör zu. Schreib die Tabelle ab und füll sie aus.**

Students listen and complete the table in German. Before playing the recording, ask students to try to anticipate some of the answers (colour and materials) by studying the photo.

Answers:

Designer	Marcel Breuer
Farbe	schwarz
Wann entworfen?	1926
Materialen	Stahlrohr, Leder

CD 1, track 32   Seite 42, Aktivität 4

Dieser Sessel ist sehr bekannt. Er ist schwarz, aus Stahlrohr und Leder.

Marcel Breuer hat dieses Objekt im Jahr 1926 entworfen. Heutzutage kann man dieses Objekt überall sehen – einfach klasse.

Marcel Breuer hat am Bauhaus in Weimar studiert.

Das Bauhaus interessiert mich. Ich bin sehr begeistert davon. Faszinierend. Dieser Sessel ist hundert Jahre alt, aber so modern. Unglaublich!

2 Mein Zuhause

5 📖 Lies den Artikel über das Bauhaus und finde die passenden Ausdrücke (a–g) auf Deutsch.

Students read the article about Bauhaus and find in the text the German equivalents of the English phrases.

Answers: **a** Viel Glas, viel Beton; **b** in großen Buchstaben; **c** Das Bauhausgebäude; **d** ist heute ein Museum; **e** hat eine Kunstschule gegründet; **f** Heute sind Bauhausmöbel Kultobjekte. **g** Weltweit

6 📖 Read the article again. Are the statements true (T) or false (F)?

Students choose if the statements are true or false, based on the information in the text. Students will need to refer to the fact box on Walter Gropius to decide whether statement e is true or false.

Answers: **a** F; **b** F; **c** T; **d** T; **e** F

➕ Students correct the false sentences.

Answers:
a One hundred years ago a new style was invented.
b Walter Gropius founded an art school.
e Walter Gropius was an architect.

7 ✏️ Präsentiere ein modernes Möbelstück oder ein Bauhaus-Objekt. Such im Internet Informationen über das Objekt und den Designer/die Designerin. Mach Notizen und schreib eine kurze Beschreibung.

Using the example as support, students write a presentation in German about a modern item of furniture or a Bauhaus object. They should make notes first, using the headings listed to help them. Refer students to the *Tipp* box for some additional ideas.

Example answer:
Dieses Objekt ist sehr bekannt.
Das ist ein Teppich aus Wolle und die Farben sind grau, gelb, weiß, rot und schwarz.
Der Stil ist geometrisch.
Es wurde im Jahr 1926 von Anni Albers entworfen.
Ich finde dieses Objekt schön, weil es so bunt ist.

2 Sprachlabor

Objectives
- Separable verbs in the present tense
- Using *es gibt* with the accusative case
- Prepositions with the dative case
- The future tense with *werden*
- Pronunciation: o and ö

Resources
- Student Book, pages 44–45
- CD 1, tracks 33–34
- Grammar, Vocabulary and Translation Workbook, pages 14–23
- Kerboodle, Unit 2

Grammatik

Separable verbs in the present tense

Write a separable verb on the board and label the prefix and main verb. Model how and where the prefix moves to, more than once if needed, and with longer sentences to demonstrate that it can move further and further away from the main verb but always moves to the end of the clause.

1 Put the words in the correct order. Start each sentence with the word in bold.

Answers:
a Ich trockne jeden Tag ab.
b Meine Mutter räumt mein Zimmer auf.
c Ich wasche nicht gern ab.
d Mein Vater steht um sechs Uhr auf.
e Ich gehe mit meinen Freunden aus.
f Wir sehen im Wohnzimmer fern.

2 Complete the sentences with the correct separable prefix.

Answers: **a** ab; **b** zu; **c** an; **d** fern

57

2 Mein Zuhause

⭐ Provide a list of prefixes for students to choose from, including distractors if appropriate.

3 Write <u>four</u> sentences to say who does each of these chores in your home.

Remind students to use the third person form of verbs where needed.

Aa Grammatik
Using *es gibt* with the accusative case

Before starting this section, ask students to recall the indefinite article for the three genders and remind or elicit that only the masculine *ein* changes after *es gibt*. If appropriate for the class, explain that this rule also applies for using the different forms of *kein*.

4 Complete the sentences with *einen*, *eine* or *ein*.

Answers: **a** einen; **b** eine; **c** ein; **d** ein; **e** einen; **f** eine

5 Translate the sentences into German. Check the gender or plural form of the noun if you need to.

Suggested translations:
a Es gibt ein Café. **b** Es gibt keinen Zoo. **c** Es gibt eine Bushaltestelle. **d** Es gab viele Kirchen. **e** Es gab einen Park. **f** Es gab keinen Flughafen.

Aa Grammatik
Prepositions with the dative case

Before starting this section, check that students understand the term 'preposition' and see if they can give any examples (they have focused on *in* and *zu* in this unit). They may also remember the contractions *im*, *zum* and *zur*.

6 Complete the sentences with the correct <u>indefinite</u> article.

Ensure that students know what the indefinite article is.

Answers: **a** einer; **b** einem; **c** einem

7 Complete the sentences with the correct <u>definite</u> article.

Ensure that students know what the definite article is.

Answers: **a** der; **b** dem; **c** dem; **d** In dem/Im

Aa Grammatik
The future tense with *werden*

Remind students that the future tense in English can be expressed as 'I will' or 'I'm going to', but this is expressed with just one verb (a form of *werden*) in German.

8 Complete the sentences with the correct form of *werden*. Then translate the sentences into English.

Answers/Suggested translations:
a werde – I will live in Switzerland.
b wirst – Where will you live?
c wird – My house will have a big garden.
d werdet – You will live in a bungalow.
e werden – We will buy a new sofa.

➕ Students change the sentences into the present tense for additional conjugation practice once finished.

9 Rewrite the sentences in the future tense.

Answers:
a Ich werde in einem Hochhaus wohnen.
b Mein Haus wird einen Balkon haben.
c Mein Vater wird einen neuen Computer kaufen.
d Meine Freunde werden an der Küste wohnen.

⭐ Provide students with the infinitive for each sentence, so they can focus on the forms of *werden*.

Aussprache: o and ö

These tasks require lots of teacher demonstration to provide students with an excellent pronunciation model. You can also play the audio files to demonstrate correct pronunciation.

10 Listen and repeat. Then practise with your partner.

Isolate the sounds first, then move on to using the words that include the sounds.

2 Mein Zuhause

🎵 **CD 1, track 33 Seite 45, Aktivität 10**

See Student Book, page 45, for audio script.

11 Practise saying the tongue twister.

Depending on the ability of the class, you could play some games with this; for example, partners saying alternate words in the sentence, whole-class repetition using different volumes or speeds, or trying to learn the tongue twister-style sentence off by heart.

➕ Students create their own sentence(s).

🎵 **CD 1, track 34 Seite 45, Aktivität 11**

See Student Book, page 45, for audio script.

2 Was kann ich schon?

Resources
- Student Book, pages 46–47
- CD 1, tracks 35–37
- Kerboodle, Unit 2

Reading

1 📖 Was passt zusammen? Verbinde die Fragen (1–10) mit den Antworten (a–j).

Students match the questions and answers. Remind them to look carefully at the tenses and pronouns in each question and answer, as this will help them match them up correctly.

Answers: **1** j; **2** f; **3** d; **4** a; **5** b; **6** h; **7** c; **8** g; **9** e; **10** i

2 📖 Füll die Lücken aus.

Students fill each gap with the correct word, choosing from those provided.

Answers: **1** Stadt; **2** Küste; **3** Deutschland; **4** schön; **5** ein; **6** Zoo; **7** wohne; **8** der; **9** werde; **10** Garten

Listening

3 🎧 GCSE Hör zu. Notiere die Meinung (1–5): positiv (P), negativ (N) oder beides (P+N).

Students listen and decide whether each speaker's opinion of where they live is positive, negative or both.

Answers: **1** P; **2** P+N; **3** N; **4** N; **5** P

🎵 **CD 1, track 35 Seite 46, Aktivität 3**

1 Ich wohne in einem Dorf in den Alpen und ich liebe es, weil es total idyllisch ist.
2 Ich wohne in Berlin. Es gibt hier alles: Kinos, Geschäfte, Cafés, Parks, alles, aber es ist oft sehr laut.
3 Ich wohne auf dem Land, aber ich finde das sehr langweilig. In der Zukunft werde ich in einer Großstadt wohnen, denn dort kann man viel machen!
4 Ich wohne in einem Hochhaus. Leider ist es sehr alt und nicht sehr schön. Außerdem ist unsere Wohnung zu klein.
5 Ich wohne in einem Haus in der Nähe von Hamburg. Das Haus ist klein, aber wir haben einen großen Garten und mein Zimmer ist echt cool. Ich finde mein Haus perfekt.

4 🎧 GCSE Listen to Bilal talking about his present, past and future homes. For each home, write the location, his opinion and any details about the home in English. Include <u>two</u> details about his present home.

It may be easier for students to note down this information in table form. You could pre-print this for them, to save time.

59

2 Mein Zuhause

Answers:

Present: *location – village in south of Germany; opinion – charming, lots of friends, super weather; details about home – (any two details) detached house, 3 bedrooms, 2 bathrooms, (beautiful) garden*

Past: *location – Stuttgart; opinion – too noisy; details about home – tower block, no garden*

Future: *location – America/San Diego; opinion – loves the coast, perfect; details about home – modern flat on outskirts of town*

CD 1, track 36   Seite 46, Aktivität 4

Ich wohne in einem Dorf im Süden von Deutschland. Ich finde das Dorf charmant. Ich habe viele Freunde hier und das Wetter ist super. Wir wohnen in einem Einfamilienhaus. Es gibt drei Schlafzimmer, zwei Badezimmer und einen schönen Garten.

Früher haben wir in Stuttgart gewohnt, aber ich fand die Stadt zu laut. Wir haben in einem Hochhaus gewohnt und wir hatten keinen Garten.

In der Zukunft werde ich in Amerika wohnen. Ich werde in einer modernen Wohnung am Stadtrand von San Diego wohnen, weil ich die Küste liebe. Es wird perfekt sein.

5 Hör zu (1–5) und schreib die richtigen Buchstaben (a–e) auf. Beginne am Pfeil. *(Start at the arrow.)*

Students listen and follow on the map the directions mentioned in each audio extract, starting at the arrow. They note down the letter of the correct end destination each time.

Answers: **1** c; **2** b; **3** e; **4** d; **5** a

CD 1, track 37   Seite 46, Aktivität 5

1 – Wie komme ich am besten zum Museum?
– Gehen Sie geradeaus und nehmen Sie die dritte Straße rechts. Das Museum ist auf der rechten Seite.

2 – Wie komme ich am besten zum Kino?
– Nehmen Sie die erste Straße links und gehen Sie dann nach rechts. Das Kino ist auf der linken Seite.

3 – Hallo. Wie komme ich am besten zum Bahnhof?
– Zum Bahnhof nehmen Sie die zweite Straße rechts und der Bahnhof ist am Ende der Straße.

4 – Guten Tag. Wie komme ich am besten zum Schwimmbad?
– Gehen Sie hier nach links und das Schwimmbad ist auf der rechten Seite. Es ist nicht weit.

5 – Wie komme ich am besten zum Café Mozart, bitte?
– Ähm… Gehen Sie geradeaus. Das Café ist am Ende der Straße.

Writing

6 GCSE Beschreib das Bild. Schreib <u>fünf</u> Sätze.

Students write five sentences in German to describe the photo of a bedroom. For each sentence, award one mark for communication and one for accuracy. Refer them to the *Tipp* box for a reminder of *im*.

Suggested answers (any five of):
Im Zimmer gibt es ein Bett, einen Sessel, einen Teppich, einen Kleiderschrank, eine Lampe und ein Fenster.
Über dem Bett ist ein Fenster./Das Fenster ist über dem Bett.
Vor dem Bett ist ein Teppich./Der Teppich ist vor dem Bett.
Neben dem Bett gibt es eine Lampe (auf einem Tisch)./Die Lampe ist neben dem Bett.
Hinter dem Sessel ist ein Kleiderschrank./Der Kleiderschrank ist hinter dem Sessel.

7 GCSE Übersetz die Sätze ins Deutsche.

Students translate the sentences into German. There are two marks available for each sentence. Award one mark if there are any minor mistakes.

Suggested translations:

a *Ich wohne/lebe gern in Berlin, weil es viele Geschäfte und Cafés gibt.*
b *Wir wohnen in einer großen Wohnung, aber wir haben keinen Garten.*
c *Früher/Vorher habe ich auf dem Land gewohnt, aber ich fand das langweilig/ich habe das langweilig gefunden.*
d *Jeden Tag decke ich den Tisch und ich wasche ab.*
e *Nächste Woche werde ich eine Lampe kaufen.*

2 Mein Zuhause

2 Vorankommen!

Resources
- Student Book, pages 48–49
- CD 1, tracks 38–40
- Kerboodle, Unit 2

Bronze

1 📖 **Choose the correct answer to complete each sentence.**

Encourage students to think about meaning and sense, as well as grammatical accuracy, when working out which is the correct option to complete each sentence.

Answers: **a** einer; **b** einen; **c** Schreibtisch; **d** decke; **e** Früher; **f** grün

2 🎧 **Listen to the people (1–5) asking for directions. Choose the correct place (a–d) and route (e–h).**

Explain to students that each letter can only be used once.

Answers: **1** d, f; **2** b, e; **3** a, g; **4** c, h

〰️ **CD 1, track 38   Seite 48, Aktivität 2**

1 – Hallo, wie komme ich am besten zum Park?
– Nehmen Sie die erste Straße rechts.

2 – Guten Tag, wie komme ich zum Museum?
– Gehen Sie links, dann rechts.

3 – Guten Morgen, wie komme ich zur Kirche?
– Gehen Sie geradeaus. Die Kirche ist auf der linken Seite.

4 – Grüß Gott, wie komme ich am besten zum Bahnhof?
– Nehmen Sie die zweite Straße links. Sie sind in fünf Minuten dort.

---

3 ✏️ **Write sentences in German using the words.**

Suggested answers:
a Ich wohne in einer Stadt./Meine Stadt ist schön/groß/klein/laut.
b Mein Zimmer ist schön/groß/klein./Ich mag mein Zimmer./In meinem Zimmer gibt es/habe ich…
c Früher habe ich in einem Dorf/einem Hochhaus/in den Bergen gewohnt.
d In meiner Stadt/meinem Dorf gibt es kein Kino./Früher gab es kein Kino.
e In meinem Haus gibt es eine Küche./In der Küche wasche ich ab./Die Küche ist schön/groß/klein/modern.

Silber

4 📖 **GCSE Read about Oliver's home now and in the past. Complete the sentences in English.**

Answers: **a** campervan; **b** on/by the coast, in the mountains; **c** living room, dining room; **d** (very) comfortable; **e** (beautiful) semi-detached house; **f** I do what I want and when I want

5 🎧 **GCSE Listen to Ralf talking about his family's spring clean and the tasks for Ralf, his brother, his father and his mother. Copy and complete the table in English.**

You may wish to remind students that they will hear the future tense, as this is about future plans. Explain that they may have to infer answers from other information given if an activity is not specifically mentioned.

61

2 Mein Zuhause

Answers:

Person	Place	Activity
father	bathroom	clean shower and toilet
mother	garage	tidy up
brother	garden	cut the grass/mow the lawn
Ralf	kitchen	vacuum and clean cabinets

CD 1, track 39   Seite 48, Aktivität 5

Morgen wird meine Familie Frühjahrsputz machen. Das wird ganz schön anstrengend, aber wir werden alle helfen.

Mein Vater wird das Badezimmer putzen, weil er das besser macht als wir alle. Er wird die Dusche und die Toilette putzen.

Meine Mutter wird die Garage aufräumen. Wir haben viele alte Sachen in der Garage!

Mein Bruder wird im Garten arbeiten, weil das Gras viel zu lang ist.

Ich werde in der Küche Staub saugen und die Schränke putzen.

Unser Haus wird so sauber und ordentlich aussehen wie schon lange nicht mehr!

6 ✏ **Schreib fünf Sätze über deine Zukunftspläne. Benutz die Wörter und schreib längere Sätze mit ‚weil'.** Write five sentences about your future plans. Use the words and write longer sentences with *weil*.

Remind students of the word order rules with *weil*, if necessary.

Suggested answers:
Ich werde in einem Schloss wohnen (, weil das toll ist).
Ich werde einen Hund haben (, weil ich Hunde/Tiere liebe).
Ich werde an der Küste wohnen (, weil ich das Meer liebe/weil das toll ist).
Ich werde nie Staub saugen (, weil das anstrengend/langweilig ist).
Mein Schlafzimmer wird (nicht) rosa sein (, weil Rosa meine Lieblingsfarbe ist, weil ich Rosa nicht mag).

Gold

7 📖 GCSE **Lies den Text. Richtig (R), falsch (F) oder nicht im Text (NT)?**

Students read the text and decide whether each statement is true, false or not in the text. They may need extra help to distinguish between 'false' and 'not in the text': a statement is 'false' is if there is contradictory information in the text to make the statement obviously incorrect; a statement is 'not in the text' if we have no idea, as the text doesn't include any information about this.

Answers: **a** F; **b** F; **c** R; **d** NT; **e** NT; **f** R; **g** F; **h** R

8 🎧 **Hör zu. Lara war letztes Wochenende in Basel. Bring die Bilder (a–h) in die richtige Reihenfolge.**

Students put the images in the order in which they are mentioned in the recording.

Answer: c, h, a, b, d, f, g, e

CD 1, track 40   Seite 49, Aktivität 8

Letztes Wochenende bin ich mit meiner Freundin Petra mit dem Zug nach Basel gefahren: das ging echt schnell – in einer Stunde waren wir da. Wir waren zum ersten Mal in der Stadt und es war super. Basel ist echt cool! Wir sind vom Bahnhof geradeaus in die Stadtmitte gegangen. In der Stadtmitte gibt es keine Autos, das ist wirklich toll. Es gibt da viele Geschäfte, aber sie waren ein bisschen teuer. Ich habe nur ein paar Tafeln Schweizer Schokolade gekauft. Wir sind dann nach rechts zum Rhein gegangen und haben in einem Café am Fluss Cola getrunken. Ich fand das sehr entspannend. Das nächste Mal werden wir in Basel auch ins Museum und in den Zoo gehen.

🎁 **Extra**

It may be more appropriate for some students to concentrate on the adjectives without the intensifiers.

Answers: (echt) schnell – (really) quick; super – super/great; (echt) cool – (really) cool; (wirklich) toll – (really) great; (ein bisschen) teuer – (a bit) expensive; (sehr) entspannend – (very) relaxing

9 ✏ GCSE **Schreib einen Text (zirka 80 Wörter) zum Thema „Mein Zuhause".**

Students write approximately 80 words on the topic of 'my life at home', guided by the bullet points: bedroom, chores, where they used to live and where they will live in the future. Remind them to check their work carefully, especially the past and future tenses.

3 Das Alltagsleben

Unit overview				
Page reference	**Vocabulary**	**Grammar**	**Strategy**	**Key language**
54–55 3.1 Meine Alltagsroutine	Talking about daily routines	Using reflexive verbs in the present tense	Checking your written work for errors	aufwachen, aufstehen, sich waschen, sich duschen, sich rasieren, sich anziehen, sich entspannen, ins Bett gehen, einschlafen, sich amüsieren, sich interessieren (für etwas) Wie ist deine Alltagsroutine? Um wie viel Uhr wachst du auf? Ich wache um … (Uhr) auf. Um wie viel Uhr stehst du auf? Ich stehe um … (Uhr) auf.
56–57 3.2 Willst du woanders zur Schule gehen?	Talking about daily life in the German-speaking world	Using sequencers with reflexive and separable verbs	Including cultural knowledge in your work	zuerst, dann, nach (der Pause/ dem Mittagessen/dem Abendessen/ der Schule), danach, später, am Abend Die Schule beginnt um (acht Uhr). Ich entspanne mich. Ich gehe in die (Informatik)-AG. Ich mache meine Hausaufgaben. Ich gehe in die Mensa. Ich sehe Netflix. Ich gucke auf mein Handy.
58–59 3.3 Wollen wir uns treffen?	Making plans and excuses	Using *wollen* + the infinitive	Reacting to the unpredictable	Willst du…? Wollen wir…? Wollt ihr…? ein Videospiel machen, ins Café gehen, in die Stadt gehen, in den Park gehen, Skateboard fahren, einkaufen gehen, angeln gehen, Backgammon spielen Wollen wir uns treffen? Willst du mit (ins Kino) kommen? Ich kann nicht (mitkommen). Es tut mir leid. Leider kann ich nicht. Ja! Gerne. Ach nein! Das ist schade. Wieso denn? Ach Quatsch! Das gibt's nicht. Keine Chance! Ich bin super enttäuscht. Ich muss mich um meine Schwester kümmern/meine Oma besuchen/ meine Hausaufgaben machen/ mit meinem Hund spazieren gehen. Ich habe kein Geld.

63

3 Das Alltagsleben

Unit overview				
Page reference	**Vocabulary**	**Grammar**	**Strategy**	**Key language**
60–61 3.4 Projekt: Gesund leben	Talking about healthy living	Revising *man soll* and *man muss*	Writing without support	Was ist dein Rezept für ein gesundes Leben? Man soll Tai Chi oder Yoga machen/ Sport treiben/aktiv sein/nachts nicht auf das Smartphone gucken/positiv denken. Man muss genug schlafen/Zeit mit Freunden oder der Familie verbringen/ gesund essen/viel Wasser trinken/ manchmal eine Pause machen. Ich nehme mir ein bisschen Zeit für mich. Das ist für mich wichtig/unwichtig. Das macht mich glücklich/unglücklich. Das stresst mich (nicht). Das nervt mich (gar nicht). Das ist richtig/falsch. Das stimmt (nicht).
62–63 3.5 Wer macht was bei euch?	Comparing chores in different families	Revising subordinate clauses with *weil* and *wenn*	Recycling language	kochen, die Papiermüllkiste rausbringen, meinen/meine/mein … sauber machen, für meine Familie einkaufen gehen, Autos waschen, das Badezimmer putzen …wenn/weil meine Eltern arbeiten. …wenn/weil meine Mutter/mein Vater spät nach Hause kommt. …weil ich Geld dafür kriege. …wenn/weil meine Eltern sehr viel zu tun haben. …weil ich für einen/eine/ein … spare. Wer macht was bei euch? Bekommst du Geld? Wie findest du die Rollenverteilung? Das finde ich ganz fair. Das finde ich in Ordnung. Das finde ich total unfair. in unserem Haushalt

3 Das Alltagsleben

3 Los geht's!

Starter
- Students practise reading aloud the unfamiliar vocabulary in activity 1. They could also try to work out the meanings of the compound nouns.

Plenary
- Ask students to summarise some of the new things that they have learnt in this lesson in a 3–2–1 activity: three key words, two interesting facts and one difference between school in England and in German-speaking countries. They can share these with the class or with a partner.

1 In der Mensa (*canteen*). Lies den Speiseplan eines liechtensteinischen Gymnasiums (the *menu from a secondary school in Liechtenstein*) und finde die passenden Wörter (a–f) auf Deutsch.

Students find on the menu the German equivalents for the English food-related words. Encourage them to use their language detective skills; for example, are they looking for a noun or an adjective? Can they see any (near-) cognates? Can they use the context for help? You could mention that *Semmel* is a regional word used for 'bread roll' (for example, in southern Germany), and discuss the other specialities mentioned.

Answers: **a** *pikant;* **b** *hausgemacht;* **c** *täglich;* **d** *frisch;* **e** *zum Mitnehmen;* **f** *Früchtekorb*

⭐ Tell students which day to look at to find the correct answers; for example, 'homemade' = Monday or Thursday.

2 Lies den Speiseplan noch einmal. Was wählst du für jeden Tag aus? (*What do you choose for each day?*)

Students read the menu again to decide what they would choose for each day of the week. They then create sentences in German, using the example sentence starter as support. They could do this individually in writing or could work in pairs and take turns to tell their partner what they would choose. Remind students of the 'verb-second' rule when they place the time expression at the start of the sentence.

Kultur

You could see how much students recall from *Echt 1* by asking them what they remember about the school day in Germany: early start and finish times, break times, not necessarily eating lunch at school, etc.

3 Read the facts about the sleeping habits of German people. Complete the sentences in English.

You may wish to pre-teach *schlafen* and the third person form *schläft*. You could ask students if they are surprised by the facts presented in the text.

Answers: **a** *8, 12;* **b** *28;* **c** *219,000, third;* **d** *5, 12;* **e** *sleep in pyjamas*

➕ Students write out the numbers from the text (492; 28; 219,000; 75; 47) in full words in German.

4 Lies den Text über die Schweizer Bahnhofsuhr und wähl die richtige Antwort.

Students read the text and choose the correct option to complete each sentence. You may wish to discuss the word *Uhr*. Students might recognise it (meaning 'o'clock') from learning to tell the time in *Echt 1*. Explain that it is a false friend and does not mean 'hour' in this context.

Answers: **a** *Bahnhof;* **b** *die Uhr entworfen;* **c** *rot*

➕ Students translate the text into English.

Suggested translation:
The Swiss railway station clock is world-famous. Hans Hilfiker designed the clock in 1944. Hilfiker was influenced by the Bauhaus movement. In this clear, reduced/minimalist design, you see black lines for the minutes and hours on a white background, with black minutes and hours hands and a red second hand. Three colours: black, red, white. An absolute classic.

65

3.1 Meine Alltagsroutine

Objectives
- Vocabulary: Talking about daily routines
- Grammar: Using reflexive verbs in the present tense
- Strategy: Checking your written work for errors

Resources
- Student Book, pages 54–55
- CD 1, tracks 41–43
- Grammar, Vocabulary and Translation Workbook, pages 28–29
- Kerboodle, Unit 3

Key language
- aufwachen, aufstehen, sich waschen, sich duschen, sich rasieren, sich anziehen, sich entspannen, ins Bett gehen, einschlafen, sich amüsieren, sich interessieren (für etwas)
- Wie ist deine Alltagsroutine? Um wie viel Uhr wachst du auf? Ich wache um … (Uhr) auf. Um wie viel Uhr stehst du auf? Ich stehe um … (Uhr) auf.

Homework and self-study
- Student Book, page 55, activity 9
- Grammar, Vocabulary and Translation Workbook, pages 28–29

Starter
- To revise telling the time, students draw a rough, blank clock and label it in German with as much detail as they can recall (numbers 1–12, numbers 5–25, quarter, half, to, past, at, o'clock). They could also add numbers 13–23 for the 24-hour clock.

Plenary
- In their books as rough work, students work in pairs or small groups to play Hangman in German. The phrases should be based on the language covered in the lesson and can be made more challenging by adding times, which therefore requires correct spelling of numbers.

1 Was passt zusammen?

Students match the daily-routine sentences with the images of Snow White and the Seven Dwarves. You could also ask them to note down another very useful (non topic-specific) reflexive verb: *sich interessieren für* (to be interested in). Give them the following sentences and ask them to translate them: *Ich interessiere mich für Sport. Sie interessiert sich für Science-Fiction.*

Answers: **1** g; **2** f; **3** h; **4** a; **5** b; **6** d; **7** c; **8** e

Students note down which verbs are reflexive, which are separable and which are both. They could do this as a Venn diagram.

Grammatik

It would be useful to go over this information before students start activity 2. Explain that German and English behave differently when it comes to these verbs, and that a direct translation isn't always possible. For example, *mich* means 'myself', but we don't say 'I shower myself'. Conversely, 'I have a shower' in German doesn't use the verb *haben*.

2 Füll die Lücken aus.

Students fill the gaps with the correct pronoun, reflexive pronoun or verb. They adapt the verbs in brackets for sentences d and e. Refer them to the *Grammatik* box for support, particularly for adapting the separable verb (*sich anziehen*) in sentence e.

Answers: **a** dich; **b** mich; **c** Wir; **d** entspannen, uns; **e** zieht, sich, an

Provide students with the correct answers to choose from, including distractors if appropriate.

3 Translate the sentences from activity 2 into English.

Suggested translations:
a You (have a) shower at seven o'clock.
b I shave at quarter past seven.
c We have fun all day.
d We relax after dinner.
e He gets dressed at half (past) seven.

3 Das Alltagsleben

4 🎧 **Hör zu. Wie ist Ninas Alltagsroutine (1–6)? Schreib die richtigen Buchstaben aus Aktivität 1 (a–h) auf.**

Students listen to Nina describing her daily routine and note down the letters of the activities from activity 1 that she mentions. Point out to students that the first audio extract requires two letters. You may wish to pre-teach (and leave on the board for reference) the questions *Um wie viel Uhr…?* and *Was machst du sonst?*

Answers: **1** g, f; **2** b; **3** c; **4** h; **5** d; **6** e

➕ Students also note down the times mentioned.

Answers: **1** 6 a.m.; **2** 6.10 a.m.; **3** 8 p.m.; **4** 9.30 p.m.; **5** 10.30 p.m., 10.45 p.m.; **6** all day

CD 1, track 41   Seite 54, Aktivität 4

1 – Um wie viel Uhr wachst du auf?
   – Ich wache um sechs Uhr auf und ich stehe sofort auf.

2 – Um wie viel Uhr ziehst du dich an?
   – Ich ziehe mich um zehn nach sechs an und dann verlasse ich das Haus.

3 – Wann entspannst du dich?
   – Ich entspanne mich nach dem Abendessen um acht Uhr abends.

4 – Um wie viel Uhr duschst du dich?
   – Ich dusche mich um halb zehn.

5 – Um wie viel Uhr gehst du ins Bett?
   – Ich gehe um 22 Uhr 30 ins Bett und schlafe um 22 Uhr 45 ein.

6 – Was machst du sonst?
   – Ich amüsiere mich den ganzen Tag! Jeden Tag!

5 💬 **Macht Dialoge. Partner A stellt Fragen und Partner B antwortet. Dann tauscht die Rollen.**

Using the example as support, students create dialogues, asking for and giving information about daily routines. You could model the task structure and pronunciation beforehand with a confident volunteer. You may wish to write on the board a list of questions if students are likely to struggle to manipulate the verbs into questions.

6 📖 **Listen and read. Find six reflexive verbs in the text and translate them into English.**

Once students have listened to the recording, you could exploit the text further by asking them to read (sections of) it aloud. They could do this alone, with a partner or as a whole-class task.

Answers/Suggested translations (in any order):
ich ziehe mich an – I get dressed;
ich dusche mich – I (have a) shower;
ich amüsiere mich – I have fun;
ich interessiere mich für – I'm interested in;
ich wasche mich – I (have a) wash;
ich entspanne mich – I relax

➕ Students could try this as a listening task, without looking at the text.

CD 1, track 42   Seite 55, Aktivität 6

See Student Book, page 55, for audio script.

7 📖 **GCSE Read the text again. Copy and complete the table for Kurt and Mindy in English.**

Answers:

Name	Daily routine	Other details
Kurt	gets up at 6.00; gets dressed (puts on spacesuit and helmet); showers once a week	works in control centre (for the Mars mission); takes photos; does experiments, has fun on Mars – it's (really) cool; is interested in the planet and his work
Mindy	wakes at 5.00; goes to bed at midnight; washes (in the craters); relaxes with friends in the evening	astronauts don't know she is there; interested in the astronauts and robots; the atmosphere on Mars is no problem for her

67

3 Das Alltagsleben

8 🎧 **Listen to Ronald the Robot talking about his daily routine. In your table from activity 7, complete another row in for Ronald in English.**

Answers:

Name	Daily routine	Other details
Ronald	wakes up; doesn't shave; doesn't get dressed; never goes to bed; prepares the food/cleans the room at midday; plays music (the latest Mars hits) for the astronauts after dinner	lives in the Mars Village with the astronauts; doesn't have to wake up in the morning because he never sleeps; works in the Mars Village

〰️ CD 1, track 43   Seite 55, Aktivität 8

Hallo. Ich heiße Ronald und bin ein Roboter. Ich wohne hier auf dem Mars im Marsdorf mit den Astronauten.

Morgens muss ich nicht aufwachen, denn ich schlafe nie ein!

Ich rasiere mich nicht. Ich ziehe mich nicht an.

Ich gehe nie ins Bett, weil ich ein Roboter bin!

Ich arbeite hier im Marsdorf. Mittags zum Beispiel bereite ich das Essen vor oder putze das Zimmer. Nach dem Abendessen spiele ich die neuesten Mars-Hits für die Astronauten.

9 ✏️ **Stell dir vor (*Imagine*), du wohnst auf der Venus. Bist du Astronaut/Astronautin, Venusmensch oder Roboter? Schreib einen Blogeintrag über deine Alltagsroutine.**

Students imagine that they are an astronaut, alien or robot living on Venus, and describe their daily routine in German. They should use the texts from activity 6 as a model.

⭐ Students write about life on earth, explaining their daily routine to someone from another planet.

➕ Students write their blog entry in the third person; for example, *Vera ist Venusmensch. Sie wohnt in den Venusbergen…*

⚙ Strategie

Before students declare their written work for activity 9 'finished', tell them to use this checklist. They could also swap with a partner and peer-assess each other's work. Alternatively, while you are circulating, you could point out or mark errors in relation to the checklist in the *Strategie* box.

3 Das Alltagsleben

3.2 Willst du woanders zur Schule gehen?

Objectives

- Vocabulary: Talking about daily life in the German-speaking world
- Grammar: Using sequencers with reflexive and separable verbs
- Strategy: Including cultural knowledge in your work

Resources

- Student Book, pages 56–57
- CD 1, tracks 44–46
- Grammar, Vocabulary and Translation Workbook, pages 30–31
- Kerboodle, Unit 3

Key language

- zuerst, dann, nach (der Pause/dem Mittagessen/dem Abendessen/der Schule), danach, später, am Abend
- Die Schule beginnt um (acht Uhr). Ich entspanne mich. Ich gehe in die (Informatik)-AG. Ich mache meine Hausaufgaben. Ich gehe in die Mensa. Ich sehe Netflix. Ich gucke auf mein Handy.

Homework and self-study

- Student Book, page 57, activity 6

- Grammar, Vocabulary and Translation Workbook, pages 30–31

Starter

- To revise vocabulary from Lesson 3.1 and prepare for the grammar focus in this lesson, students recall key verbs from Lesson 3.1 and write them out in two lists: reflexive and separable. Or, for a more formalised task, you could provide a list of the verbs from Lesson 3.1 as a vocabulary quiz (half to translate into English, half into German) and once completed, ask them to note down whether the verbs are reflexive or separable.

Plenary

- To practise word-order rules with sequencers, students work in pairs. One student starts the sentence by saying a sequencer (for example, *zuerst*), then their partner adds one suitable word (for example, *wache*) to continue the sentence. The first partner adds a logical third word and the pair continues to add alternate single words until they have created a complete, accurate German sentence.

1 Listen and read Mathea's description of her school life. Are the statements true (T) or false (F)?

Students listen and read the text and decide whether the statements are true or false. As background to this activity, you could provide students with some additional cultural information about Liechtenstein or show some images or a map. It's a German-speaking principality (ruled by a prince), bordered by Switzerland and Austria. It's a rich, land-locked country with the highest gross domestic product per capita in the world. It's very mountainous and is a popular winter sports destination. The capital city is Vaduz and the currency is the Swiss franc.

Answers: **a** F; **b** F; **c** F; **d** T; **e** F; **f** T

➕ Students correct the false sentences.

Answers: **a** Mathea goes to school in Liechtenstein. **b** She gets up at 6.15 a.m. **c** Break lasts 20 minutes. **e** Mathea does have a mobile phone.

CD 1, track 44   Seite 56, Aktivität 1

See Student Book, page 56, for audio script.

Grammatik

It would be useful to go over this information before students start activity 2. See if they can recall these sequencers in both languages without looking at the box. Remind them or elicit that the verb is always the second idea, but not necessarily the second word.

2 Rewrite the text using the sequencers in brackets. Then translate the text into English.

Suggested answer/translation:
Wie ist meine Alltagsroutine? Zuerst wache ich um sieben Uhr auf. Dann stehe ich um zehn nach sieben auf. Danach dusche ich mich und dann ziehe ich mich an. Später mache ich meine Hausaufgaben.

69

3 Das Alltagsleben

What is my daily routine? First, I wake up at seven o'clock. Then I get up at ten past seven. After that, I have a shower and then I get dressed. Later, I do my homework.

3 🎧 GCSE **Listen to Kwame talking about a typical school day (1–4). Copy and complete the table in English.**

Answers:

	Time/Sequencer	Activity
1	6.30 a.m. first after that	gets up makes his bed has a shower and gets dressed
2	7.45 a.m. then 12.00 p.m./ midday	school begins, he has three lessons has break goes to canteen (eats pizza or sandwich)
3	after school later	does homework plays video games
4	after dinner/ evening meal 10 p.m.	looks at phone goes to bed

⭐ An alternative format for this task would be to provide students with a partly filled-in table (half times/sequencers, half activities). They can then have practice with both sets of vocabulary but do not need to record as much information.

🎵 **CD 1, track 45   Seite 56, Aktivität 3**

Hallo, ich heiße Kwame und bin in der zehnten Klasse.
1. Ich stehe um halb sieben auf. Zuerst mache ich mein Bett und danach dusche ich mich und ziehe mich an.
2. Die Schule beginnt um Viertel vor acht. Ich habe drei Stunden und dann eine Pause. Um zwölf Uhr gehe ich in die Mensa. Ich esse eine Pizza oder ein belegtes Brötchen.
3. Nach der Schule mache ich meine Hausaufgaben. Später spiele ich Videospiele.
4. Nach dem Abendessen gucke ich auf mein Handy. Ich gehe um 22 Uhr ins Bett.

4 📖 GCSE **Listen and read Victor's description of his German school in Lagos, Nigeria. Answer the questions in English.**

You may wish to pre-teach *Gast* ('host') in the context of school exchanges.

Answers: **a** two months; **b** because he is going to bed earlier; **c** Do you have internet there? **d** yes; **e** his parents, his host family, many students and teachers

🎵 **CD 1, track 46   Seite 57, Aktivität 4**

See Student Book, page 57, for audio script.

🎭 **Kultur**

You could also point out Nigeria and Lagos on a map.

5 💬 **Macht ein Interview mit Mathea oder Victor.**

Using the phrases provided as support, students conduct interviews as either Mathea or Victor from activities 1 and 4. You could model the task structure and pronunciation beforehand with a confident volunteer. Students may need preparation time to note down their answers.

Aussprache: *ie*, *ei* and *au*

Once students have practised saying the words, they could move on to sentences; for example:
Ich stehe auf und dann ziehe ich mich an.
Im Liechtensteinischen Gymnasium sind meine Lieblingsfächer Biologie und Chemie.
Ich bin fleißig. Ich mache immer meine Hausaufgaben.
They could also try some tongue twisters; for example:
Dreihundertdreiunddreißig Reiter ritten dreihundertdreiunddreißigmal um das große runde Rastenburger Rathaus.
Kleine Kinder können keine Kirschkerne knacken.

6 ✏️ **Stell dir vor, du wohnst in einem deutschsprachigen Land. Schreib einen Blogeintrag über deine Alltagsroutine.**

Students imagine that they live in a German-speaking country and write a blog about their daily routine. Encourage them to use the texts from activities 1 and 4 as a model.

⚙️ **Strategie**

Before students start the writing task, brainstorm as a class any facts that students may know about German-speaking countries that they could include in their work; for example, timings of the school day or typical food and drink.

3 Das Alltagsleben

3.3 Wollen wir uns treffen?

Objectives
- Vocabulary: Making plans and excuses
- Grammar: Using *wollen* + the infinitive
- Strategy: Reacting to the unpredictable

Resources
- Student Book, pages 58–59
- CD 1, tracks 47–48
- Grammar, Vocabulary and Translation Workbook, pages 32–33
- Kerboodle, Unit 3

Key language
- *Willst du...? Wollen wir...? Wollt ihr...?*
- *ein Videospiel machen, ins Café gehen, in die Stadt gehen, in den Park gehen, Skateboard fahren, einkaufen gehen, angeln gehen, Backgammon spielen*
- *Wollen wir uns treffen? Willst du mit (ins Kino) kommen?*
- *Ich kann nicht (mitkommen). Es tut mir leid. Leider kann ich nicht. Ja! Gerne. Ach nein! Das ist schade. Wieso denn? Ach Quatsch! Das gibt's nicht. Keine Chance! Ich bin super enttäuscht.*
- *Ich muss mich um meine Schwester kümmern/ meine Oma besuchen/meine Hausaufgaben machen/mit meinem Hund spazieren gehen. Ich habe kein Geld.*

Homework and self-study
- Student Book, page 59, activity 7
- Grammar, Vocabulary and Translation Workbook, pages 32–33

Starter
- To revise key verbs in preparation for this lesson, provide students with a list of nouns, each followed by a gaps to which students should add a suitable infinitive; for example, *Ins Kino _____, Meine Oma _____*. Based on the Lesson 3.3 content, the most useful verbs are *spielen, gehen, fahren, treffen, kommen, besuchen* and *machen*.

Plenary
- Provide a short 'tangled translation' text or some sentences for students to complete (or they could create their own for a partner). The text should be written with sentences containing both languages; for example, *Ich kann nicht* come with you. *Es tut mir leid,* but I have to *meine Hausaufgaben machen*. Students write out the correct version either in English, in German or in both languages.

---

1 🎧 **Hör zu. Was wollen sie machen (1–8)? Schreib die richtigen Buchstaben (a–h) auf.**

Students listen and note down the letter of the correct photo for each speaker. They may not be familiar with the game Backgammon, so you may wish to explain what this is before they start the task. As preparation, students could also note down any German vocabulary they already know related to the photos; for example, e – *Kino, Filme*.

Answers: **1** d; **2** g; **3** b; **4** h; **5** c; **6** a; **7** e; **8** f

➕ Students note down in English when each activity is planned for. Challenge them also to spot the reflexive verb used: *sich treffen* in number 8.

Answers: **1** this evening; **2** at the weekend; **3** later; **4** later; **5** at the weekend; **6** tomorrow; **7** on Sunday; **8** at the weekend

CD 1, track 47   Seite 58, Aktivität 1

1. Willst du heute Abend ein Videospiel spielen?
2. Willst du am Wochenende in die Stadt gehen?
3. Wollen wir später Skateboard fahren?
4. Wollen wir später in den Park gehen?
5. Willst du am Wochenende angeln gehen?
6. Willst du morgen Backgammon spielen?
7. Willst du am Sonntag mit ins Kino kommen?
8. Wollen wir uns am Wochenende treffen?

3 Das Alltagsleben

2 📖 **Was passt zusammen? Verbinde die Fragen (1–8) mit den Bildern aus Aktivität 1 (a–h).**

Students match the questions to the photos from activity 1.

> Answers: **1** a; **2** g; **3** b; **4** f; **5** c; **6** d; **7** e; **8** h

➕ Students translate the questions into English. Explain that *Wollen wir...?* is translated as 'Shall we...?' rather than 'Do we want to...?'

> *Suggested translations:*
> 1 Do you want to play Backgammon tomorrow?
> 2 Do you want to go into town at the weekend?
> 3 Shall we go skateboarding later?
> 4 Shall we meet (up) at the weekend?
> 5 Do you want to go fishing at the weekend?
> 6 Do you want to play a video game this evening?
> 7 Do you want to go to the cinema on Sunday?
> 8 Shall we go to the park later?

Sprachmuster

Depending on the ability of the class, you could also elicit or recap what these phrases would be in the dative case, i.e. when talking about being in a place already (*in dem/im Park, in der Stadt, in dem/im Kino*).

Grammatik

Ensure that students understand the term 'infinitive', eliciting or providing examples if needed, and that they understand that the suggestion *Wollen wir...?* ('Shall we...?') is not translated as 'Do we want to...?'.

3 🎧 GCSE **Listen to the questions and answers (1–6). Copy and complete the table in English.**

Answers:

	When?	Activity
1	at the weekend	go skateboarding
2	tomorrow	go to the cinema
3	at the weekend	go into town
4	tomorrow	go to the café
5	later	play a video game
6	at the weekend	go fishing

⭐ An alternative format for this task would be to provide students with a partly filled-in table (half time markers, half activities). They can then have practice with both sets of vocabulary but do not need to record as much information.

➕ Students also note down the reasons given for not accepting the invitation.

> Answers: **1** is visiting grandma; **2** has to look after sister; **3** has to walk the dog; **4** has no money; **5** has to do homework; **6** –

🎵 **CD 1, track 48   Seite 58, Aktivität 3**

1 – Willst du am Wochenende Skateboard fahren?
  – Ich kann nicht. Ich besuche meine Oma.
  – Ach nein! Das ist schade.
2 – Willst du morgen ins Kino gehen?
  – Ach nein, leider muss ich mich um meine Schwester kümmern.
  – Keine Chance!
3 – Willst du am Wochenende in die Stadt gehen?
  – Ich kann nicht mitkommen. Ich muss mit meinem Hund spazieren gehen.
  – Das tut mir leid.
4 – Wollen wir morgen ins Café gehen?
  – Es tut mir leid. Ich habe kein Geld.
  – Wieso denn?
5 – Willst du später ein Videospiel spielen?
  – Ach nein! Ich muss meine Hausaufgaben machen.
  – Ach, ich bin super enttäuscht.
6 – Willst du am Wochenende angeln gehen?
  – Ja! Gerne.

4 📖 GCSE **Read @Piachen's invitation and the responses. Answer the questions with the correct username.**

Remind students that they won't always see the answer in the text in exactly the same words as in the questions. For example, for question e ('Who has to clean the house?'), @Ove doesn't specifically say *Ich muss das Haus sauber machen*, but he does mention various cleaning tasks, from which students can infer that he has to clean the house.

> Answers: **a** @Piachen; **b** @Dannyboy; **c** @Lasse; **d** @Lasse; **e** @Ove; **f** @Lasse

3 Das Alltagsleben

5 🔄 GCSE **Übersetz die Sätze ins Deutsche.**

Students translate the sentences into German. You may wish to use these sentences to demonstrate the time–manner–place rule. This is covered in more detail in Unit 5.

> *Suggested translations:*
> *a Ich will am Donnerstag ins Kino gehen.*
> *b Sie wollen schwimmen gehen.*
> *c Wollen wir ein Videospiel spielen?*
> *d Er will später Skateboard fahren.*

> ✱ **Strategie**
>
> Model and practise pronunciation of these useful phrases as preparation for activity 6, and demonstrate that intonation is also important.
>
> The following reactions appear in the conversations in activities 3 and 4:
>
> *Ach nein. Das ist schade.*
>
> *Wieso denn?*
>
> *Keine Chance!*
>
> *Das/Es tut mir leid.*
>
> *Ich bin super enttäuscht.*

6 💬 **Macht drei Dialoge.**

Using the example as support, students create three dialogues, making and responding to invitations based on the information provided in the table. You could model the task structure and pronunciation beforehand with a confident volunteer.

⭐ An alternative format for this task would be to provide students with full sentences, which they complete as a 'trapdoor'-style task. Students read the text aloud, trying to guess their partner's chosen option in each sentence. If they guess correctly, they move on to the next one, but if they guess incorrectly, they swap over and start again. This allows them to practise speaking without having to formulate their own sentences.

🎁 **Extra**

Once students have completed activity 6, they could revisit their dialogues and try to add the reactions from the *Strategie box*.

7 ✏️ **Deine Mutter will mit dir einkaufen gehen und du hast keine Lust. Schreib die längstmögliche Entschuldigung.** (*Write the longest possible excuse.*)

Students write the longest possible excuse for not going shopping, drawing on the excuses covered in this lesson. This could be developed further as a speaking activity or memory game, in which students give an excuse and the next person in the group repeats it and adds their own, as many times as possible. If anyone forgets an excuse, they start the task again from the beginning.

3.4 Projekt: Gesund leben

Objectives

- Vocabulary: Talking about healthy living
- Grammar: Revising *man soll* and *man muss*
- Strategy: Writing without support

Resources

- Student Book, pages 60–61
- CD 1, tracks 49–50
- Grammar, Vocabulary and Translation Workbook, pages 34–35
- Kerboodle, Unit 3

Key language

- *Was ist dein Rezept für ein gesundes Leben?*
- *Man soll Tai Chi oder Yoga machen/Sport treiben/aktiv sein/nachts nicht auf das Smartphone gucken/positiv denken.*
- *Man muss genug schlafen/Zeit mit Freunden oder der Familie verbringen/gesund essen/viel Wasser trinken/manchmal eine Pause machen.*
- *Ich nehme mir ein bisschen Zeit für mich. Das ist für mich wichtig/unwichtig. Das macht mich glücklich/unglücklich. Das stresst mich (nicht). Das nervt mich (gar nicht). Das ist richtig/falsch. Das stimmt (nicht).*

Homework and self-study

- Student Book, page 61, activity 7
- Grammar, Vocabulary and Translation Workbook, pages 34–35

Starter

- Students create two columns in their books (as rough work, if necessary) for *Gesund* and *Ungesund* and then note down relevant vocabulary in German. They will probably include food, drink and activities, and the vocabulary could be nouns, verbs and possibly adjectives (for example, *faul, sportlich*). This is useful revision for the activities in this lesson and can be referred back to in the freer practice provided in activity 7.

Plenary

- Select a key phrase from the lesson (for example, *Man soll positiv denken*), or allow students to choose their own. It can be from any activity. Students then add to the phrase in three different ways: once with *aber* (for example, *...aber ich bin manchmal negativ*), once with *und* and once with *denn* or *weil*.

1 Was ist ein Rezept für ein gesundes Leben? Füll die Lücken aus.

Students complete the tips on healthy living by filling each gap with the correct word from those provided. You may wish to revise the meaning of *man muss* and *man soll* before students start this activity.

> Answers: **a** *Yoga machen;* **b** *Sport, aktiv;* **c** *nachts, Smartphone;* **d** *schlafen;* **e** *muss, Familie;* **f** *essen, Wasser* **g** *positiv;* **h** *Pause*

2 Hör zu. Ist alles richtig?

Students listen to the recording to check their answers from activity 1. Ensure that they correct any mistakes. After listening, you could do some whole-class, individual and/or paired reading aloud to practise pronunciation.

CD 1, track 49   Seite 60, Aktivität 2

a   Man soll Tai-Chi oder Yoga machen.
b   Man soll Sport treiben oder irgendwie aktiv sein.
c   Man soll nachts nicht auf das Smartphone gucken.
d   Man muss genug schlafen.
e   Man muss Zeit mit Freunden oder der Familie verbringen.
f   Man muss gesund essen und viel Wasser trinken.
g   Man soll positiv denken.
h   Man muss manchmal eine Pause machen.

3 Das Alltagsleben

3 🎧 **Hör zu. Katja und Medi reden über das Rezept für ein gesundes Leben. Bring die Tipps aus Aktivität 1 (a–h) in die richtige Reihenfolge. Ist Medis Meinung dazu positiv (✓) oder negativ (✗)?**

Students listen to the recording and arrange the tips from activity 1 in the order in which they are mentioned. They then decide if Medi's opinion of each tip is positive or negative. Allow students time to read and digest the opinion phrases in the key language box before they start the activity, and to do some pronunciation practice if time allows. It would be useful to split the task into two distinct parts: firstly, listening out for the order of the tips, and then secondly, noting down the opinion.

Answer: f ✓, g ✗, b ✓, h ✗, a ✗, c ✓, d ✗, e ✓

⭐ Instead of ordering the tips and adding a tick or cross, students simply note down in English all of the tips they hear, in no particular order.

〰️ CD 1, track 50   Seite 60, Aktivität 3

– Wie findest du das Rezept für ein gesundes Leben, Medi?
– Man muss gesund essen und viel Wasser trinken. Das ist mir wichtig. Ich esse immer gesund und ich trinke viel Wasser.
– Man soll positiv denken.
– Das nervt mich und ist mir nicht wichtig. Manchmal kann man negativ sein.
– Man soll Sport treiben oder irgendwie aktiv sein.
– Das stresst mich nicht. Ich bin immer aktiv.
– Man muss manchmal eine Pause machen.
– Nein, das ist falsch. Manchmal will ich keine Pause machen.
– Man soll Tai-Chi oder Yoga machen.
– Das macht mich unglücklich. Ich will kein Yoga machen.
– Man soll nachts nicht auf das Smartphone gucken.
– Ja, das ist richtig. Das nervt mich gar nicht.
– Man muss genug schlafen.
– Das ist mir eigentlich nicht wichtig. Ich schlafe ungefähr fünf Stunden.
– Man muss Zeit mit Freunden oder der Familie verbringen.
– Ja, natürlich. Das macht mich glücklich.

4 💬 **Macht Dialoge.**

Using the example as support, students create a dialogue, asking for and giving tips on healthy living. You could model the task structure and pronunciation beforehand with a confident volunteer. Remind students of the importance of intonation when responding to the statements.

Aa Grammatik

You may wish to revisit how to translate *man*, and recap or elicit what an infinitive is.

5 📖 **Lies die Blogeinträge über ein gesundes Leben. Finde die passenden Sätze (a–e) auf Deutsch.**

Students read the blog entries about healthy living and find in the text the German equivalents for the English phrases listed.

Answers:
a Das war keine gute Idee!
b Dann habe ich mir ein bisschen Zeit für mich genommen.
c Total ungesund. Nein, danke.
d Es gibt so viele Regeln.
e Man soll keine süßen Getränke trinken.

⭐ Provide students with the first word(s) of each German phrase.

➕ Students translate one or more of the sections into English. Ahmed and Soleya's entries offer additional practice with the perfect tense.

Suggested translations:
Ahmed: *Normally I'm very active and always eat healthily. You should do sport and be active. I find that important. But yesterday I was (together) with friends and I ate four hamburgers. I also drank a litre of cola. That wasn't a good idea!*
Soleya: *Yesterday I did yoga and then I took a bit of time for myself. (You should have a break at some point anyway.) But today it was different. I worked the whole day and that stressed me out so much. Totally unhealthy. No, thanks.*

3 Das Alltagsleben

Melda: There are so many rules: you should eat and drink healthily every day. You should eat vegan or vegetarian food. You shouldn't drink sweet drinks. You should eat vegetables regularly. That annoys me/gets on my nerves. I want to live how I want to!

6 GCSE Read the blog posts again. Are the statements true (T), false (F) or not in the text (NT)?

Remind students of the distinction between 'false' (there is contradictory information in the text to make the statement obviously incorrect) and 'not mentioned' (we have no idea, as the text doesn't include any information about this).

Answers: **a** NT; **b** T; **c** T; **d** F; **e** NT; **f** T

Extra

Once students have completed the *Extra* task, they could highlight, underline or make a note of the past tense verbs and translate them.

Answers:
Past: ich war, ich habe … gegessen, ich habe … getrunken, das war, ich habe … gemacht, ich habe … genommen, es war, ich habe … gearbeitet, das hat … gestresst
Present: ich bin, (ich) esse, man soll, ich finde, man muss, es gibt, das nervt, ich will

Strategie

Before student start activity 7, ask them to come up with their own plan for the task and to see if any of their points match those covered in this box.

7 Was ist *dein* Rezept für ein gesundes Leben?

Students write their own tips for healthy living, using the language covered in the lesson for support.

⭐ Before starting the writing task, look at the plan provided in the *Strategie* box together and come up with some sentence starters for each point, so students have an example of planning their own structure alongside some key vocabulary.

3 Das Alltagsleben

3.5 Wer macht was bei euch?

Objectives

- Vocabulary: Comparing chores in different families
- Grammar: Revising subordinate clauses with *weil* and *wenn*
- Strategy: Recycling language

Resources

- Student Book, pages 62–63
- CD 1, track 51
- Grammar, Vocabulary and Translation Workbook, pages 36–37
- Kerboodle, Unit 3

Key language

- *kochen, die Papiermüllkiste rausbringen, meinen/meine/mein … sauber machen, für meine Familie einkaufen gehen, Autos waschen, das Badezimmer putzen*
- *…wenn/weil meine Eltern arbeiten. …wenn/weil meine Mutter/mein Vater spät nach Hause kommt. …weil ich Geld dafür kriege. …wenn/weil meine Eltern sehr viel zu tun haben. …weil ich für einen/eine/ein … spare.*
- *Wer macht was bei euch? Bekommst du Geld? Wie findest du die Rollenverteilung? Das finde ich ganz fair. Das finde ich in Ordnung. Das finde ich total unfair. in unserem Haushalt*

Homework and self-study

- Student Book, page 63, activity 6
- Grammar, Vocabulary and Translation Workbook, pages 36–37

Starter

- To revise key language from Lesson 3.4 alongside the grammar point covered in this lesson ('Revising subordinate clauses with *weil* and *wenn*'), provide students with two short sentences; for example, *Ich bin gesund. Ich schlafe viel.* Students then join these up and rewrite them using *weil* or *wenn*, whichever is most suitable.

Plenary

- Students return to the tweets in activity 1 and change at least one element in the sentences that use *weil* or *wenn*; for example: *…, weil ich für ein **Videospiel** spare.* This can be done verbally or as a written task, in pairs or alone.

---

1 🎧 **Lies die Tweets und dann hör zu. Wer spricht (1–6)? Finde den passenden Hashtag in den Tweets.**

Students listen and match the speakers to the hashtags in the tweets. Before playing the recording, allow students time to read the tweets thoroughly and encourage them to identify key words to listen out for. Clarify that the audio extracts will not be identical to the tweets, but that students need to listen to the gist of what is said and then work out which of the tweets covers similar information.

Answers: **1** *#Haushalt;* **2** *#Regenbogenfamilie;* **3** *#Geld;* **4** *#Modernefamilie;* **5** *#Recyceln;* **6** *#Patchworkfamilie*

🎵 **CD 1, track 51   Seite 62, Aktivität 1**

1   Ich habe zwei Kaninchen. Ich mache meinen Kaninchenstall sauber, weil ich Geld dafür bekomme. Das finde ich in Ordnung. Ich liebe meine Kaninchen und sie müssen sauber sein.

2   Wir sind vier in meiner Familie: ich, meine zwei Mütter und mein Bruder. Kochen gefällt mir. Ich koche, wenn meine Eltern arbeiten. Das finde ich okay. Ich muss den Tisch für das Frühstück oder das Abendessen decken.

3   Ich muss unbedingt ein Handy haben. Alle meine Freunde haben schon eins. Ich wasche Autos und ich staubsauge sie, weil ich für ein Handy spare.

4   Ich gehe ganz oft für meine Familie einkaufen, weil meine Eltern sehr viel zu tun haben. Sie arbeiten ganz viel.

77

3 Das Alltagsleben

5   Recyceln ist ganz wichtig. Wir müssen uns um unseren Planeten kümmern. Wenn ich die Papiermüllkiste rausbringe, kriege ich Geld. Recyceln ist wichtig in unserem Haushalt.

6   Meine Mutter und mein Stiefvater verstehen sich gut. Aber mein Stiefbruder... er macht alles, was er will. Ich muss das Badezimmer putzen, weil er das Auto waschen will. Das finde ich unfair.

2 📖 **Find examples of these structures in the tweets in activity 1.**

Answers:
opinions: *Das finde ich okay. Das finde ich in Ordnung. Das finde ich nicht so fair.*
modal verb + infinitive: *ich muss ... decken, ich muss ... putzen; ...mein Stiefbruder das Auto waschen will.*
nouns: *(any five) Müttern, Bruder, Tisch, Frühstück, Abendessen, Eltern, Papiermüllkiste, Geld, Recyceln, Haushalt, Meerschweinchenstall, Ordnung, Familie, Autos, Handy, Mutter, Stiefvater, Badezimmer, Stiefbruder, Auto*

➕ Rather than students just identifying nouns, provide them with a list in English and ask them to find the German equivalents in the tweets, thereby working out their correct meaning.

Aa Grammatik

On the board, model and explain how to use *weil* and *wenn* and the subsequent verb order.

Start with two separate sentences (for example, *Ich putze das Badezimmer. Meine Eltern arbeiten.*) and demonstrate how they should be combined with the correct word order (for example, *Ich putze das Badezimmer, weil meine Eltern arbeiten.*) You could contrast these with coordinating conjunctions, such as *und* and *aber*, to demonstrate the different word-order rules.

3 ✏️ **Verbinde die Sätze. Benutz die Konjunktion in Klammern (*brackets*).**

Students join the sets of sentences using *weil* or *wenn*, as specified in brackets. If necessary, remind students again of the word-order rule after *weil* and *wenn* (the verb goes to the end of the clause).

Answers:
a *Ich gehe einkaufen, weil meine Eltern arbeiten.*
b *Ich wasche Autos, weil ich Geld dafür bekomme.*
c *Luis kocht, wenn seine Mutter spät nach Hause kommt.*

⭐ Tell students which words in each of the second sentences are verbs, so they know which word moves to the end.

➕ As an additional or alternative task, students start their sentences with the subordinating conjunction. This is more challenging as it also requires them to rearrange the information and use the 'verb–comma–verb' rule.

Answers:
a *Weil meine Eltern arbeiten, gehe ich einkaufen.*
b *Weil ich Geld dafür bekomme, wasche ich Autos.*
c *Wenn seine Mutter spät nach Hause kommt, kocht Luis.*

4 📖 GCSE **Read the article about family roles. Choose the correct answer to complete each sentence.**

You may wish to pre-teach *Rolle(n)*.

Answers: **a** children; **b** earns; **c** 20; **d** mothers; **e** roles; **f** new

5 💬 **Macht Dialoge.**

Using the example as support, students create dialogues asking for and giving information about household chores. You could model the task structure and pronunciation beforehand with a confident volunteer. Students may need some time to prepare and make notes.

6 ✏️ **Schreib einen Tweet über die Rollenverteilung in deinem Haushalt. Benutz ungefähr 280 Zeichen (*characters*).**

Guided by the bullet points, students write a tweet about how chores are allocated in their house. Remind them that the information doesn't need to be true. Encourage them to adhere to the 280-character limit, as this will help them write more succinctly and accurately.

➕ Students include information in the perfect tense and/or imperfect tense and come up with a hashtag for their tweet.

3 Das Alltagsleben

> ⚙ **Strategie**
>
> Before students declare their written work for activity 6 'finished', tell them to use this checklist. They could also swap with a partner and peer-assess each other's work. Alternatively, while you are circulating, you could point out improvements or note down examples of good work in relation to the checklist in the *Strategie* box.

3 Kultur

> **Resources**
> - Student Book, pages 64–65
> - CD 1, tracks 52–54

1 📖 GCSE **Listen and read the article about Jürgen Klopp. Complete the sentences in English.**

Students fill the gaps based on the information in the text. To exploit this task further, you could ask students to listen to the recording before reading the text, and to make notes of anything they can understand. They can then check this information by reading the text. You may need to explain who Jürgen Klopp is: a former *Bundesliga* (German national football league) player, who now manages Liverpool Football Club. You may also wish to pre-teach *Freibad* ('outdoor pool') and contrast it with *Schwimmbad* ('indoor pool').

> Answers: **a** Kloppo; **b** best-known German, best trainer; **c** two sisters, parents; **d** swimming, the summer/Glatten/an outdoor swimming pool; **e** football player; **f** football trainer, Liverpool

⭐ Provide the answers for students to choose from, adding several plausible distractors to increase challenge, if appropriate.

> 〰 **CD 1, track 52   Seite 64, Aktivität 1**
>
> See Student Book, page 64, for audio script.

2 🎧 **Hör zu. Sind die Meinungen zu Jürgen Klopp (1–4) positiv (P) oder negativ (N)? Welche Adjektive hörst du?**

Students listen to the opinions about Jürgen Klopp and note down whether they are positive or negative. They also note down the adjectives that they hear about him.

> Answers: **1** P – der beste, gar nicht arrogant;
> **2** N – langweilig, (zu) perfekt;
> **3** P – (total) normal; **4** N – guter Trainer, nicht so spannend

⭐ Students note down the adjectives in English rather than German.

> 〰 **CD 1, track 53   Seite 64, Aktivität 2**
>
> 1 Hallo, ich bin Simone und ich bin ein großer Fan vom ‚Kloppo'. Er ist der beste Trainer der Welt und ist gar nicht arrogant.
>
> 2 Ich heiße Klaus und mag Jürgen Klopp gar nicht. Seinen Stil finde ich langweilig, und er ist irgendwie zu perfekt.
>
> 3 Hallo, ich heiße Silvia. Ich komme aus Glatten und wohne immer noch hier. Für uns hat Jürgen Klopp Helden-Status. Er sieht auch total normal aus und das gefällt mir.

3 Das Alltagsleben

4 Ich bin Jens. Klopp ist nicht für mich. Guter Trainer, ja. Aber der Fußballstil ist nicht so spannend.

3 📖 Hör zu und lies. Finde die passenden Wörter (a–l) auf Deutsch.

Students read the text and find the German equivalents of the English vocabulary in the text. As in activity 1, you could exploit this task further by asking students to listen to the recording before reading the text and to make notes of anything they can understand. They can then check this information by reading the text.

Answers: **a** Beziehung; **b** in der Nähe von; **c** Ferienhaus; **d** Insel; **e** pünktlich; **f** schnell; **g** während; **h** SMS; **i** ermutigen; **j** engagiert sich; **k** gegen den Rassismus; **l** Helden-Status

🎵 CD 1, track 54   Seite 65, Aktivität 3
See Student Book, page 65, for audio script.

4 📖 GCSE Read the text again and answer the questions in English.

Answers: **a** his second wife; **b** seven bedrooms, three living rooms and a cinema; **c** on the island of Sylt (in Germany); **d** early; **e** he has hero status

5 💬 Macht ein Interview mit Jürgen Klopp.

Using the questions provided, students conduct an interview with Jürgen Klopp. You could model the task structure and pronunciation beforehand with a confident volunteer. Assign roles, if necessary, to decide who will ask the questions and who will answer. Then remind students to swap roles when appropriate.

6 ✏️ Schreib einen Artikel über oder ein Interview mit Martina Voss-Tecklenburg.

Based on the information in the profile, students write about Martina Voss-Tecklenburg, either in the first or third person. If they are writing an interview, they should use (and adapt, with teacher support if necessary) the questions from activity 5.

3 Sprachlabor

Objectives

- Reflexive verbs in the present tense
- Using *wollen* + the infinitive
- Revising *man soll* and *man muss*
- Revising subordinate clauses with *weil* and *wenn*
- Pronunciation: *sch*, *sp* and *st*

Resources

- Student Book, pages 66–67
- CD 1, tracks 55–56
- Grammar, Vocabulary and Translation Workbook, pages 28–37
- Kerboodle, Unit 3

Aa Grammatik

Reflexive verbs in the present tense

Before starting this section, see if students can recall any reflexive pronouns. Explain or elicit that reflexive verbs in German don't always have direct English translations; for example, a literal translation of *ich dusche mich* would not make sense. Remind students to conjugate the verb and to use the correct reflexive pronoun.

1 Which of these are reflexive verbs in German? Write the *ich* form.

Answers: **a** to have a wash – ich wasche mich; **c** to relax – ich entspanne mich; **d** to have a shower – ich dusche mich; **e** to shave – ich rasiere mich; **h** to have fun – ich amüsiere mich

3 Das Alltagsleben

2 Complete the text with the correct reflexive pronouns.

Answers: **1** sich; **2** mich; **3** mich; **4** sich; **5** sich; **6** sich

Aa Grammatik
Using wollen + the infinitive

Before starting this section, remind students that the second verb is an infinitive, which goes to the end of the clause. You may wish to remind students that *ich will* ('I want') does not mean 'I will'.

3 Complete the sentences with the correct form of *wollen*.

Answers: **a** Willst; **b** wollen; **c** will; **d** will; **e** wollen; **f** Wollt

4 Write sentences with the words and the correct form of *wollen*. For an extra challenge, try to include time markers in your sentences.

Answers (*indicates where a time marker could go):
a Ich will * Fußball spielen.
b Willst du * ins Kino gehen?
c Kim will * in die Stadt gehen.
d Wir wollen * ein Videospiel spielen.
e Ich will * Pizza essen.
f Tanja und Mesut wollen * Skateboard fahren.

Aa Grammatik
Revising man soll and man muss

Before starting this section, remind students that the second verb is an infinitive which goes to the end of the clause.

5 Put the words in the correct order. Start each sentence with the word in bold.

Answers:
a Man soll Yoga machen.
b Man muss viel Wasser trinken.
c Man soll 8 bis 10 Stunden schlafen.
d Man muss viel Obst essen.
e Man soll Sport treiben.
f Man soll manchmal eine Pause machen.

6 Translate the sentences into German.

Suggested translations:
a Man soll jeden Tag Gemüse essen.
b Man soll Freunde treffen.
c Man soll zwei Liter Wasser pro Tag trinken.
d Man muss gesund essen.
e Man muss genug schlafen.
f Man muss positiv denken und aktiv sein.

★ Provide students with the infinitive that they will need in each sentence.

Aa Grammatik
Revising subordinate clauses with weil and wenn

Elicit or explain that *weil* and *wenn* only affect the verbs which appear <u>after</u> them in the clause. When used with modal verbs, this may result in two verbs at the end of the clause.

7 Combine the two sentences using *weil* or *wenn*.

Answers:
a Ich esse Kekse, weil/wenn ich Hunger habe.
b Ich höre Rockmusik, weil das meine Lieblingsmusik ist.
c Meine Eltern entspannen sich, wenn sie fernsehen.
d In Deutschland trägt man keine Uniform, wenn man zur Schule geht.

3 Das Alltagsleben

8 Put the words in the second half of each sentence in the correct order.

> Answers: **a** weil ich zu Hause helfen muss; **b** wenn meine Mutter arbeiten muss; **c** wenn er zu Hause ist; **d** weil er immer faulenzen will

⭐ Provide students with the last word in each sentence and remind them that the first word after the comma will be the subordinating conjunction (*weil* or *wenn*).

9 Translate the sentences from activity 8 into English.

> *Suggested translations:*
> **a** I can't go out today because I have to help (out) at home.
> **b** I help a lot at home when/if my mother has to work.
> **c** My father likes cooking when/if he's at home.
> **d** Ralf doesn't like helping (out) at home because he always wants to laze around.

> **Aussprache: *sch*, *sp* and *st***
>
> These tasks require lots of teacher demonstration to provide students with an excellent pronunciation model. You can also play the audio files to demonstrate correct pronunciation.

10 Listen and repeat. Then practise with your partner.

Isolate the sounds first, then move on to using the words that include the sounds.

> 〰️ **CD 1, track 55   Seite 67, Aktivität 10**
>
> See Student Book, page 67, for audio script.

11 Practise saying the tongue twister.

Depending on the ability of the class, you could play some games with this; for example, partners saying alternate words in the sentence, whole-class repetition using different volumes or speeds, or trying to learn the tongue twister-style sentence off by heart.

➕ Students create their own sentence(s).

> 〰️ **CD 1, track 56   Seite 67, Aktivität 11**
>
> See Student Book, page 67, for audio script.

3 Was kann ich schon?

> **Resources**
>
> - Student Book, pages 68–69
> - CD 1, tracks 57–58
> - Kerboodle, Unit 3

Reading

1 📖 Choose the correct heading for each sentence.

> Answers: **before school:** a, c, g, j; **at school:** d, h, i; **after school:** b, e, f

2 📖 GCSE Wer sagt das: Pilot Anton (PA), Prinzessin Beate (PB) oder Piratin Clara (PC)?

When completing this activity, students should use their common sense and knowledge of what life is like for a pilot (male in this instance), a princess and a pirate (female in this instance).

> Answers: **a** PA; **b** PC; **c** PA; **d** PC; **e** PB; **f** PA; **g** PC; **h** PB; **i** PC; **j** PB

3 Das Alltagsleben

Listening

3 🎧 **Listen to the advice for healthy living (1–10). Decide if each piece of advice is good (✓) or bad (✗).**

Answers: 1 ✗; 2 ✗; 3 ✓; 4 ✓; 5 ✗; 6 ✗; 7 ✓; 8 ✓; 9 ✓; 10 ✗

〜〜 **CD 1, track 57   Seite 68, Aktivität 3**

1 Man soll jeden Tag Schokolade essen.
2 Man soll viel Limonade trinken.
3 Man soll Sport treiben.
4 Zur Entspannung soll man Yoga machen.
5 Man soll nur vier Stunden schlafen.
6 Man soll in der Nacht das Handy benutzen.
7 Man soll positiv denken.
8 Man muss viel Wasser trinken.
9 Man muss manchmal eine Pause machen.
10 Man soll kein Obst und Gemüse essen.

---

4 🎧 **Listen to Otto's daily routine and complete the sentences in English.**

Answers: **a** eight to nine; **b** 7.45; **c** 6.30; **d** gets dressed; **e** eat breakfast; **f** with friends in a café; **g** salad, vegetables and fish; **h** basketball; **i** cinema; **j** social networks/social media

---

〜〜 **CD 1, track 58   Seite 68, Aktivität 4**

Normalerweise schlafe ich zwischen acht und neun Stunden.
Bei uns beginnt die Schule um Viertel vor acht.
Morgens stehe ich um halb sieben auf.
Ich dusche mich und ich ziehe mich an.
Man soll ein gesundes Frühstück essen, aber normalerweise habe ich keine Zeit zum Frühstücken.
Zu Mittag esse ich mit meinen Freunden in einem Café.
Normalerweise esse ich ziemlich gesund: Ich esse gern Salat, Gemüse und Fisch.
Nach der Schule gehe ich in die Basketball-AG, weil ich sehr sportlich bin.
Am Wochenende treffe ich meine Freunde im Park oder wir gehen zusammen ins Kino.
Ich benutze mein Handy zum Chatten und Telefonieren, aber ich benutze soziale Netzwerke nicht oft.

Writing

5 ✏️ **Du machst mit einem Freund/einer Freundin Pläne für das Wochenende. Schreib einen Dialog.**

Students write a dialogue for making weekend plans. Students should award themselves two marks per sentence: one for communicating the correct message and one for accuracy.

Suggested answer:
– Hallo, willst du am Samstag ins Kino gehen?/ Wollen wir am Samstag ins Kino gehen?
– Ich kann nicht, weil ich meine Oma besuche.
– Kannst/Willst du mit am Sonntag kommen?/ Hast du am Sonntag Zeit?
– Ja. Wollen wir uns um drei Uhr treffen?
– Super/Toll, gute Idee!

6 ✏️ **Was ist dein Rezept für ein gesundes Leben? Was soll/muss man machen? Schreib fünf Sätze. Benutz die Ideen unten.**

Students write five tips for a healthy lifestyle.

Suggested answer:
Man soll/muss … aktiv sein/viel Wasser trinken/ genug schlafen/positiv denken/Yoga oder Tai-Chi machen/gesund essen/Sport treiben/Obst und Gemüse essen.

7 ✏️ **GCSE Übersetz die Sätze ins Deutsche.**

Award one mark for a fully correct answer or half a mark if there are minor mistakes. Sentences a and c are longer, so divide them into two sections and award each section a mark, as detailed above.

Suggested translations:
a Ich stehe um sieben Uhr auf, weil die Schule um halb neun/acht Uhr dreißig beginnt.
b Mein Bruder duscht sich jeden Morgen.
c Farida geht zum Park, wenn es sonnig ist.

83

3 Vorankommen!

Resources
- Student Book, pages 70–71
- CD 1, tracks 59–61
- Kerboodle, Unit 3

Bronze

1 📖 [GCSE] Read Frau Fit's description of her daily routine and answer the questions in English.

Answers: **a** does yoga; **b** goes jogging; **c** eats chocolate; **d** eat vegetables; **e** plays computer games; **f** drinks beer; **g** drink water

2 🎧 [GCSE] Listen to the voicemails (1–5). Copy and complete the table in English.

Students complete the table with the day and suggested activity mentioned in each voicemail.

Answers:

	Day	Suggested activity
1	Saturday	go to the cinema
2	Friday	go to eat pizza
3	Tuesday	play computer games
4	Monday	go skateboarding (in park)
5	Sunday	go fishing

〰️ CD 1, track 59   Seite 70, Aktivität 2

1 Hi Rosa! Ich bin's, Maike. Willst du mit mir am Samstag ins Kino gehen? Ruf mich an. Ciao!
2 Hi! Ich will am Freitagabend in die Pizzeria essen gehen. Willst du mitkommen? Schick mir eine SMS!
3 Grüß dich, willst du am Dienstag zu mir nach Hause kommen und mit mir Computerspiele spielen? Ich habe heute ein neues Spiel gekauft. Es ist super!
4 Hallo! Willst du am Montag mit mir im Park Skateboard fahren?
5 Hi! Willst du mit mir am Sonntag angeln gehen? Ruf mich an!

3 ✏️ Complete the conversation about free-time plans.

Point out to students that the number of gaps for each word corresponds to the number of missing letters.

Answers:
- Hi Thomas. **Willst** du am Sonntag **ins** Kino g**ehen**?
- Hi Yanis. Gute Idee, aber ich m**uss** meine **Hausaufgaben** m**achen**.
- Schade. Wann h**ast** du **Z**eit?
- Ich k**ann** am **F**reitag kommen.
- Cool, bis dann!

Silber

4 📖 [GCSE] Read the leaflet about cats. Are the statements true (T), false (F) or not in the text (NT)?

Answers: **a** NT; **b** T; **c** F; **d** T; **e** NT; **f** F

84

3 Das Alltagsleben

5 🎧 Listen to Jamilah talking about her life with the circus. What does she do at each time? Note the activity and any extra information in English.

Answers:

	Activity	Extra information
a 5.30 a.m.	gets up	has lots to do
b 5.45 a.m.	washes and gets dressed	small bath in caravan
c 6.00 a.m.	training	acrobat, trains on trampoline
d 8.00 a.m.	break and breakfast	hungry, trains for five hours every day
e 4.00 p.m.	cleans tent	for their show
f 8.00 p.m.	eats dinner/ evening meal	almost never watches TV, but that's OK

🎵 **CD 1, track 60   Seite 70, Aktivität 5**

Hi! Ich heiße Jamilah und ich lebe in einem Zirkus. Ich stehe sehr früh auf, um halb sechs, weil ich viel zu tun habe.

Um Viertel vor sechs wasche ich mich und ziehe mich an. Wir haben ein kleines Bad in unserem Wohnwagen.

Dann um sechs Uhr beginnt das Training. Ich bin Akrobatin und trainiere auf dem Trampolin.

Um acht Uhr machen wir eine Pause, weil ich Hunger habe, dann esse ich Frühstück. Ich trainiere jeden Tag fünf Stunden.

Am Nachmittag um vier Uhr helfe ich, das Zelt für unsere Show zu putzen.

Nach der Show um acht Uhr essen wir zu Abend – ich sehe fast nie fern, aber das ist okay.

6 ✏️ Füll die Lücken mit deinen eigenen Ideen aus. Complete the sentences with your own ideas.

Students complete the sentences with information of their choice. Remind them that the sentences need to make sense, based on the conjunction they choose.

Gold

7 📖 Lies Heikos Blogeintrag und wähl die richtige Antwort.

Students read the article and choose the correct option to complete each sentence.

Answers: **a** ein schlechter Tag; **b** zum Essen; **c** Bus; **d** seine Badehose; **e** hat er kein Handy; **f** früher ins Bett gehen

8 ✏️ Übersetz die unterstrichenen Ausdrücke aus Aktivität 7 ins Englische.

Students translate the underlined phrases in Heiko's blog entry in activity 7 into English.

Answers: eine totale Katastrophe – a total disaster/catastrophe; geschlafen habe – slept; Bushaltestelle – bus stop; Nachhausefahrt – the way/journey home; anrufen – to call/phone/telephone; wiederfinden – to find again

9 🎧 GCSE Hör einen Podcast mit Tipps für Schüler. Beantworte die Fragen auf Englisch.

Students listen to the podcast about tips for students and answer the questions in English. Remind students that they do not need to answer in full sentences for this type of task.

Answers: **a** good organisation/being organised; **b** listen to the teachers; **c** watch TV or play computer games; **d** it aids relaxation; **e** get up at 6 a.m. and have a healthy breakfast; **f** someone who has a positive mindset/who thinks positively

🎵 **CD 1, track 61   Seite 71, Aktivität 9**

Part A

Um Erfolg in der Schule zu haben, ist es wichtig, gut organisiert zu sein. Natürlich muss man in der Schule den Lehrern zuhören und zu Hause Hausaufgaben machen, aber das ist nicht alles.

85

3 Das Alltagsleben

Part B

Man braucht eine gute Routine! Man soll nicht zu spät ins Bett gehen und soll vor dem Schlafen nicht fernsehen oder Computerspiele spielen. Studien zeigen, dass man besser schläft, wenn man abends ein Buch liest, weil Lesen einem hilft, sich zu entspannen.

Part C

Man soll jeden Tag um sechs Uhr aufstehen und ein gesundes Frühstück essen. Während des Tages soll man auf jeden Fall zwei Liter Wasser trinken und Obst essen. Man soll auch Pausen machen und positiv denken. Wer positiv denkt, hat bessere Chancen, gute Noten zu bekommen.

10 GCSE Schreib einen Blogeintrag (zirka 80 Wörter) über „Meine Vorsätze für das neue Jahr".

Students write approximately 80 words about their New Year's resolutions, guided by the bullet points: healthy lifestyle, helping at home, school and hobbies.

Extra

Before students declare their written work 'finished', tell them to check the *Extra* box and to follow the suggestions to ensure that their writing is the best it can possibly be. They could also peer-assess each other's work.

4 Meine Klamotten

Unit overview				
Page reference	Vocabulary	Grammar	Strategy	Key language
76–77 4.1 Was trägst du gern?	Saying what you are wearing and like to wear	Using verbs with the vowel change 'a' to 'ä' in the present tense	Translating into German	das Kleidungsstück, Was trägst du (gern)? Welches Kleidungsstück trägst du immer/nie? Ich trage (gern/immer/nie)..., Am Wochenende/Meistens trage ich... der Rock, der Pullover, der Kapuzenpullover, der Mantel, die Hose, die Jacke, das Cap, das T-Shirt, das Hemd, das Kleid, die Jeans, Turnschuhe (pl), Stiefel (pl)
78–79 4.2 Wie ist dein Stil?	Talking about your style	Using accusative adjective endings	Revising gern, lieber and am liebsten	Ich trage gern/lieber/am liebsten..., die Mode der Hut, der Ring, die Tasche, die Sonnenbrille, die Kette, die Armbanduhr, die Krawatte, das Accessoire, Ohrringe (pl), Sneakers (pl) bunt, kariert, gestreift, golden, kurz, lang, groß, blau, schwarz, grün, braun, rot, grau, weiß, gelb Wie ist dein Modestil? Mein Modestil ist lässig/cool/klassisch/sportlich/romantisch/alternativ. Wie findest du meinen Stil? Ich finde deinen Stil (total) okay/nicht zu schrecklich/furchtbar. Wie sehe ich aus? Du siehst super/(nicht so) gut/elegant aus. Was ist deine Lieblingsmarke? Welche Farbe trägst du am meisten? Welches Accessoire vergisst du nie? Wie findest du Piercings? Interessierst du dich für Trends?

4 Meine Klamotten

Unit overview

Page reference	Vocabulary	Grammar	Strategy	Key language
80–81 4.3 Wo kaufst du lieber deine Klamotten?	Talking about your shopping habits	Using possessive adjectives in the accusative case	Improving your reading skills	Wo kaufst du lieber deine Klamotten? Wo gehst du am liebsten shoppen? die Kleidung, Klamotten (pl) Ich kaufe lieber meine Klamotten…, Ich gehe am liebsten … shoppen. Ich gehe nicht gern … shoppen. Meine Eltern kaufen alle meine Klamotten. auf dem Flohmarkt, in großen Städten, in kleinen Läden, in Boutiquen, im Internet, in Secondhandläden, in Designerläden, im Einkaufszentrum Letztes Wochenende bin ich (im Einkaufszentrum) shoppen gegangen. Ich habe (meine weißen Turnschuhe) gekauft. Ich habe es (toll) gefunden. Das hat mir gut gefallen.
82–83 4.4 #Shoppen	Talking about shopping for clothes	Revising the future tense with *werden*	Using *ich möchte* + the infinitive	Ich möchte zuerst (ein schwarzes T-Shirt) finden/kaufen. Ich möchte (Ohrringe) aussuchen. Ich suche einen Hut. Ich werde (eine Kette) suchen. Ich werde ganz viel Geld (für ein Paar Stiefel) ausgeben. (Die Jacke) wird teuer sein. Das könnte interessant sein. Das muss (alternativ) wirken. die Lederjacke, das Paar (Sneaker), die silberne Kette
84–85 4.5 Party!	Talking about special occasions	Revising the perfect tense with *haben* and *sein*	Using three tenses together	Letztes Jahr/Letzten Sommer/Letzte Woche bin ich nach … gefahren. Ich habe (ein Hemd/eine Jeans/ein Kleid) getragen/(Currywurst/Pommes) gegessen/(Cola/Wasser) getrunken. Es gab (eine große Party). Es hat Spaß gemacht. Das Wetter war (gut). Nächstes Jahr/Nächsten Sommer/Nächste Woche werde ich nach … fahren. Ich werde … besuchen. die Party, die Feier, die Einladung, das Fußballspiel, die Stimmung, die Veranstaltung, das Fest/Festival, das Konzert, dort, Absatzschuhe

4 Los geht's!

4 Meine Klamotten

Starter

- Students match the German and English for five key verbs from the lesson: *behalten* (to keep), *tragen* (to wear), *brauchen* (to need), *kaufen* (to buy) and *dauern* (to last). These can be printed out or just displayed on the board.

Plenary

- Students summarise some of the new things they have learnt in the lesson in a 3–2–1 activity: three key words, two traditional German items of clothing and one interesting fact. They can share these with the class or with a partner.

1 Quiz! Was weißt du über Kleidung in deutschsprachigen Ländern? Rate mal!

Students complete the quiz about clothes in German-speaking countries. Encourage them to use (near-) cognates in the text, the glossary box and the photos to help them.

Answers: **1** c; **2** b; **3** b; **4** a; **5** a and b; **6** b; **7** c

2 Look at the bar chart showing how long people keep various items of clothing. Are the statements true (T) or false (F)?

Answers: **a** T; **b** T; **c** F

➕ Students correct the false sentence.

Answer: **c** People keep skirts and dresses for longer than they keep trousers.

3 Wie kann man Textilmüll vermeiden? *(How can you avoid textile waste?)* Was passt zusammen?

Students match the sentences about avoiding textile waste (1–3) with the correct photo (a–c).

Answers: **1** c; **2** b; **3** a

4 Macht Dialoge über Kleidung in einer kleinen Gruppe. Stellt und beantwortet folgende Fragen.

Students work in groups to ask and answer the questions about clothing.

⭐ Provide students with sentence starters for each answer.

4.1 Was trägst du gern?

Objectives

- Vocabulary: Saying what you are wearing and like to wear
- Grammar: Using verbs with the vowel change 'a' to 'ä' in the present tense
- Strategy: Translating into German

Resources

- Student Book, pages 76–77
- CD 2, tracks 2–3
- Grammar, Vocabulary and Translation Workbook, pages 38–39
- Kerboodle, Unit 4

Key language

- *das Kleidungsstück, Was trägst du (gern)? Welches Kleidungsstück trägst du immer/nie? Ich trage (gern/immer/nie)…, Am Wochenende/ Meistens trage ich…*
- *der Rock, der Pullover, der Kapuzenpullover, der Mantel, die Hose, die Jacke, das Cap, das T-Shirt, das Hemd, das Kleid, die Jeans, Turnschuhe (pl), Stiefel (pl)*

Homework and self-study

- Student Book, page 77, activity 7
- Grammar, Vocabulary and Translation Workbook, pages 38–39

Starter

- Students take turns to spell out a word from activity 1 for their partner, who then says the correct German word. They could also work out what the words mean in English. This provides practice of the alphabet and pronunciation of unknown words, as well as preparing students for activity 1.

Plenary

- Students create sentences about clothing. Provide them with a prescriptive number of words for each sentence; for example, for a four-word sentence they could say, *Ich trage gern Stiefel*; for a six-word sentence they could say, *Ich trage Stiefel und ein Hemd*. This can be done as a written or verbal task, individually or in pairs, for as many sentences as you wish. They could also include colours, if appropriate for the ability of the class.

---

1 🎧 **Hör zu. Was tragen sie gern (1–6)? Finde die passenden Bilder (a–l).**

Students note down the letters of the items of clothing mentioned by each speaker. You may wish to model the pronunciation of the vocabulary before students start the activity so they know what to listen for. It would also be useful to pre-teach the key question and answer phrases: *Was trägst du gern?* and *Ich trage…*

Answers: **1** a, c; **2** b, d; **3** i, e; **4** l, f; **5** h, j; **6** j, g, k

〰️ **CD 2, track 2   Seite 76, Aktivität 1**

1 – Was trägst du gern?
 – Nun, ich trage gern einen Rock und einen Mantel.
2 – Was trägst du gern?
 – Ich trage gern einen Kapuzenpullover und eine Hose.
3 – Was trägst du gern?
 – Ich trage gern ein Kleid und eine Jacke.
4 – Was trägst du gern?
 – Ich trage gern Stiefel und ich habe auch immer ein Cap auf.
5 – Was trägst du gern?
 – Ich trage gern ein Hemd und Jeans.
6 – Was trägst du gern?
 – Ich trage gern Jeans, ein T-Shirt und Turnschuhe.

Sprachmuster

Remind students that the indefinite article only changes in the accusative case with <u>masculine</u> nouns.

2 🎧 **Listen to Torsten. Which item of clothing in the picture below does he <u>not</u> mention that he's wearing? Answer in English.**

Answer: *cap*

90

4 Meine Klamotten

🎵 CD 2, track 3 Seite 76, Aktivität 2

– Was trägst du?
– Ich trage eine Jacke, einen Pullover, ein Hemd, Jeans und Stiefel.

3 💬 Macht Dialoge.

Using the example as support, students create dialogues, asking for and giving information about clothing. You could model the task structure and pronunciation beforehand with a confident volunteer. You may wish to give students time to make notes and prepare beforehand.

Aussprache: a and ä

Isolate and model the sounds first, then move on to words which include the sounds. Depending on the ability of the class, you could play some games with the sentences; for example, partners saying alternate words in each sentence, whole-class repetition using different volumes or speeds, or trying to learn the sentences off by heart.

4 ✏️ Was trägt Torsten? Schreib einen Satz über das Bild aus Aktivität 2. Benutz die ‚er'-Form.

Students write about Torsten (from activity 2) in the third person form.

Suggested answer:
Er trägt ein Cap, eine Jacke, einen Pullover, ein Hemd, Jeans und Stiefel.

🎁 Extra

This could also be done as a written task first, which students then pass to their partner to draw.

Aa Grammatik

Check students' understanding by asking them to write on mini-whiteboards the affected forms of the verbs listed in the *Grammatik* box (*fahren, waschen, schlafen, laufen*). You could also practise the pronunciation of these different forms.

If appropriate for the ability of the class, tell students that there are two other types of verbs with vowel changes: e → ie and e → i. These are covered later in the unit.

5 🔄 GCSE Übersetz die Sätze ins Deutsche.

Students translate the sentences into German. Check that they are not applying the vowel change to every verb and that they understand that only the second and third person singular forms are affected.

Suggested translations:
a *Sie tragen Jeans und ein T-Shirt.*
b *Was trägst du gern?*
c *Sie schläft, aber er läuft.*
d *Wir waschen Jeans, aber du wäschst einen Rock.*
e *Ich fahre mit dem Zug. Wie fährst du?*

⚙️ Strategie

Students may recall key phrases, such as *Ich heiße…* and *Ich habe am … Geburtstag*, which also demonstrate that not everything can be translated word for word.

6 📖 Wer trägt was in Sabrinas Wohngemeinschaft (*houseshare*)? Was passt zusammen?

Students match the sentence halves about activities and the clothing worn for them. Pre-teach the less familiar words such as *Gummihandschuhe* and *Helm*.

Answers: **1** *b;* **2** *d;* **3** *a;* **4** *c*

⭐ How many verbs with the vowel change a → ä can students spot in the sentences?

Answers: fährt, trägt, wäscht ab, lädt, schläft

➕ Students write an alternative ending to each sentence, using vocabulary of their own choice.

7 ✏️ Schreib einen Blogeintrag. Beschreib deine Kleidung.

Using the sentence starters as support, students write in German a blog entry about their clothing.

🎁 Extra

Remind students that the a → ä vowel change will apply to these verbs if used in the third person.

4.2 Wie ist dein Stil?

Objectives
- Vocabulary: Talking about your style
- Grammar: Using accusative adjective endings
- Strategy: Revising *gern*, *lieber* and *am liebsten*

Resources
- Student Book, pages 78–79
- CD 2, tracks 4–5
- Grammar, Vocabulary and Translation Workbook, pages 40–41
- Kerboodle, Unit 4

Key language
- *Ich trage gern/lieber/am liebsten..., die Mode*
- *der Hut, der Ring, die Tasche, die Sonnenbrille, die Kette, die Armbanduhr, die Krawatte, das Accessoire, Ohrringe (pl), Sneakers (pl)*
- *bunt, kariert, gestreift, golden, kurz, lang, groß, blau, schwarz, grün, braun, rot, grau, weiß, gelb*
- *Wie ist dein Modestil? Mein Modestil ist lässig/cool/klassisch/sportlich/romantisch/alternativ. Wie findest du meinen Stil? Ich finde deinen Stil (total) okay/nicht zu schrecklich/furchtbar. Wie sehe ich aus? Du siehst super/(nicht so) gut/elegant aus.*
- *Was ist deine Lieblingsmarke? Welche Farbe trägst du am meisten? Welches Accessoire vergisst du nie? Wie findest du Piercings? Interessierst du dich für Trends?*

Homework and self-study
- Student Book, page 79, activity 8
- Grammar, Vocabulary and Translation Workbook, pages 40–41

Starter
- To revise colours alongside the vocabulary from Lesson 4.1, students write some simple sentences about their uniform; for example, *Das Hemd ist weiß. Die Hose ist schwarz.*

Plenary
- To consolidate and practise the vocabulary from the lesson, students return to the accessories covered in the key language box at the top of page 78. For each one, they write a simple opinion using *gern/lieber/am liebsten* plus the verb *tragen*. They then circulate in the classroom, reading aloud a sentence of their choice to classmates and trying to find someone who has written exactly the same phrase.

1 📖 **Lies die Kommentare und finde die passenden Bilder (a–d).**

Students read the comments and match each one to the correct set of pictures.

> Answers: **Aysun** d; **Zelig** a; **Ismail** c; **Irma** b

2 📖 **Lies die Kommentare aus Aktivität 1 noch einmal und finde die passenden Wörter (a–d) auf Deutsch.**

Students reread the texts and find the German equivalents for the four words. Point out the adjective endings so that students can recognise the stem forms of the adjectives.

> Answers: **a** bunt(e); **b** kariert(es); **c** gestreift(en); **d** golden(e)

3 🎧 [GCSE] **Listen to Ada, Achim and Johanna discussing clothes and styles. For each person, note in English what they like to wear, their style and what the interviewer thinks.**

There are two questions posed to each speaker. You may wish to pre-teach these: *Was trägst du gern?* and *Wie ist dein Modestil?*

> Answers:
> **Ada:** likes to wear: checked dress, black trainers, bag, sunglasses; style: casual; interviewer's opinion: cool
> **Achim:** likes to wear: blue trousers, blue T-shirt, striped cap; style: (quite) sporty; interviewer's opinion: OK, not too terrible, cool
> **Johanna:** likes to wear: long, bright skirt, black boots, hippy sunglasses, a big hat; style: romantic; interviewer's opinion: not bad, elegant

4 Meine Klamotten

⭐ Provide students with the answers and ask them, instead, to match the answers to the correct speaker.

> 🎵 **CD 2, track 4   Seite 78, Aktivität 3**
> – Ada, was trägst du gern?
> – Ich trage gern ein kariertes Kleid und schwarze Turnschuhe. Ich habe immer eine Tasche und auch eine Sonnenbrille.
> – Wie ist dein Modestil?
> – Mein Modestil ist lässig. Wie findest du meinen Stil?
> – Ich finde deinen Stil total cool. Du siehst super aus.
> – Achim, was trägst du gern?
> – Ich trage am liebsten eine blaue Hose und ein blaues T-Shirt. Ich trage auch ein gestreiftes Cap.
> – Wie ist dein Modestil?
> – Mein Modestil ist ziemlich sportlich. Wie findest du meinen Stil?
> – Na, ja, ich finde deinen Stil okay. Nicht zu schrecklich. Du siehst cool aus.
> – Johanna, was trägst du gern?
> – Ich trage meistens einen langen bunten Rock und ich trage gern schwarze Stiefel. Meistens trage ich auch eine Hippie-Sonnenbrille und ich habe auch einen großen Hut.
> – Wie ist dein Modestil?
> – Nun…mein Modestil ist…romantisch? Wie findest du meinen Stil?
> – [hesitates] Nicht schlecht. Du siehst elegant aus.

🅰 Grammatik

Revise the terms 'noun' and 'gender', and the concept of the accusative case. If students have learnt other languages previously, there may be some misconceptions around the position of adjectives. German is the same as English: they come <u>before</u> the noun.

✲ Strategie

Remind students that *gern*, *lieber* and *am liebsten* are not verbs; for example, *ich gern eine Kette* is incorrect German. They are adverbs, which means that they must be used with a verb (which will most likely be *tragen* in this lesson).

4 ✏ **Schreib die Sätze mit den Adjektiven in Klammern. Benutz die richtigen Adjektivendungen.**

Students rewrite the sentences using the adjectives in brackets, adding the correct adjective endings.

> Answers:
> **a** Er trägt gern ein <u>rotes</u> T-Shirt und einen <u>grauen</u> Mantel.
> **b** Ich trage lieber eine <u>karierte</u> Jacke und eine <u>schwarze</u> Hose.
> **c** Sie trägt meistens einen <u>langen</u> Rock und einen <u>gestreiften</u> Pullover.
> **d** Er trägt am liebsten ein <u>weißes</u> Hemd und eine <u>grüne</u> Krawatte.
> **e** Trägst du einen <u>gelben</u> Kapuzenpullover und <u>blaue</u> Turnschuhe?

➕ Students translate the sentences into English.

> Suggested translations:
> **a** He likes to wear a red T-shirt and a grey coat.
> **b** I prefer to wear a checked jacket and black trousers.
> **c** She mostly wears a long skirt and a striped jumper.
> **d** He likes to wear a white shirt and a green tie most/best.
> **e** Are you wearing a yellow hoodie and blue trainers?

5 🎧 **Hör zu. Mila und Jens machen das Mode-Quiz. Wie antworten sie auf die Fragen (1–6)? Schreib die Tabelle ab und füll sie aus.**

Students listen to a discussion about the fashion quiz and note the speakers' responses (a, b or c). Allow students some preparation time to read and digest the questions and answers before they start this activity.

Answers:

	Mila	Jens
1	a	b
2	c	b
3	a	b
4	c	a
5	b	a
6	a	b

93

4 Meine Klamotten

CD 2, track 5   Seite 79, Aktivität 5

– Nummer 1. Wie ist dein Modestil, Mila?
– Mein Modestil ist…hmm…lässig. Und du, Jens? Wie ist dein Modestil?
– Mein Modestil ist sportlich. Jetzt Nummer 2. Was ist deine Lieblingsmarke?
– Meine Lieblingsmarke ist…Ich weiß nicht…Ja, ich habe keine. Und du? Was ist deine Lieblingsmarke?
– Nike, selbstverständlich, weil ich so sportlich bin. Nummer 3. Welche Farbe trägst du am meisten?
– Am meisten trage ich…blau. Und welche Farbe trägst du am meisten?
– Am meisten trage ich rot. Nummer 4. Welches Accessoire vergisst du nie?
– Ich vergesse nie meine Tasche. Und du?
– Ich trage immer einen Ring. Nummer 5. Wie findest du Piercings?
– Ich finde Piercings total furchtbar.
– Ich finde, ein oder zwei Piercings sind okay. Nummer 6. Interessierst du dich für Trends?
– Ja, total!
– Ich, überhaupt nicht!

6 Lies das Quiz noch einmal und notiere deine eigenen Antworten. Welcher Modetyp bist du? Finde die Quiz-Resultate rechts.

Students note their own answers to the quiz and then read the results at the bottom of Student Book page 79 (upside-down in the blue box).

7 Macht Dialoge.

Using the bulleted example sentences provided, students create a dialogue about their fashion and style preferences. You could model the task structure and pronunciation beforehand with a confident volunteer, and collate a class mind map of adjectives and intensifiers that they could use (adjectives: *romantisch/elegant/alternativ/umweltfreundlich/ minimalistisch/lässig/sportlich/klassisch/cool/toll/ schön/elegant/schick/okay*; intensifiers: *total/echt/ nicht so/ziemlich*). Students should be encouraged to keep their opinions on each other's style positive!

8 Wie ist dein Stil? Schreib deine Antworten aus Aktivität 7 als Blogeintrag auf.

Students write a blog post about clothing and style, using the answers they gave in activity 7 as a basis. Remind them to recycle language, wherever possible, to improve their answers.

4.3 Wo kaufst du lieber deine Klamotten?

4 Meine Klamotten

Objectives
- Vocabulary: Talking about your shopping habits
- Grammar: Using possessive adjectives in the accusative case
- Strategy: Improving your reading skills

Resources
- Student Book, pages 80–81
- CD 2, tracks 6–7
- Grammar, Vocabulary and Translation Workbook, pages 42–43
- Kerboodle, Unit 4

Key language
- *Wo kaufst du lieber deine Klamotten? Wo gehst du am liebsten shoppen?*
- *die Kleidung, Klamotten (pl)*
- *Ich kaufe lieber meine Klamotten…, Ich gehe am liebsten … shoppen. Ich gehe nicht gern … shoppen. Meine Eltern kaufen alle meine Klamotten.*
- *auf dem Flohmarkt, in großen Städten, in kleinen Läden, in Boutiquen, im Internet, in Secondhandläden, in Designerläden, im Einkaufszentrum*
- *Letztes Wochenende bin ich (im Einkaufszentrum) shoppen gegangen. Ich habe (meine weißen Turnschuhe) gekauft. Ich habe es (toll) gefunden. Das hat mir gut gefallen.*

Homework and self-study
- Student Book, page 81, activity 6
- Grammar, Vocabulary and Translation Workbook, pages 42–43

Starter
- Students make a list or mind map of as many German question words as they can remember. Tell the class that these words will be useful in various activities in this lesson (particularly *Was…?, Wer…?, Wie…?* and *Wo…?*). Question words will be covered in more detail in Lesson 5.2.

Plenary
- Students demonstrate their learning by producing three sentences about clothing: one including *meinen*, one including *meine* and one including *mein*. They will need to understand gender and cases to do this correctly. Some students may produce more advanced sentences and some will keep them fairly simple.

1 🎧 **Hör zu. Wo kaufen sie lieber ihre Klamotten (1–6)? Finde die passenden Bilder (a–f).**

Students listen and decide which of the photos of shopping locations corresponds to where each speaker says they prefer to buy their clothes. Tell students that each shopping location can only be used once.

Answers: **1** c; **2** a; **3** b; **4** e; **5** f; **6** d

➕ Students note down the additional information for numbers 4 and 6.

Answers: **4** not everything has to be new; **6** shopping online is practical

〰️ **CD 2, track 6   Seite 80, Aktivität 1**

1 – Wo kaufst du lieber deine Klamotten?
  – Ich kaufe meine Klamotten lieber in kleinen Läden oder Boutiquen.

2 – Wo kaufst du lieber deine Klamotten?
  – Ich kaufe meine Klamotten lieber auf dem Flohmarkt.

3 – Wo gehst du am liebsten shoppen?
  – Ich gehe am liebsten in großen Städten shoppen.

4 – Wo kaufst du lieber deine Klamotten?
  – Ich kaufe meine Klamotten lieber in Secondhandläden. Nicht alles muss neu sein.

5 – Wo gehst du am liebsten shoppen?
  – Ich gehe am liebsten im Einkaufszentrum shoppen.

6 – Wo kaufst du lieber deine Klamotten?
  – Ich kaufe meine Klamotten lieber im Internet, weil es so praktisch ist.

4 Meine Klamotten

2 🔄 **Translate the sentences into English.**

Students revised *gern*, *lieber*, and *am liebsten* in the *Strategie* box in Lesson 4.2. Remind them that these are not verbs; for example, *ich lieber im Einkaufszentrum* is grammatically incorrect; they are adverbs, which means that they must be used with a verb (which will most likely be *kaufen* in this lesson).

Suggested translations:
a I like going shopping in shopping centres best/ most (of all).
b We prefer to buy our clothes in designer shops.
c She prefers to go shopping in flea markets.
d He likes to buy his clothes in big towns/cities best/most (of all).
e My parents buy all (of) my clothes.

3 💬 **Macht eine Klassenumfrage.**

Using the bulleted question and example answer, students interview their classmates about where they prefer to buy clothes and where they like shopping most of all. You could model the task structure and pronunciation beforehand with a confident volunteer. Remind students that If they begin a sentence with *am liebsten*, the verb will be the second idea in the clause.

➕ Students add extra detail to their sentences, using *und*, *aber* or *denn*.

🎚 Sprachmuster

You could remind students about compound nouns and explain that words such as *Kleider-* and *Buch-* can be added as prefixes to the words for 'shop'.

4 🎧 **Listen to Matilda and Marcus talking about shopping trips. Find and correct the mistake in each sentence.**

Answers:
a Matilda went to OutletCity on <u>Saturday</u>.
b She bought <u>trainers</u> and a denim jacket.
c She likes shopping in big shopping centres because there are so many <u>shops</u>.
d Marcus went to the <u>flea market</u> by bus.
e He bought a <u>watch</u> and his black bag.
f He liked it because there was a lot to <u>see</u>.

⭐ Tell students what and/or where the error is (for example, **a** the day is incorrect), so that they can concentrate on listening for the correct information.

➕ Students listen again and note down all of the present and perfect tense verbs in the recording. For extra challenge, they could also note down the one example of the imperfect tense.

Answers:
Present tense: *ich bin, ich gehe, es gibt, ich finde*
Perfect tense: *ich habe besucht, ich habe gekauft, ich bin gefahren, das hat mir gefallen*
Imperfect tense: *es gab*

🎵 **CD 2, track 7   Seite 81, Aktivität 4**

– Hallo! Ich bin Matilda. Am Samstag habe ich OutletCity Metzingen besucht. Ich habe meine weißen Turnschuhe und eine schöne Jeansjacke gekauft. Ich gehe am liebsten in ein großes Einkaufszentrum, weil es so viele Läden gibt. Ich finde es toll.

– Ich bin Marcus. Schöne Grüße aus Wien. Am Sonntag bin ich mit dem Bus zum Flohmarkt Wienerberg gefahren. Ich habe eine Armbanduhr und meine schwarze Tasche gekauft. Das hat mir gut gefallen, weil es viel zu sehen gab. Echt cool.

Aa Grammatik

Remind students that the accusative case only affects the articles of <u>masculine</u> nouns. They may be able to recall *ein → einen* and therefore predict the pattern of *mein → meinen*. Remind them, too, that the gender of the possessive adjective depends on the owner, not the item. For example: *sein**e** Schwester* ('his sister'), *ihr**en** Hund* ('her dog'). Depending on the ability of the class, you could draw on the board a table with the headings in place and ask students to help complete it. Alternatively, ask students to write all of the German forms for 'your', 'his' and 'her in the accusative case.

⚙ Strategie

It would be useful to read the *Strategie* box in preparation for the reading task in activity 5. Before students read the *Strategie* box, ask them to discuss their most effective reading strategies with their partner. You could then collate these on the board and see if they match any of those listed in the box.

4 Meine Klamotten

5 📖 **Read the article about what happens to old clothes in Germany. Are the statements true (T) or false (F)? Correct the false statements.**

Encourage students to use the reading strategies from the *Strategie* box. To exemplify these suggestions, you could model how to find the first answer and narrate your thought process as you use these skills and strategies.

> Answers: **a** F – Every **year**, around a million tonnes of old clothes end up in clothes recycling banks in Germany. **b** F – The article asks who gets the old **trousers** and T-shirts. **c** T; **d** F – The remaining 50 per cent are **recycled** or burnt. **e** T

➕ Students write four questions in English about the text for their partner to answer. They should write the answers too, so they can check their partner's responses.

6 ✏️ [GCSE] **Schreib einen kurzen Text über das Shoppen.**

Guided by the bullet points, students write about a recent shopping trip or experience and their shopping habits. Remind them that the information doesn't need to be true.

⭐ Provide a sentence starter for each bullet point.

4.4 #Shoppen

Objectives

- Vocabulary: Talking about shopping for clothes
- Grammar: Revising the future tense with *werden*
- Strategy: Using *ich möchte* + the infinitive

Resources

- Student Book, pages 82–83
- CD 2, track s 8–9
- Grammar, Vocabulary and Translation Workbook, pages 44–45
- Kerboodle, Unit 4

Key language

- *Ich möchte zuerst (ein schwarzes T-Shirt) finden/ kaufen. Ich möchte (Ohrringe) aussuchen. Ich suche einen Hut. Ich werde (eine Kette) suchen. Ich werde ganz viel Geld (für ein Paar Stiefel) ausgeben. (Die Jacke) wird teuer sein.*
- *Das könnte interessant sein. Das muss (alternativ) wirken.*
- *die Lederjacke, das Paar (Sneaker), die silberne Kette*

Homework and self-study

- Student Book, page 83, activity 7
- Grammar, Vocabulary and Translation Workbook, pages 44–45

Starter

- Write on the board a 'starter sentence' linked to clothing, such as *Ich trage lieber sportliche Kleidung*. Students then need to 'grow, change, shrink' the sentence, by writing three new sentences based on yours: adding more information ('grow'), changing a noun, verb or adjective ('change') and removing information so that it still makes sense ('shrink'). This can be done with as many 'starter sentences' as you wish.

Plenary

- Students create three sentences using key verbs from this unit: *kaufen, tragen* and *finden*. They should use these infinitives with either *ich möchte* or *ich werde*. If time permits, they can dictate their German sentence to their partner to practise listening and spelling.

---

1 📖 **GCSE** Read the web page for the TV programme *Shopping-Marathon!* and answer the questions in English.

Encourage students to read all of the headings and sections of the web page in order to understand the context: that this is a fashion competition on TV.

Answers: **a** five hours; **b** 1000 euros; **c** Scottish, checked/tartan; **d** (a pair of) boots and a bag; **e** sporty; **f** totally uncool; **g** He would like to buy it first./It will be quite expensive. **h** at the flea market

2 📖 Lies die Webseite noch einmal und finde die passenden Sätze auf Deutsch.

Students read the text again and find the German equivalents for the English sentences.

Answers:
a *Das könnte interessant sein.*
b *Ich werde ganz viel Geld für ein Paar Stiefel und eine Tasche ausgeben.*
c *Das muss alternativ wirken.*
d *Es wird Spaß machen.*
e *Ich werde auf einem Flohmarket ein Paar Stiefel suchen.*

⭐ Direct students to the correct speech bubble to find each answer and inform them that the English sentences are in the same order as in the German text.

🅰 Grammatik

Students met the future tense in Lesson 2.5. Remind them that English has two forms of the future ('will' and 'going to'), but German uses just one verb to express both of these: a form of *werden*. You may come across the misconception that 'going to' involves *gehen zu*.

4 Meine Klamotten

3 🎧 **Hör zu. Adnan ist dritter Kandidat im *Shopping-Marathon!* Bring die Klamotten und Accessoires (a–f) in die richtige Reihenfolge.**

Students listen to the information about a third candidate in the fashion competition and note the order in which they hear the clothing and accessories mentioned.

Answer: d, c, b, e, f, a

⭐ Provide students with a list of clothing and accessories in German or English (including distractors), which they then tick off as they hear them mentioned, rather than putting them in the correct order.

CD 2, track 8   Seite 83, Aktivität 3

– Adnan Uddin ist 25 Jahre alt. Er ist ein Schweizer Fotograf. Er wohnt mit seiner Partnerin in Zürich.
– Also, Punk-Look: los geht's! Zuerst möchte ich eine silberne Kette und dann ein weißes T-Shirt finden. Hm… Ich möchte ein Paar Sneaker kaufen. Ich werde das vielleicht in einem Secondhandladen machen. Dann möchte ich eine Jeans und ein schwarzes Cap aussuchen. Ich werde ganz viel Geld für eine schwarze Lederjacke ausgeben. Dann ist mein Punk-Look komplett. Es wird Spaß machen. Ich möchte 1000 Euro gewinnnen!

4 🎧 **Hör noch einmal zu. Schreib Adnans Profil ab und füll die Lücken mit Wörtern aus Aktivität 3 aus.**

Students listen again and complete the profile in German with the clothing and accessories vocabulary from activity 3.

Answers: **1** *eine silberne Kette;* **2** *ein weißes T-Shirt;* **3** *ein Paar Sneaker;* **4** *Jeans;* **5** *ein schwarzes Cap;* **6** *eine schwarze Lederjacke*

CD 2, track 9   Seite 83, Aktivität 4

See activity 3 for audio script.

Strategie

Explain that *ich möchte* means 'I would like' and recap the word-order rule for modal verbs: the infinitive goes to the end of the clause.

5 GCSE **Übersetz die Sätze ins Deutsche.**

Students translate the sentences into German. Explain that they will need to use *möchten* or the future tense.

Suggested translations:
a *Er möchte ein kariertes Hemd kaufen.*
b *Sie möchte eine schwarze Sonnenbrille finden.*
c *Ich möchte Accessoires kaufen.*
d *Wir werden Turnschuhe kaufen.*
e *Sie werden eine Sonnenbrille finden.*

6 💬 **Du bist vierter Kandidat/vierte Kandidatin im *Shopping-Marathon!* und du suchst ein Outfit aus. Das Thema: ‚Hip-Hop-Look'. Stell dich vor.**

Using the example key phrases as support, students imagine that they are a candidate for the competition, and write about their clothes in German. Allow some preparation time before they make their presentation to their partner.

⭐ Students base their presentation on one of the images of the famous German artists provided at the bottom of page 83, rather than thinking of their own outfit. Before they start, collate with them a mind map of the key vocabulary for each image; for example, colours and the nouns for the clothing and accessories shown.

7 ✏️ **Stell dich in einem kurzen Text als Kandidat/Kandidatin vor.**

Students write in German the candidate profile they have created for activity 6.

99

4.5 Party!

Objectives

- Vocabulary: Talking about special occasions
- Grammar: Revising the perfect tense with *haben* and *sein*
- Strategy: Using three tenses together

Resources

- Student Book, pages 84–85
- CD 2, tracks 10–12
- Grammar, Vocabulary and Translation Workbook, pages 46–47
- Kerboodle, Unit 4

Key language

- *Letztes Jahr/Letzten Sommer/Letzte Woche bin ich nach … gefahren. Ich habe (ein Hemd/ eine Jeans/ein Kleid) getragen/(Currywurst/ Pommes) gegessen/(Cola/Wasser) getrunken. Es gab (eine große Party). Es hat Spaß gemacht. Das Wetter war (gut).*
- *Nächstes Jahr/Nächsten Sommer/Nächste Woche werde ich nach … fahren. Ich werde … besuchen.*
- *die Party, die Feier, die Einladung, das Fußballspiel, die Stimmung, die Veranstaltung, das Fest/Festival, das Konzert, dort, Absatzschuhe*

Homework and self-study

- Student Book, page 85, activity 6
- Grammar, Vocabulary and Translation Workbook, pages 46–47

Starter

- To revise previously learnt vocabulary and prepare for this lesson, students create two mind maps based on the German words *Fußballspiel* and *Party*. They should add as many nouns, verbs and adjectives as they can think of. You could refer back to these mind maps later on, to see if any of the vocabulary listed appears in the activities for this lesson.

Plenary

- Students use the key verb *tragen* from this lesson to create three sentences: one in each tense (past, present and future). If time permits, they can dictate their German sentences to their partner to practise listening and spelling.

---

1 🎧 **Hör zu und lies den Blogeintrag.**

For this activity, students simply read (and listen to) the information, before answering questions about the text in activity 2. Before moving on to the questions, you could exploit the text further by asking students to read (sections of) it aloud. They could do this alone, with a partner or as a whole-class task.

> **CD 2, track 10   Seite 84, Aktivität 1**
> See Student Book, page 84, for audio script.

2 📖 [GCSE] **Read the blog post again and complete the sentences in English.**

> Answers: **a** the atmosphere was (really) electric;
> **b** cap; **c** curried sausage/Currywurst with chips; **d** it didn't rain;
> **e** the France–Germany football match;
> **f** the Eiffel Tower

4 Meine Klamotten

🎁 **Extra**

Remind students that not every verb will need to change, only those in the *ich* form.

Answers:
Letztes Jahr ist er nach Dortmund gefahren und er hat dort im Westfalenstadion das Fußballspiel Deutschland gegen England gesehen. Es war toll, weil die Stimmung total elektrisierend war.
Er hat sein Mannschaftscap, seine Mannschaftshandschuhe und seinen Mannschaftsschal getragen.
In der Halbzeitpause hat er eine Bratwurst gegessen und das hat 2,80 Euro gekostet – nicht so teuer. Sein Vater hat Currywurst mit Pommes gegessen und ein Bier getrunken.

Grammatik

Before working through the *Grammatik* box, see how much students can remember about forming the perfect tense. This could be done as a 'think, pair, share' task or a mini-quiz.

3 🎧 **Hör zu. Hannah ist zur Berlinale gegangen. Bring die Bilder (a–f) in die richtige Reihenfolge.**

Students listen to Hannah describing her experience at the *Berlinale*. They note the letters of the photos in the order in which they are mentioned on the recording. You could take this opportunity to give students some cultural background about the *Berlinale* (the Berlin International Film Festival): it is a world-renowned film festival, held every year in February in Berlin. The top award is the Golden Bear (*Goldener Bär*).

Answer: e, c, a, f, d, b

⭐ Provide students with the German words to listen out for, rather than the images.

CD 2, track 11   Seite 85, Aktivität 3

Hallo. Mein Name ist Hannah. Ich bin siebzehn Jahre alt und ich wohne in einem Reihenhaus in Berlin.

Ich interessiere mich für Filme und letztes Jahr habe ich eine Einladung zur Berlinale als junge Journalistin bekommen. Ich habe ein schwarzes Kleid und Absatzschuhe getragen. Ich war so nervös! Ich bin mit der U-Bahn gefahren.

Nach der Preisverleihung gab es eine große Party. Ich habe Canapés gegessen, vegan und vegetarisch. Ich habe Fruchtsaft getrunken. Die Party war so elegant!

Nächstes Jahr werde ich noch einmal hingehen. Ich werde vielleicht einen Frauen-Tuxedo-Anzug anziehen. Ich freue mich schon darauf. Es wird toll.

⚙ **Strategie**

See if students can conjugate any other verbs in all three tenses. You may also wish to go over the impersonal verb *geben*, as it is commonly used and very useful, but often difficult for students.

4 🎧 **Listen again. Which tense does Hannah use to talk about the item in each picture (a–f) in activity 3? Write P (past), PR (present) or F (future).**

Answers: **a** P; **b** F; **c** P; **d** P; **e** PR; **f** P

CD 2, track 12   Seite 85, Aktivität 4

See activity 3 for audio script.

5 💬 **Macht Dialoge.**

Using the key language box as support, students ask and answer questions about attending a special event. You could model the task structure and pronunciation beforehand with a confident volunteer.

6 ✏ **GCSE Schreib einen Text über eine Veranstaltung (event).**

Guided by the bullet points, students write about a special event they have attended. They can make it up or imagine that they went to the *Berlinale*.

⭐ Provide a sentence starter for each bullet point.

101

4 Kultur

> **Resources**
> - Student Book, pages 86–87
> - CD 2, track 13

1 📖 **Lies die Fakten über traditionelle Kleidung und finde die passenden Wörter (a–h) auf Deutsch.**

Students read the facts and find the corresponding German words for the English words and phrases. Remind them that *Tracht* refers to traditional dress/costumes.

> Answers: **a** *Arbeitshosen*; **b** *Handwerker*; **c** *jahrelang*; **d** *Feiertag*; **e** *Schürze*; **f** *einfarbig*; **g** *Blumenmuster*; **h** *Hochzeiten*

⭐ Provide students with the start of each word; for example, *Arbeits-, Hand-, jahre-*.

2 📖 **Read the facts again and complete the sentences in English.**

After they have completed the activity, ask students to read the information box next to activity 2. Ask students if they know of any similar trends in the UK where traditional clothes are worn for celebrations, are enjoying renewed popularity or have been reinvented by modern fashion designers.

> Answers: **a** *work*; **b** *knee*; **c** *comfortable, warm*; **d** *years*; **e** *apron, blouse*; **f** *work dress*; **g** *wash*; **h** *weddings, folk festivals, family celebrations*

3 🎧 **Hör zu. Bring die Fragen und Antworten (a–h) in die richtige Reihenfolge.**

Students listen to the dialogue and note down the letters of the questions and answers, in the order in which they are stated in the dialogue. If additional preparation is needed, they could match the questions and answers before listening.

> Answer: *c, f, h, a, b, e, g, d*

CD 2, track 13   Seite 87, Aktivität 3

– Dirndl oder Lederhosen, was trägst du lieber?
– Ich habe ein Paar Lederhosen, aber ich trage lieber ein Dirndl. Das finde ich cool.
– Trägst du Lederhosen?
– Ja, ich trage meine Lederhosen am Wochenende, zum Wandern oder Radfahren. Nicht nur an Feiertagen!
– Welche Accessoires trägst du?
– Ich trage fast immer einen Hut mit einer Feder.

4 💬 **Macht Dialoge. Stellt und beantwortet die Fragen. Sagt eure Meinung!**

Students read the two extracts from the *Alpenmädel* and *Noh Nee* websites. Using the questions above each website and the key language box below for support, students then ask for and give opinions about the images of modern-day versions of the *Dirndl* and traditional waistcoat. More images are available on the *Alpenmädel* and *Noh Nee* websites.

5 📖 **Was passt zusammen?**

Students match the questions and answers.

> Answers: **1** *d*; **2** *c*; **3** *b*; **4** *a*

6 ✏️ **Du bist Designer! Wie sieht dein Dirndl oder deine Lederhose aus? Schreib Sätze.**

Guided by the bullet points, students imagine they are a designer and write about their own design of a *Dirndl* or *Lederhosen*.

4 Sprachlabor

4 Meine Klamotten

Objectives

- Irregular verbs in the present tense
- Accusative adjective endings
- Possessive adjectives in the accusative case
- Revising the perfect tense with *haben* and *sein*
- Pronunciation: vowel changes in irregular verbs

Resources

- Student Book, pages 88–89
- CD 2, tracks 14–15
- Grammar, Vocabulary and Translation Workbook, pages 38–47
- Kerboodle, Unit 4

Aa Grammatik

Irregular verbs in the present tense

Remind students that the vowel changes only apply to the second and third person singular forms.

1 Choose the correct form of the verb to complete each sentence.

Answers: **a** trägt; **b** vergisst; **c** fahre; **d** liest; **e** fahren; **f** Siehst

2 Complete the sentences with the correct form of the verb in brackets.

Students may need support with question **c** due to the separable verb. Remind them that the main verb is conjugated as normal and the prefix moves to the end of the clause.

Answers: **a** Fährst; **b** trägt; **c** sieht, aus; **d** sehen; **e** isst; **f** vergisst

Aa Grammatik

Accusative adjective endings

Before starting this section, draw a blank version of the table containing the accusative case adjective endings and elicit the correct endings, to see how much students can recall.

3 Divide each chain of letters into separate words and write the sentences. Underline any indefinite articles (a) and circle the adjectives in each sentence.

Answers:
a Er trägt <u>einen</u> (schwarzen) Kapuzenpullover.
b Sie kauft <u>einen</u> (weißen) Mantel und <u>eine</u> (blaue) Hose.
c In der Schule tragen wir <u>eine</u> (graue) Uniform.
d Sie hat <u>eine</u> (schöne rote) Tasche aus Leder.
e Ich trage (braune) Stiefel und (warme) Handschuhe.
f Wir tragen im Sommer (bunte) Klamotten.

➕ Students translate the sentences into English. Remind them that some items of clothing, such as trousers, are singular in German but plural in English and so will not require an indefinite article in their translations.

Suggested translations:
a He wears a black hoodie.
b She buys/is buying a white coat and blue trousers.
c At school we wear a grey uniform.
d She has a beautiful red leather bag/red bag made from leather.
e I wear brown boots and warm gloves.
f We wear colourful clothes in summer.

4 Complete the sentences with the correct ending for each article and adjective. (Sometimes you won't have to add anything.) Then translate the sentences into English.

Answers/Suggested translations:
a Er hat ein**en** schrecklich**en** Stil. – He has (a) terrible style.
b Sie trägt ein**e** bunt**e** Jacke. – She wears/is wearing a colourful jacket.
c Anke kauft ein**en** sehr elegant**en** blau**en** Mantel. – Anke buys/is buying a very elegant blue coat.
d Ich habe ein schön**es** schwarz**es** Kleid. – I have a beautiful black dress.
e Trägst du neu**e** Turnschuhe? – Are you wearing new trainers?

103

4 Meine Klamotten

Aa Grammatik

Possessive adjectives in the accusative case

Before starting this section, draw a blank version of the table containing the accusative case possessive adjectives and elicit the correct forms, to see how much students can recall. Once the first row has been completed, they should be able to recall or identify the pattern and/or the similarity with the indefinite article.

5 Complete the sentences with the correct possessive adjective in the correct form.

Answers: **a** meinen; **b** deine; **c** seine; **d** deine; **e** ihren; **f** ihre

6 Translate the sentences into English.

Suggested translations:
a She often wears her favourite skirt.
b Where did you buy your hoodie?
c He finds his clothes very comfortable.
d I found my chain at the flea market.

7 Rewrite the sentences in activity 6 (a–d), changing the words indicated. Change the possessive adjective endings too.

Answers:
a Sie trägt oft **ihre Lieblingshose**.
b Wo hast du **deine Jacke** gekauft?
c Er findet **sein Hemd** sehr bequem.
d Ich habe **mein Kleid** auf dem Flohmarkt gefunden.

Aa Grammatik

Revising the perfect tense with haben and sein

Before students start activity 8, ask them what they remember about auxiliary verbs and past participles. All students should recall that: most verbs take *haben* as their auxiliary verb; verbs of movement take *sein*; regular past participles are formed by adding *ge-* and replacing the *-en* of the infinitive with *-t*. Some students may remember that *bleiben* is a notable exception to the 'verbs of movement' rule, and also how to form irregular past participles.

8 Copy and complete the table with the past participles according to the auxiliary verb they take in the perfect tense.

Answers:

haben	sein
gehört	gelaufen
gelesen	geschwommen
gekauft	gegangen
gefunden	gekommen
besucht	geflogen
vergessen	
gewonnen	

Aussprache: vowel changes in irregular verbs

These tasks require lots of teacher demonstration to provide students with an excellent pronunciation model. You can also play the audio files to demonstrate correct pronunciation.

9 Listen and repeat. Then practise with your partner.

Isolate the sounds first, then move on to using the words that include the sounds.

CD 2, track 14   Seite 89, Aktivität 9
See Student Book, page 89, for audio script.

10 Practise saying the tongue twisters.

Depending on the ability of the class, you could play some games with this; for example, partners saying alternate words in each sentence, whole-class repetition using different volumes or speeds, or trying to learn the tongue twister-style sentences off by heart.

CD 2, track 15   Seite 89, Aktivität 10
See Student Book, page 89, for audio script.

4 Was kann ich schon?

4 Meine Klamotten

Resources
- Student Book, pages 90–91
- CD 2, tracks 16–17
- Kerboodle, Unit 4

Reading

1 Was passt zusammen? Verbinde die Fragen (1–10) mit den Antworten (a–j).

Students match the questions and answers.

Answers: **1** b; **2** d; **3** f; **4** h; **5** i; **6** c; **7** j; **8** a; **9** g; **10** e

2 Füll die Lücken aus.

Students fill the gaps with the correct word from those provided.

Answers: **1** Mode; **2** lässig; **3** Turnschuhe; **4** Sonnenbrille; **5** Boutiquen; **6** Internet; **7** bin; **8** habe; **9** goldene; **10** findest

Listening

3 GCSE Listen to Anja talking about her party outfit. Complete the sentences in English.

Answers: **a** checked, (really) elegant; **b** shopping centre; **c** Brands/Labels, right colour; **d** yellow; **e** jacket, party; **f** designer shop, spend a lot of money

CD 2, track 16   Seite 90, Aktivität 3

Ich bin Anja. Letzte Woche bin ich auf eine Party gegangen und habe mein kariertes Kleid getragen. Meine Freunde haben gesagt, dass es total elegant war. Sie denken, ich habe das Kleid in einem Designerladen gekauft, aber ich habe es im Einkaufszentrum gefunden.

Marken sind mir nicht so wichtig, weil sie zu teuer sind. Aber die richtige Farbe ist mir wichtig. Ich finde, dass gelb am besten zu mir passt.

Für die nächste Party möchte ich eine neue Jacke. Ich habe im Internet gesucht, aber ich werde die Jacke in einem Designerladen kaufen. Aber ich möchte nicht viel Geld ausgeben.

4 Listen to five teenagers talking about fashion. Are the statements true (T) or false (F)?

Answers: **a** F; **b** F; **c** F; **d** T; **e** T; **f** T; **g** T; **h** F; **i** T; **j** F

CD 2, track 17   Seite 90, Aktivität 4

– Mein Name ist Britta. Ich kaufe meine Klamotten immer in Secondhandläden, weil ich umweltbewusst bin. Ich mag jeden Stil, aber gestreifte Klamotten mag ich am liebsten.

– Ich heiße Jörg. Ich habe letzte Woche ein Hemd im Internet gesucht, aber nichts gefunden. Ich habe also mein Hemd in einer Boutique gekauft. Es hat 52 Euro gekostet.

– Ich bin Zeki. Ich bin gestern einkaufen gegangen. Ich war im Kaufhaus, aber sie hatten keinen roten Pullover. Daher habe ich keinen Pullover gekauft. Ich habe aber eine Hose gefunden und gekauft.

– Ich heiße Ilka. Für mich sind Accessoires ganz wichtig. Am liebsten trage ich große Ohrringe. Meine Schwester findet meinen Stil schrecklich.

– Ich bin's, Daniel. Ich denke, mein Modestil ist ziemlich alternativ. Letzte Woche habe ich auf einer Party ein schwarzes T-Shirt mit einer silbernen Kette getragen. Ich habe viele Komplimente bekommen.

Writing

5 Bring die Wörter in die richtige Reihenfolge. Beginn mit dem **fettgedruckten** (bold) Wort.

Students rearrange the words to form an accurate sentence, starting with the word in bold each time.

4 Meine Klamotten

Answers:
a Ich gehe am liebsten in Designerläden shoppen.
b Was trägst du gern auf einer Party?
c Er trägt fast immer schwarze Klamotten.
d Ich interessiere mich für Trends.
e Sie interessiert sich überhaupt nicht für Mode.
f Sie kaufen ihre Klamotten am liebsten im Internet.
g Wir sind zum Flohmarkt gefahren.
h Ich habe den Flohmarkt in Berlin besucht.
i Ich möchte warme Handschuhe kaufen.
j Was wirst du tragen?

6 ✏️ **Was trägst du? Schreib Sätze auf Deutsch.**

Students write a sentence describing what they are wearing, based on each of the pictures provided.

Answers:
a Ich trage einen roten Mantel.
b Ich trage schwarze Stiefel.
c Ich trage eine gestreifte Hose.
d Ich trage ein kariertes Hemd.

7 ✏️ [GCSE] **Übersetz die Sätze ins Deutsche.**

Students translate the sentences into German. Award one mark for a fully correct sentence or half a mark if there are minor mistakes.

Suggested translations:
a Ich trage einen blauen Pullover.
b Karin trägt ein neues Kleid.
c Ich werde eine grüne Jacke tragen.
d Ich habe ein graues T-Shirt gekauft.
e Haben Sie ein gestreiftes Hemd?
f Er geht am liebsten auf dem Flohmarkt shoppen.

4 Vorankommen!

Resources

- Student Book, pages 92–93
- CD 2, tracks 18–20
- Kerboodle, Unit 4

Bronze

1 📖 **Read Sabine's email about clothes. Choose the correct answer to complete each sentence.**

Answers: **a** friend; **b** a shopping centre; **c** nothing; **d** colourful; **e** terrible

2 🎧 [GCSE] **Listen and complete the table in English with the clothes each person (1–3) mentions.**

Encourage students to try to note down the adjectives as well, although these are not necessary to gain a mark.

Answers:

	Normally	Last week	Next week
1	jogging bottoms/joggers	(new) shoes	sunglasses
2	T-shirt	jacket	(black) shirt
3	trainers	(striped) jumper	(brown) boots

106

4 Meine Klamotten

🎵 CD 2, track 18 Seite 92, Aktivität 2

1 Also, normalerweise trage ich am Wochenende eine Jogginghose. Das ist bequem. Letztes Wochenende habe ich auf einer Party meine neuen Schuhe getragen. Cool. Und nächste Woche? Ja, da wird es sonnig. Ich werde meine Sonnenbrille tragen.

2 Letzte Woche habe ich meine Großeltern besucht. Ich habe meine Jacke getragen, weil es kalt war. Normalerweise ist mein Stil ganz einfach. Ich trage immer ein T-Shirt. Nächste Woche werde ich auf ein Konzert gehen. Ich werde ein schwarzes Hemd tragen.

3 Nun, es ist Dezember. Nächste Woche werden wir Schnee haben und ich werde meine braunen Stiefel tragen. Normalerweise hasse ich Stiefel und ich trage lieber meine Turnschuhe, aber im Schnee sind sie nicht praktisch. Letzte Woche habe ich einen gestreiften Pullover gekauft.

3 ✏️ **Complete the sentences in German. Then translate them into English.**

Students complete the sentences with their own information. They could also swap with a partner and translate each other's sentences.

Silber

4 📖 GCSE **Read Svenja's blog post about recycling old clothes and answer the questions in English.**

Remind students to pay attention to the number of details required for each answer and to ensure that they provide the required information.

Answers:
a fashion (1 mark) and the environment (1 mark);
b at the flea market; c (really) strange/odd;
d Are the clothes dirty? (1 mark) Are the clothes damaged? (1 mark); e His style is relaxed/casual (1 mark) and he has really cool clothes (1 mark).

5 🎧 **Listen to Mohammed talking about his shopping trip. Complete the text in English.**

Answers: 1 broken; 2 second-hand shop; 3 super; 4 plastic; 5 colour; 6 nothing

🎵 CD 2, track 19 Seite 92, Aktivität 5

Hallo. Ich bin Mohammed. Gestern bin ich in die Stadt gegangen, weil ich einen neuen Pullover und eine Tasche wollte. Ich brauche eine neue Tasche, weil meine alte Tasche kaputt ist.

Ich mag Vintage-Sachen und bin kein Fan von großen Einkaufszentren und deshalb bin ich in einen Secondhandladen gegangen. Ich habe eine super Tasche gefunden, aber sie war aus Plastik und ich wollte eine Tasche aus Leder.

Dann habe ich noch einen Pullover gesucht. Ich habe einen gefunden, aber er hatte nicht die richtige Farbe. Er war blau, aber ich wollte lila. Also, bin ich wieder nach Hause gegangen und habe nichts gekauft.

6 ✏️ **Beschreib Andre (30–40 Wörter). Gib folgende Informationen auf Deutsch.** Describe Andre (30–40 words). Give the following information in German.

Guided by the bullet points, students describe the picture of Andre.

Suggested answer:
Andre trägt blaue Jeans, ein weißes T-Shirt, ein blau-gelb kariertes Cap, eine braune Armbanduhr, rot-weiß Turnschuhe und rot-weiß-grün gestreifte Socken. Ich finde seinen Stil sehr lässig und cool.

Gold

7 📖 **Lies den Artikel über Raphaels Arbeit als Modedesigner. Wähl die richtige Antwort.**

Students read the article and choose the correct option to complete each sentence. Encourage them to refer to the glossary box for help.

Answers: a sport; b clothes shop; c talented; d after a while; e abroad; f small shop; g natural

8 ✏️ GCSE **Übersetz die unterstrichenen Sätze in dem Artikel ins Englische.**

Students translate the underlined sentences in the text in activity 7 into English.

107

4 Meine Klamotten

Suggested translations:
I studied fashion design in Paris and London.
I liked that a lot, but now I am in Austria. Here, I have a small shop on the ground floor with a fashion studio on the first floor.

9 🎧 GCSE Hör zu. Mia spricht über ihren Besuch auf dem Oktoberfest. Wähl die <u>vier</u> richtigen Sätze.

Students listen to Mia's account of her visit to *Oktoberfest* and choose the four correct sentences. Ensure students know what *Oktoberfest* is before they start this activity.

Answer (in any order): a, b, d, g

CD 2, track 20   Seite 93, Aktivität 9

Ich heiße Mia und bin 23 Jahre alt. Ich bin letztes Wochenende aufs Oktoberfest gegangen. Ich gehe jedes Jahr aufs Oktoberfest.

Alle meine Freunde tragen Tracht, also ein Dirndl oder Lederhosen, denn das ist Tradition. Aber ich mag das nicht und habe nur meine normalen Klamotten getragen. Ich finde es eine blöde Idee, wenn man nur einmal im Jahr Tracht trägt.

Wir waren am Nachmittag auf dem Oktoberfest. Wir sind ziemlich früh angekommen, aber es waren schon so viele Menschen da. Sie haben gesungen, getanzt und natürlich Bier getrunken.

Ich trinke keinen Alkohol, aber ich habe die Stimmung total fantastisch gefunden. Nächstes Jahr werde ich reisen und kann leider nicht aufs Oktoberfest gehen.

10 ✏️ GCSE Du bist Modedesigner/Modedesignerin. Schreib einen Text (zirka 80 Wörter).

Guided by the bullet points, students imagine that they are a fashion designer and write a text of about 80 words about clothing and style.

🎁 **Extra**

This could be done as an extension or homework task.

5 Virtuelle und reelle Welt

Unit overview				
Page reference	**Vocabulary**	**Grammar**	**Strategy**	**Key language**
98–99 5.1 Kino, Kino	Talking about TV and film	Using subordinate clauses with *weil* and *da*	Inferring meaning	*Was für Fernsehsendungen siehst du gern/am liebsten?* *der Krimi, der Zeichentrickfilm, die Dokumentarsendung, die Nachrichten (pl), die Reality-TV-Serie, die Sportsendung* *Was willst du heute Abend sehen? Ich will (Tatort) sehen, da ich (Krimis) mag. Ich liebe Krimis, weil sie spannend sind. Ich gehe nicht oft ins Kino, da es so teuer ist.* *Was sind deine Lieblingsfilme? Was für Filme siehst du gern? Was für Filme siehst du nicht gern? Welcher Film hast du als letztes gesehen? Wie hast du den Film gefunden?* *Meine Lieblingsfilme sind... Ich sehe (nicht) gern..., Ich mag (nicht)..., Mir gefallen (nicht)..., Für mich sind (Horrorfilme) zu ...* *der Abenteuerfilm, der Bollywoodfilm, der fremdsprachige Film, der Horrorfilm, der Science-Fiction-Film, die romantische Komödie* *Ich finde (Science-Fiction-Filme) romantisch/lustig/spannend/ unterhaltsam/interessant/faszinierend/ gruselig/schrecklich/furchtbar/ kompliziert/langweilig/kindisch/blöd/ nervig/unrealistisch.*
100–101 5.2 Musik liegt in der Luft	Talking about different types of music	Using time–manner–place word order	Learning the question words	*Was für Musik hörst du (nicht) gern? Wer ist dein Lieblingssänger oder deine Lieblingssängerin? Wann/Wie/Wo hörst du Musik? Was hast du als letztes gehört? Wann bist du zuletzt auf ein Konzert gegangen?* *der Deutschrap, der Hip-Hop, der Pop, der Schlager, die Dance-Musik, die klassische Musik, die Rockmusik, die Volksmusik* *mit meinen Freunden, allein, in meinem Zimmer/Bett, auf meinem Handy, mit Kopfhörern* *auf ein Konzert gehen, mitsingen, die Melodie, Texte (pl), (Hip-Hop) hat einen tollen Rhythmus* *melodisch, entspannend, lebendig, rhythmisch, beliebt, laut*

5 Virtuelle und reelle Welt

Unit overview				
Page reference	Vocabulary	Grammar	Strategy	Key language
102–103 5.3 Sicher im Internet	Talking about the internet and social media	Expressing opinions using *dass*	Building more complex sentences	*Wie oft benutzt du das Internet? Ich benutze das Internet eine Stunde/ zwei Stunden pro Tag/nie.* *Was machst du im Internet? Musik runterladen, mit Freunden/der Familie chatten, Computerspiele spielen, Klamotten/Geschenke/Make-up kaufen, soziale Medien benutzen* *Wie findest du das? Ich finde das gut/ praktisch/zu lang.* *der Vorteil, der Nachteil* *Man kann mit Freunden sprechen/ unabhängig sein/mit Freunden im Ausland in Kontakt bleiben. Man findet immer den Weg. Man findet viele Informationen. Man ist nicht aktiv genug. Man verbringt nicht genug Zeit mit Freunden und der Familie. Man schläft nicht genug. Man spricht vielleicht mit Fremden. Es gibt Cyber-Mobbing.* *Ich denke/glaube, dass… Ein Vorteil/ Ein Nachteil ist, dass… Meine Eltern denken, dass… Meine Mutter glaubt, dass…*
104–105 5.4 Technologie heute und damals	Talking about technology today and in the past	Recognising and using the imperfect tense	Narrating events in the past	*damals, heutzutage, in den 1970er/1980er/1990er Jahren* *Es gab fast überall/keine/nicht so viel(e)/ mehr/wenig…* *Ich ging (ins Internetcafé). Ich hatte (kein Smartphone). Ich hörte (Musik). Ich interessierte mich (für Umweltschutz). Ich las (Zeitschriften). Ich schrieb (Postkarten). Ich spielte (Computerspiele).* *auf dem Handy, auf Musikplattformen, im Heft, im Internet, im Radio*
106–107 5.5 Ich engagiere mich	Talking about volunteering projects	Revising the use of different tenses	Recognising and using compound nouns	*der Tierschutz, der Umweltschutz, die Behindertenhilfe, die Altenhilfe, die Obdachlosenhilfe, die Flüchtlingshilfe, das Projekt* *(Umweltschutz) ist mir sehr wichtig. Ich denke, dass (Flüchtlingshilfe) total wichtig ist. (Obdachlosenhilfe) interessiert mich.* *Ich verkaufe Kuchen. Ich arbeite in einem Tierheim. Ich spende Geld. Ich helfe Menschen. Ich unterrichte Deutsch. Ich gehe einkaufen. Ich sammle Geld. Ich sammle Abfall auf.* *Ich habe … verkauft/gearbeitet/gespendet/ geholfen/unterrichtet. Ich bin … gegangen.* *Ich werde … verkaufen/arbeiten/ spenden/helfen/unterrichten/gehen.*

5 Los geht's!

5 Virtuelle und reelle Welt

Starter

- To help students revise key verbs used in this lesson, provide a list of gapped infinitives for them to fill in; for example, h _ _ e n (*hören*), m _ _ h _ n (*machen*). Choose a selection of six to eight verbs from activities 1 and 3.

Plenary

- Students study the image and verbs in activity 1 for a minute, and then test each other in pairs to see how much they can remember. They take turns to say the English and elicit the German from their partner, or vice versa.

---

1 Was machen Jugendliche mit dem Smartphone? Was passt zusammen? Verbinde die deutschen Verben (1–9) mit den Apps (a–i).

Students match the German verbs with the app icons. Confirm the correct English translations of the verbs in the lozenges and what each app icon represents before moving on (students sometimes interpret pictures differently).

Answers: **1** e; **2** a; **3** d; **4** b; **5** g; **6** i; **7** c; **8** f; **9** h

2 Was machst du mit deinem Handy? Was machst du nicht? Schreib mindestens <u>drei</u> Sätze. Beginne damit, was du am meisten machst. (*Start with what you do most.*)

Using the example and the key language box as support, students write at least three sentences about what they do and don't do on their mobile phone. They should start with the thing they do most frequently.

Tipp

To exemplify the 'verb-second' rule, give a simple example sentence (such as *Ich schicke SMS*) and then place an adverb of frequency at the start to demonstrate the change of word order.

3 Wie benutzen Jugendliche in Deutschland Technologie? Füll die Lücken mit der richtigen Prozentzahl aus.

Students fill the gaps with the correct percentages, based on the statistics provided with the images.

Answers: **a** 96%; **b** 12%; **c** 26%; **d** 90%; **e** 44%; **f** 65%

➕ Students write the German percentages in full.

Answers: **a** sechsundneunzig Prozent; **b** zwölf Prozent; **c** sechsundzwanzig Prozent; **d** neunzig Prozent; **e** vierundvierzig Prozent; **f** fünfundsechzig Prozent

Kultur

You may wish to discuss the #FridaysforFuture movement with the children and show them images online of previous protests from young people in Germany.

4 Match the German TV programmes (1–6) to their British equivalents (a–f).

Answers: **1** c; **2** e; **3** a; **4** f; **5** b; **6** d

➕ Students work out the literal translations of the German titles; for example, 'The big bake'.

Suggested translations:
1 –; **2** I am a star – get me out of here!; **3** Who becomes a millionaire?; **4** The big bake; **5** The super-talent; **6** We help children

Kultur

You could show some clips of these programmes on YouTube and see if students can understand any of the dialogue. Students could also write sentences, giving their opinions of the programmes.

111

5.1 Kino, Kino

Objectives
- Vocabulary: Talking about TV and film
- Grammar: Using subordinate clauses with *weil* and *da*
- Strategy: Inferring meaning

Resources
- Student Book, pages 98–99
- CD 2, tracks 21–23
- Grammar, Vocabulary and Translation Workbook, pages 52–53
- Kerboodle, Unit 5

Key language
- *Was für Fernsehsendungen siehst du gern/am liebsten?*
- *der Krimi, der Zeichentrickfilm, die Dokumentarsendung, die Nachrichten (pl), die Reality-TV-Serie, die Sportsendung*
- *Was willst du heute Abend sehen? Ich will (Tatort) sehen, da ich (Krimis) mag. Ich liebe Krimis, weil sie spannend sind. Ich gehe nicht oft ins Kino, da es so teuer ist.*
- *Was sind deine Lieblingsfilme? Was für Filme siehst du gern? Was für Filme siehst du nicht gern? Welcher Film hast du als letztes gesehen? Wie hast du den Film gefunden?*
- *Meine Lieblingsfilme sind…, Ich sehe (nicht) gern…, Ich mag (nicht)…, Mir gefallen (nicht)…, Für mich sind (Horrorfilme) zu …*
- *der Abenteuerfilm, der Bollywoodfilm, der fremdsprachige Film, der Horrorfilm, der Science-Fiction-Film, die romantische Komödie*
- *Ich finde (Science-Fiction-Filme) romantisch/lustig/spannend/unterhaltsam/ interessant/faszinierend/gruselig/schrecklich/ furchtbar/kompliziert/langweilig/kindisch/ blöd/nervig/unrealistisch.*

Homework and self-study
- Student Book, page 99, activity 9
- Grammar, Vocabulary and Translation Workbook, pages 52–53

Starter
- Provide students with five simple sentences about watching films and/or TV (for example, *Ich sehe Filme auf meinem Computer. Ich sehe auf meinem Smartphone fern.*), using key words for devices from *Los geht's!* Students copy out the sentences, adding an adverb of frequency in an appropriate place to describe their own usage; for example, *Ich sehe **oft** Filme auf meinem Computer.*

Plenary
- Students create sentences about their TV- and film-viewing habits. Provide them with a prescriptive number of words for each sentence; for example, for a three-word sentence they could say *Ich hasse Sportsendungen*; for a four-word sentence they could say, *Ich sehe nie Sportsendungen*. To practise *weil* and *da*, give them a higher number of words. This can be done as a written or verbal task, individually or in pairs, for as many sentences as you wish.

1 📖 **Was passt zusammen? Verbinde die Fernsehsendungen (1–6) mit den Bildern (a–f).**

Students match the German TV programme-types with the corresponding photos. Confirm the correct English translations before moving on (students sometimes interpret pictures differently).

Answers: **1** c; **2** a; **3** f; **4** d; **5** b; **6** e

2 🎧 **Listen. What type of TV programme does each person like (1–6)? Make notes in English.**

Model the pronunciation of the programme types before students start the activity, so they know what to listen for.

Answers: **1** crime series; **2** reality TV series; **3** cartoons; **4** documentaries; **5** sports programmes; **6** the news

5 Virtuelle und reelle Welt

CD 2, track 21　Seite 98, Aktivität 2

1. Meine Lieblingssendungen sind Krimis, weil die so spannend sind.
2. Ich mag Reality-TV-Sendungen echt gern, weil sie mir Spaß machen.
3. Ich finde Zeichentrickfilme toll, da sie so lustig sind.
4. Da ich mich für die Umwelt und Tiere interessiere, mag ich Dokumentarsendungen sehr gern.
5. Ich sehe fast jeden Tag Sportsendungen, weil Schwimmen, Fußball, Basketball mir gefallen.
6. Die Nachrichten sind meine Lieblingssendung, weil ich mich für Politik interessiere.

Extra

Answers: **1** they're exciting; **2** they're fun; **3** they're (so) funny; **4** interested in the environment and animals; **5** likes swimming, football and basketball; **6** interested in politics

Grammatik

To avoid students producing incorrect sentences such as *Ich Sportsendungen mag, weil/da...*, remind them that subordinate clauses only affect the verbs which come <u>after</u> them.

3 💬 **Ihr seht heute Abend fern. Macht Dialoge.**

Using the example as support, students create dialogues asking for and giving information about watching TV. You could model the task structure and pronunciation beforehand with a confident volunteer. Explain to students that they can name English programmes without translating them if there is no German equivalent.

4 📖 **Lies die Blogeinträge. Finde die passenden Ausdrücke (a–d) auf Deutsch.**

Students read the blog entries and find the German equivalents for the English film genres.

Answers: **a** romantische Komödien; **b** Abenteuerfilme; **c** fremdsprachige Filme; **d** Horrorfilme

Strategie

You may need to explain what 'infer' means (working out information that is not directly stated). Remind students to look for synonyms and equivalent phrases when completing activity 5.

5 📖 **GCSE Lies die Blogeinträge noch einmal. Wer sagt das: @KinoKati (KK) oder @FilmFeroza (FF)?**

Students read the blog entries again and decide who would be likely to say each of the statements.

Answers: **a** KK; **b** FF; **c** FF; **d** KK; **e** FF; **f** KK

6 💬 **GCSE Translate @FilmFeroza's blog entry into English.**

Suggested translation:
I go to the cinema every month and I like watching films in French, English or Spanish best/most (of all). I find foreign-language films fascinating because I like learning foreign languages at school. But I can't stand horror films./But horror films are not for me. I don't find these films scary/spooky, but just stupid/silly. I don't watch much TV/I don't watch TV a lot at home because my television is so small.

7 🎧 **Listen. What types of films do the teenagers (1–6) like (✓) and dislike (✗)? Make notes in English.**

Answers: **1** ✓ horror, ✗ Bollywood; **2** ✓ romcoms, ✗ foreign-language; **3** ✓ adventure, ✗ science-fiction; **4** ✓ foreign-language, ✗ romcoms; **5** ✓ science-fiction, ✗ horror; **6** ✓ Bollywood, ✗ adventure

⭐ Provide students with the film genres mentioned. They then only need to decide if the speaker likes or dislikes them.

5 Virtuelle und reelle Welt

CD 2, track 22 Seite 99, Aktivität 7

1. Ich liebe Horrorfilme, weil sie spannend sind. Meine Freunde lieben Bollywoodfilme, aber ich finde Bollywoodfilme ganz schrecklich. Ich interessiere mich nicht für Tanz.

2. Mir gefallen Filme mit viel Liebe und Gefühl, zum Beispiel romantische Komödien, denn ich bin selbst sehr romantisch. Aber fremdsprachige Filme finde ich furchtbar – viel zu kompliziert und langweilig.

3. Am liebsten sehe ich Abenteuerfilme so wie *Jumanji*, denn sie sind total unterhaltsam. Science-Fiction-Filme sind aber gar nichts für mich, da sie zu unrealistisch sind.

4. Ich sehe gern fremdsprachige Filme, denn Französisch und Spanisch sind meine Lieblingsfächer in der Schule. Meine Schwester mag romantische Komödien, aber für mich sind romantische Komödien zu blöd.

5. Meine Lieblingsfilme sind Science-Fiction-Filme, denn ich finde die Technologie so cool. Meine Freunde sehen immer Horrorfilme, aber ich mache das nicht, weil diese Filme zu gruselig sind.

6. Nummer eins sind für mich Bollywoodfilme, da ich mich für andere Kulturen interessiere. Aber Abenteuerfilme? Nein, das geht gar nicht. Ich finde sie einfach nicht spannend.

8 Listen again and write the reasons for the teenagers' (1–6) likes and dislikes in English.

Answers: **1** horror – exciting, Bollywood – (really) terrible, not interested in dance; **2** romcoms – is (very) romantic himself, foreign-language – awful/terrible, (much) too complicated and boring; **3** adventure – (really) entertaining, science-fiction – too unrealistic; **4** foreign-language – French and Spanish are favourite subjects (at school), romcoms – too stupid/silly; **5** science-fiction – technology is so cool, horror – too scary/spooky; **6** Bollywood – interested in other cultures, adventure – (simply) not exciting

⭐ Provide students with the answers in a random order for them to choose from, rather than having to note them down themselves.

CD 2, track 23 Seite 99, Aktivität 8

See activity 7 for audio script.

9 [GCSE] Schreib 40–60 Wörter für eine Diskussion auf einem sozialen Netzwerk. Was für Filme magst du (nicht) und warum?

Guided by the bullet points, students write about their film preferences.

💡 **Tipp**

Encourage students to refer to the *Tipp* box when completing activity 9 and to use a variety of phrases to express their likes and dislikes.

5 Virtuelle und reelle Welt

5.2 Musik liegt in der Luft

Objectives
- Vocabulary: Talking about different types of music
- Grammar: Using time–manner–place word order
- Strategy: Learning the question words

Resources
- Student Book, pages 100–101
- CD 2, tracks 24–25
- Grammar, Vocabulary and Translation Workbook, pages 54–55
- Kerboodle, Unit 5

Key language
- *Was für Musik hörst du (nicht) gern? Wer ist dein Lieblingssänger oder deine Lieblingssängerin? Wann/Wie/Wo hörst du Musik? Was hast du als letztes gehört? Wann bist du zuletzt auf ein Konzert gegangen?*
- *der Deutschrap, der Hip-Hop, der Pop, der Schlager, die Dance-Musik, die klassische Musik, die Rockmusik, die Volksmusik*
- *mit meinen Freunden, allein, in meinem Zimmer/Bett, auf meinem Handy, mit Kopfhörern*
- *auf ein Konzert gehen, mitsingen, die Melodie, Texte (pl), (Hip-Hop) hat einen tollen Rhythmus*
- *melodisch, entspannend, lebendig, rhythmisch, beliebt, laut*

Homework and self-study
- Student Book, page 101, activity 8
- Grammar, Vocabulary and Translation Workbook, pages 54–55

Starter
- To revise question words, provide students with a list of five with which they are most familiar. They should then create a full question for each one; for example, *Wie → Wie heißt du?; Wo → Wo wohnst du?*

Plenary
- Write some sentences on the board, one at a time, using the key vocabulary and grammar from the lesson, but give only the first letter of each word; for example, I h n V, d e i s = *Ich höre nie Volksmusik, denn es ist schrecklich.* Students write the full sentence in their books or on mini-whiteboards. For increased challenge, you could use more complex phrases from the listening transcripts. This task could be done individually, in pairs or in small groups.

---

1 🔄 **Translate the types of music on the playlist into English.**

You could play an example of *Schlager* (German pop) to demonstrate this genre.

> *Suggested translations:*
> **a** German pop; **b** classical music; **c** folk music; **d** pop; **e** hip-hop and German rap; **f** rock music

2 📖 **Was passt zusammen? Verbinde die Fragen (1–6) mit den Antworten (a–f).**

Students match the questions and answers about music. Elicit which two questions are in the past tense (5 and 6) and point out that this will help them match these questions to the correct answers. You could give them some information about German singer Mark Forster or ask them to find out who he is.

> Answers: **1** b; **2** e; **3** d; **4** c; **5** a; **6** f

⚙ Strategie
Remind students how to pronounce 'w' in German and allow them time to practise saying the question words. Recap or elicit that most question words are followed by a verb (*Wann **hörst** du Musik?*), whereas *Was für...?* is followed by a noun (*Was für **Musik** hörst du gern?*).

115

5 Virtuelle und reelle Welt

3 💬 **Stellt und beantwortet die Fragen aus Aktivität 2. Jede Person stellt drei Fragen.**

Students ask and answer three questions from activity 2. You could model the task structure and pronunciation beforehand with a confident volunteer. Depending on the ability of the class, students could either come up with their own answers (in full sentences, if possible) or simply practise reading aloud the answers listed in activity 2.

Aa Grammatik

See if students can think of any other adverbs of time, manner or place. Students often find it difficult to identify adverbs of manner; explain that these describe 'how' something is done (in contrast to 'when' for adverbs of time, and 'where' for adverbs of place).

4 📖 **Read what Kai, Nina and Lars say about music. Translate the highlighted phrases into English.**

Suggested translations:
Kai: every Wednesday, with my friends, in the cellar
Nina: mostly, alone/on my own, in my (bed)room
Lars: often, with me and my sister, to church, last week, together, to a gospel festival

➕ Students translate the whole texts.

Suggested translations:
Kai: Every Wednesday I play in a band with my friends in the cellar. We play rock music and I play (the) electric guitar.
Nina: I mostly listen to German pop alone/on my own in my (bed)room because my family finds this (type of) music terrible.
Lars: My parents often go to church with me and my sister, as my sister sings in the Gospel choir. Last week we went to a Gospel festival together.

5 ✏️ **Schreib die Sätze richtig auf.**

Students separate the letter strings into words to form correct statements.

Answers:
a Ich höre am liebsten mit meinen Freunden Musik.
b Er hört jeden Tag allein in seinem Zimmer Rockmusik.
c Ich habe zuletzt am Wochenende in meinem Bett Musik gehört.
d Ich habe als letztes auf meinem Handy einen Podcast gehört.

⭐ Provide students with the English translations or the number of words in each German sentence.

➕ Students identify the adverbs of time, manner and place, and then translate the sentences into English.

Answers/Suggested translations:
a am liebsten (M), mit meinen Freunden (M) – I like listening to music with my friends best/most (of all).
b jeden Tag (T), allein (M), in seinem Zimmer (P) – He listens to rock music alone in his (bed)room every day.
c zuletzt (T), am Wochenende (T), in meinem Bett (P) – I last listened to music in my bed at the weekend.
d als letztes (T), auf meinem Handy (m) – Most recently I listened to a podcast on my mobile phone.

6 🎧 **Hör zu. Leonie spricht über Musik, die sie hört. Wähl die richtige Antwort.**

Students listen to Leonie talking about music and choose the correct option to complete each German statement. Allow them some preparation time to read and digest the questions, and to annotate them in English, if appropriate.

Answers: **a** wichtig; **b** immer; **c** Rockmusik; **d** Nach der Schule; **e** das einen guten Rhythmus hat; **f** schlechte; **g** entspannend

5 Virtuelle und reelle Welt

CD 2, track 24 — Seite 101, Aktivität 6

Hallo. Ich bin Leonie. Für mich ist Musik sehr wichtig und gut für die Nerven. Ich höre jeden Tag Musik. Ich höre zum Beispiel Musik immer vor der Schule. Am Morgen bin ich oft sehr müde. Deshalb höre ich Rockmusik, weil sie so lebendig ist und mich aufweckt. In der Schule darf ich nicht Musik hören, aber im Auto nach der Schule höre ich Schlager, weil Schlagermusik einen tollen Rhythmus hat. Ich singe aber nicht mit, weil ich nicht gut singen kann. Bei den Hausaufgaben höre ich immer Deutschrap. Meine Mutter findet das keine gute Idee, aber es hilft mir beim Konzentrieren. Und vor dem Schlafen? Da höre ich immer klassische Musik, weil ich mich entspannen kann. Meine Freunde denken, dass klassische Musik langweilig ist, aber ich nicht.

7 GCSE Listen and read the interview with Julia. Answer the questions in English.

Remind students to pay attention to the number of details required to answer each question.

Answers: **a** guitar, drums, piano; **b** it's really not good; **c** dance, because it has rhythm/is rhythmic and is popular; **d** they're relaxing and melodic; **e** the melody; **f** it was not popular/it was out of fashion; **g** because the sound of the bass is so loud/her parents always say her music is too loud

CD 2, track 25 — Seite 101, Aktivität 7

See Student Book, page 101, for audio script.

8 Wann, wie, wo und warum hörst du Musik? Schreib einen langen Satz. Denk an die Wortstellung. (*Think about the word order.*)

Students write about when, how, where and why they listen to music.

5.3 Sicher im Internet

Objectives

- Vocabulary: Talking about the internet and social media
- Grammar: Expressing opinions using *dass*
- Strategy: Building more complex sentences

Resources

- Student Book, pages 102–103
- CD 2, track 26
- Grammar, Vocabulary and Translation Workbook, pages 56–57
- Kerboodle, Unit 5

Key language

- *Wie oft benutzt du das Internet? Ich benutze das Internet eine Stunde/zwei Stunden pro Tag/nie.*
- *Was machst du im Internet? Musik runterladen, mit Freunden/der Familie chatten, Computerspiele spielen, Klamotten/Geschenke/Make-up kaufen, soziale Medien benutzen*
- *Wie findest du das? Ich finde das gut/praktisch/zu lang.*
- *der Vorteil, der Nachteil*
- *Man kann mit Freunden sprechen/unabhängig sein/mit Freunden im Ausland in Kontakt bleiben. Man findet immer den Weg. Man findet viele Informationen. Man ist nicht aktiv genug. Man verbringt nicht genug Zeit mit Freunden und der Familie. Man schläft nicht genug. Man spricht vielleicht mit Fremden. Es gibt Cyber-Mobbing.*
- *Ich denke/glaube, dass... Ein Vorteil/Ein Nachteil ist, dass... Meine Eltern denken, dass... Meine Mutter glaubt, dass...*

Homework and self-study

- Student Book, page 103, activity 6. Remind students not to use translation websites; all of the vocabulary and structures they need are in the Student Book.
- Grammar, Vocabulary and Translation Workbook, pages 56–57

Starter

- To revise vocabulary covered so far in Unit 5, students write the alphabet from A to Z and try to think of a German word for each letter from the unit: nouns, verbs (such as *hören, sehen, lesen*) or adjectives. This could be done in pairs.

Plenary

- Ask students to close their Student Books. Read aloud some (or all, if time permits) of sentences 1–10 from activity 2 in a random order. Students listen and decide if they are an advantage or disadvantage of the internet and social media. They can feed back in various ways: by giving a thumbs up/down or by noting down a tick or a cross on mini-whiteboards. Alternatively, you could number each sentence and students note down the numbers under two headings: advantages and disadvantages. This task can be done individually, in pairs or in small groups.

1 „Wie oft benutzt du das Internet? Was machst du im Internet?" Macht eine Umfrage in kleinen Gruppen.

Using the key language box for support, students work in small groups to ask and answer questions about how they use the internet. Ensure that they know the meaning of the key language. Practise pronunciation if needed. You could model the task structure beforehand with a confident volunteer.

➕ Students write their answers in the third person form. They could then share these with the class.

Extra

Students include opinions in their responses, by adding this additional question and answer to their dialogues for activity 1.

2 Was sind die Vorteile und Nachteile (*advantages and disadvantages*) des Internets und der sozialen Medien? Verbinde die Sätze (1–10) mit den Übersetzungen (a–j).

Students match the German and English sentences describing advantages and disadvantages of the internet and social media.

5 Virtuelle und reelle Welt

Answers: **1** b; **2** i; **3** f; **4** e; **5** a; **6** c; **7** j; **8** h; **9** g; **10** d

⭐ Before matching, tell students which sentences are an advantage or disadvantage.

3 🎧 GCSE **How do the people (1–6) feel about the internet and social media? Listen and write P (positive), N (negative) or P+N (both). Listen again and write the reason in English.**

Remind students that the conjunction *aber* is often used to introduce a contrasting point of view for a 'P+N' statement.

> Answers:
> **1** P – You find a lot of information.
> **2** N – You don't sleep enough (because you look at your phone in the night).
> **3** N – You don't spend enough time with friends and family.
> **4** P+N – You can stay in contact with family abroad, but it's dangerous because you might speak with strangers.
> **5** P – You can find the way with your mobile phone and you can shop very cheaply.
> **6** P+N – You aren't active enough because you always have your phone in your hand. But you can do a lot with a mobile phone, for example when you have a disability.

⭐ Provide students with the reasons in a random order for them to choose from, rather than noting them down themselves.

> 🎵 **CD 2, track 26   Seite 102, Aktivität 3**
>
> 1 – Jaromir, was denkst du über das Internet und soziale Medien?
>   – Ich finde das Internet total gut. Ich denke, dass man viele Informationen findet.
> 2 – Und du, Kathrin? Was denkst du?
>   – Also ich denke, dass das Internet nicht gut ist. Ich glaube, dass man nicht genug schläft, weil man in der Nacht auf das Handy guckt.
> 3 – Und Bernd, wie findest du das Internet und soziale Medien?
>   – Ich denke, dass soziale Medien schlecht sind, weil man nicht genug Zeit mit Freunden und der Familie verbringt.
> 4 – Lena, was denkst du?
>   – Ich denke, dass es Vorteile und Nachteile gibt. Ein Vorteil ist, dass man mit der Familie im Ausland in Kontakt bleiben kann, aber ein Nachteil ist, dass man vielleicht mit Fremden spricht. Das ist gefährlich.
> 5 – Ruben, wie findest du soziale Medien und das Internet?
>   – Ich finde, dass sie total toll sind. Man kann den Weg mit dem Handy finden. Man kann auch sehr billig einkaufen.
> 6 – Und Sina, was ist deine Meinung?
>   – Naja, es gibt schlechte und gute Aspekte. Ich finde, dass man nicht aktiv genug ist, weil man immer das Handy in der Hand hat. Aber ich denke, dass es auch Vorteile gibt. Meine Mutter ist behindert, aber mit dem Handy kann sie viel machen.

Aa Grammatik

Remind students that *dass* and *das* are not interchangeable (learners of German often get them confused).

4 ✏️ **Bring die fettgedruckten Wörter in die richtige Reihenfolge.**

Students rearrange the bold words in the correct order.

> Answers: **a** man viele Informationen findet; **b** das Internet Nachteile hat; **c** man mit Freunden sprechen kann; **d** man nicht aktiv genug ist; **e** ich nicht mehr genug schlafe; **f** es zu viel Cyber-Mobbing gibt

➕ Students translate the sentences into English. Refer them to the English sentences in activity 2 for support.

> Suggested translations:
> **a** I think that you find a lot of information.
> **b** I believe that the internet has disadvantages.
> **c** An/One advantage is that you can speak with friends.
> **d** A/One disadvantage is that you aren't active enough.
> **e** My parents think that I no longer sleep enough/I don't sleep enough anymore.
> **f** My mother believes that there is too much cyber-bullying.

119

5 Virtuelle und reelle Welt

5 Füll die Lücken aus. Du brauchst nicht alle Wörter zu benutzen.

Students fill the gaps with a word from those provided. There are three distractors.

> Answers: **1** wichtig; **2** Nachteile; **3** Freunden; **4** nicht; **5** Handy; **6** hören; **7** Fremden

6 GCSE Translate the last two bullet points from Tobi's blog post into English.

> *Suggested translations:*
> - Many children and young people don't sleep enough. You should sleep (for) at least eight hours, but many teenagers look at the/their mobile phone in bed. Before sleeping, you can read or listen to music.
> - And of course, it's very important that you don't speak to strangers.

Strategie

Point out and/or collate ideas about how students could apply this strategy in their dialogues for activity 7.

7 Macht Dialoge.

Students ask and answer questions about the internet and social media. You could model the task structure and pronunciation beforehand with a confident volunteer. As a follow-up task, students could write their dialogues in German.

5.4 Technologie heute und damals

5 Virtuelle und reelle Welt

Objectives

- Vocabulary: Talking about technology today and in the past
- Grammar: Recognising and using the imperfect tense
- Strategy: Narrating events in the past

Resources

- Student Book, pages 104–105
- CD 2, tracks 27–28
- Grammar, Vocabulary and Translation Workbook, pages 58–59
- Kerboodle, Unit 5

Key language

- *damals, heutzutage, in den 1970er/1980er/1990er Jahren*
- *Es gab fast überall/keine/nicht so viel(e)/mehr/ wenig…*
- *Ich ging (ins Internetcafé). Ich hatte (kein Smartphone). Ich hörte (Musik). Ich interessierte mich (für Umweltschutz). Ich las (Zeitschriften). Ich schrieb (Postkarten). Ich spielte (Computerspiele).*
- *auf dem Handy, auf Musikplattformen, im Heft, im Internet, im Radio*

Homework and self-study

- Student Book, page 105, activity 6
- Grammar, Vocabulary and Translation Workbook, pages 58–59

Starter

- As preparation for activity 1 in this lesson and for general grammar revision, provide students with a print-out of sentences a–j from activity 1. Students highlight or underline the verb(s) (or write a list of them, if they don't have a print-out). They could also translate the verbs, if time permits.

Plenary

- Tell students to refer to Lesson 5.4 in their Student Books (in particular, activities 1, 2, 3 and 5), and to work in pairs. One partner reads a present tense or imperfect tense sentence from the lesson aloud; for example, *Es gab keine Smartphones*. Their partner repeats the sentence but changes the verb to the other tense; for example, *Es gibt keine Smartphones*. This provides practice of listening and speaking alongside the grammar focus of the lesson: Recognising and using the imperfect tense.

---

1 📖 **GCSE** Wer sagt das: Lili (L) oder ihre Oma (O)?

Students decide whether the statements would be more likely to apply to a teenage girl (Lili) or her grandmother. Tell students to think logically about context and what they know about life today and in the past.

Answers: **a** O; **b** L; **c** O; **d** O; **e** L; **f** O; **g** L; **h** O; **i** L; **j** L

2 🎧 Hör zu und füll die Lücken aus.

Students listen and complete the sentences with the correct German word(s). Point out to students that that some gaps require more than one word. You may wish to explain that when referring to years, 'in' is not required in German: *1970 gab es kein Internet*. When referring to decades, -er in German (as in *1970er*) is the equivalent of '-ies' in English (as in 1970s). Explain also that *als* is used to mean 'when', when talking about the past (not *wenn* or *wann*).

Answers: **a** Technologie; **b** Computer; **c** Teenager; **d** Zeitschrift; **e** Sport; **f** auf dem Handy, im Radio; **g** Technologie; **h** ein Handy, einen Laptop, einen Fernseher; **i** Sport, Umweltschutz; **j** Informationen im Internet; **k** Rockmusik, Songs

⭐ Provide the first letter of the word(s) in each gap.

〰️ **CD 2, track 27   Seite 104, Aktivität 2**

Herr Brahms, 64 Jahre alt

Es gab wenig Technologie, als ich jünger war und ich hatte keinen Computer. Ich war aber ein typischer Teenager und kaufte jede Woche eine Zeitschrift, weil ich mich für Musik und

121

5 Virtuelle und reelle Welt

Sport interessierte. Ich hörte aber Musik nie auf dem Handy, sondern nur im Radio oder auf einem Plattenspieler.

Dominik, 18 Jahre alt

Es gibt sehr viel Technologie heutzutage. Ich habe ein Handy, einen Laptop und einen Fernseher in meinem Zimmer. Ich interessiere mich für Sport, aber auch für Umweltschutz. Ich finde Informationen im Internet. Ich höre gern Rockmusik und ich kaufe Songs auf Musikplattformen.

Aussprache: r

Model the correct pronunciation and encourage students to practise saying the example sentence.

Grammatik

Students may already be familiar with common imperfect tense verbs such as *war*, *hatte* and *gab*. Explain that the imperfect tense is also often used in a more narrative sense, particularly in written German, to express the idea of 'used to'.

Tipp

Remind students to apply this reading tip when they complete activity 3.

3 Wähl das richtige Verb.

Students choose the correct verb form to complete each sentence.

Answers: **a** *gab;* **b** *haben;* **c** *interessiere;* **d** *hörte*

➕ Students create a new sentence containing each verb.

4 Hör zu. Sind die Sätze (1–8) im Präsens (P) oder Imperfekt (I)? Schreib das Verb aus jedem Satz.

Students listen and decide whether the verb in each sentence is in the present or imperfect tense. They also note down each verb in German.

Answers: **1** P – gibt; **2** P – engagiere mich; **3** I – interessierte mich; **4** I – las; **5** I – gab; **6** P – gibt; **7** P – liest; **8** I – gab

CD 2, track 28   Seite 105, Aktivität 4

1   Es gibt viel Umweltverschmutzung.
2   Ich engagiere mich für die Obdachlosenhilfe.
3   Ich interessierte mich für Umweltschutz.
4   Man las nur Zeitungen.
5   Es gab viele Fernsehkanäle.
6   Es gibt viele Fernsehkanäle.
7   Man liest oft Zeitungen im Internet.
8   Es gab nicht so viel Umweltverschmutzung.

5 GCSE Read Monika's text about life and technology in the 1990s. Answer the questions in English.

Answers: **a** *slow;* **b** *not many people had a computer at home;* **c** *very simple;* **d** *you couldn't use the phone;* **e** *there weren't any smartphones and mobile phones were very big*

Strategie

Explain to students that the imperfect tense is a past tense that is more frequently used in more formal and written German; for example, in the news on TV, online and in newspapers, as well as in novels and stories. Remind them that general word-order rules still apply in the imperfect tense; for example, with subordinating conjunctions, and the 'verb-second' and 'time–manner–place' rules.

6 Wie war die Technologie in den 1980er Jahren und wie ist sie jetzt? Such im Internet Informationen darüber und schreib 70–90 Wörter.

Students write a comparison between technology in the 1980s and technology today.

⭐ Provide a simple list of English bullet points for students to cover; for example: the internet, mobile phones, listening to music.

7 Stell dir vor, wir sind im Jahr 2050. Mach eine Präsentation.

Guided by the bullet points, students create an oral presentation about technology in the year 2050. They don't need to use the future tense, but should instead refer to today's technology using the imperfect tense.

122

5.5 Ich engagiere mich

5 Virtuelle und reelle Welt

Objectives
- Vocabulary: Talking about volunteering projects
- Grammar: Revising the use of different tenses
- Strategy: Recognising and using compound nouns

Resources
- Student Book, pages 106–107
- CD 2, track 29
- Grammar, Vocabulary and Translation Workbook, pages 60–61
- Kerboodle, Unit 5

Key language
- der Tierschutz, der Umweltschutz, die Behindertenhilfe, die Altenhilfe, die Obdachlosenhilfe, die Flüchtlingshilfe, das Projekt
- (Umweltschutz) ist mir sehr wichtig. Ich denke, dass (Flüchtlingshilfe) total wichtig ist. (Obdachlosenhilfe) interessiert mich.
- Ich verkaufe Kuchen. Ich arbeite in einem Tierheim. Ich spende Geld. Ich helfe Menschen. Ich unterrichte Deutsch. Ich gehe einkaufen. Ich sammle Geld. Ich sammle Abfall auf.
- Ich habe … verkauft/gearbeitet/gespendet/geholfen/unterrichtet. Ich bin … gegangen
- Ich werde … verkaufen/arbeiten/spenden/helfen/unterrichten/gehen.

Homework and self-study
- Student Book, page 107, activity 6
- Grammar, Vocabulary and Translation Workbook, pages 60–61

Starter
- As preparation for activity 1 and to work on the *Strategie* focus of the lesson (Recognising and using compound nouns), provide students with a print-out of sentences a–f from activity 1, completed with the correct compound nouns in German. They highlight or underline the individual nouns in each word. They could also translate the nouns, if time permits.

Plenary
- Prepare a 'trapdoor' speaking activity: write a short paragraph including key vocabulary from this and previous lessons, with three different options for key words; for example, *Ich habe **bei einem Umweltprojekt/in einem Altenheim/den Obdachlosen** geholfen. Ich **denke/finde/glaube**, dass es sehr wichtig ist.* Students choose an option for each sentence and then take turns to read the whole text aloud, trying to guess their partner's choices. If they choose correctly, they continue; if they are incorrect, they swap over and have to start again at the beginning next time.

1 🔊 **Übersetz die Wörter (a–f) ins Deutsche. Wähl den richtigen Wortanfang und das richtige Wortende.**

Students use the English translations provided to create the correct German compound nouns.

> Answers: **a** Tierschutz; **b** Umweltschutz; **c** Behindertenhilfe; **d** Altenhilfe; **e** Obdachlosenhilfe; **f** Flüchtlingshilfe

🔆 Strategie

Students may be able to recall compound nouns from other topic areas such as 'where I live' (for example, types of houses and rooms) and 'free time'. Students could also identify compound nouns used in the activity rubrics in this lesson; for example, *Wortanfang* ('beginning of word'), *Wortende* ('ending of word') and *Würfelspiel* ('dice game').

> Answers: social project; soup kitchen; nature protection;
> (synonym for Naturschutz:) Umweltschutz

123

5 Virtuelle und reelle Welt

2 📖 **Read what the young people do to support charitable causes. Translate the sentences into English.**

Suggested translations:
a I sell cakes. **b** I work in an animal shelter/home. **c** I donate money. **d** I help people. **e** I teach German. **f** I go shopping. **g** I collect money. **h** I collect rubbish.

➕ Students include extra detail in each sentence by adding a subordinate clause beginning with *denn* or *weil*.

⚠️ **Achtung!**

Elaborate on the *Achtung!* box by telling students that 'to spend' is translated as *ausgeben* for money and *verbringen* for time. You could also explain that *ausgeben* is a separable verb and *verbringen* is not.

3 🎧 [GCSE] **Listen to the teenagers (1–5) talking about a charity project. Copy and complete the table in English.**

Remind students to listen carefully to the tenses and time expressions used. They will need to note down how the speakers help, which requires answers in the present tense.

Answers:

	Charity project	How they help
1	animal protection	donates money
2	environmental protection	collects rubbish
3	helping refugees	reads German books twice a week with teenage immigrants
4	helping the elderly	goes shopping for an elderly man
5	helping homeless people	works in a soup kitchen

⭐ Provide students with a table that has half of each answer filled in; for example, **1** _____ protection, donates_____.

➕ Students add a 'What they did' column to the table and note down what each speaker did yesterday. You may wish to remind students of the word *gestern*.

Answers:

	What they did
1	saw a documentary about problems faced by gorillas
2	collected rubbish for two hours (with youth group)
3	babysat for a Syrian woman
4	cooked
5	cooked pasta with tomato sauce

🔊 **CD 2, track 29   Seite 107, Aktivität 3**

1 – Hallo, Karin. Was machst du für das Wohltätigkeitsprojekt?
– Ich liebe Tiere. Ich interessiere mich für Tierschutz. Ich spende Geld für Tiere – fünf Euro pro Monat von meinem Taschengeld. Gestern habe ich im Fernsehen einen Dokumentarfilm über die Probleme von Gorillas gesehen.

2 – Und du, Lutz, was machst du?
– Mir ist Umweltschutz sehr wichtig. Ich helfe der Umwelt und ich sammle Abfall auf. Gestern habe ich zwei Stunden Abfall mit meiner Jugendgruppe aufgesammelt.

3 – Hallo, Jenny. Was ist dein Wohltätigkeitsprojekt?
– Mir ist Hilfe für Asylsuchende wichtig. Ich engagiere mich für die Flüchtlingshilfe. Ich lese zweimal in der Woche mit jugendlichen Immigranten deutsche Bücher und gestern habe ich für eine syrische Frau Babysitting gemacht.

4 – Was machst du für das Projekt, Jonas?
– Mir ist Altenhilfe sehr wichtig. Ich helfe einem alten Mann und gehe einkaufen. Gestern habe ich auch gekocht.

5 – Und du, Amira, was machst du?
– Ich interessiere mich für Obdachlosenhilfe. Normalerweise arbeite ich in der Suppenküche. Gestern habe ich Nudeln mit Tomatensoße gekocht.

5 Virtuelle und reelle Welt

Aa Grammatik

Before working through the *Grammatik* box, use a question-and-answer session to remind students of what they already know about the three tenses: meaning, usage, formation and differences between English and German.

4 💬 **Würfelspiel! Werft den Würfel dreimal. Benutzt die Sätze aus Aktivität 2 (1–6).**

Students use a die to select an action from activity 2. They then form a sentence to tell their partner. If dice are unavailable or unsuitable, write a list of die scores on the board in a random order and students can just work through these. It may be useful to model this task beforehand with a confident volunteer.

➕ Students practise third person verb forms by writing down their partner's responses or reporting them back to the class.

Sprachmuster

To add more challenge to activity 4, students could try to complete the activity without looking at the phrases in the *Sprachmuster* box.

5 📖 **GCSE Read about three students' experiences of a class volunteering project. Are the statements true (T), false (F) or not in the text (NT)?**

Students may need extra help to distinguish between 'false' and 'not in the text': a statement is 'false' is if there is contradictory information in the text to make the statement obviously incorrect; a statement is 'not in the text' if we have no idea, as the text does not include any information about this.

> Answers: **a** F; **b** NT; **c** T; **d** F; **e** NT; **f** T

➕ Students correct the false sentences.

> Answers:
> **a** Lina worked for an <u>environmental</u> project.
> **d** Barbara wants to <u>help with an environmental project</u> in future.

6 ✏️ **Wie engagierst du dich?** (*How do you get involved in causes?*) **Beschreib ein Projekt. Das kann auch etwas sein, was du früher gemacht hast oder in Zukunft machen wirst.**

Students write a response to the question in German. Remind them to use the correct tense(s), depending on whether they choose a current, past or future project to describe. Remind them also that the information doesn't need to be true, particularly as they may have had limited opportunity to engage with any voluntary or charitable work.

5 Kultur

Resources
- Student Book, pages 108–109
- CD 2, track 30

1 📖 **GCSE Read the article about the *Pfand* system in Germany. Complete the sentences in English.**

Students should read the information box below activity 1 before starting the task, to help them understand the context. You may also wish to pre-teach the key words in the text, which are in bold.

> Answers: **a** bottle; **b** bring/take; **c** money; **d** rubbish/litter; **e** machine; **f** button; **g** shop

⭐ Provide students with a word bank to choose from, including several plausible distractors. Alternatively, point out to them that the German words in bold in the text correspond directly to the gaps in sentences a–g and are in the same order as the gaps.

125

5 Virtuelle und reelle Welt

2 🎧 **Hör zu. Fatima spricht über ihren Besuch im österreichischen Jugendparlament. Wähl die richtige Antwort.**

Students listen and choose the correct option to complete each sentence. You may wish to explain the term *Jugendparlament* ('youth parliament') and refer to the UK's equivalent Youth Parliament and MYPs, with which they may be familiar.

Answers: **a** *letztes Jahr;* **b** *Tage;* **c** *neunten;* **d** *Umweltschutz;* **e** *wichtig;* **f** *Jugendliche;* **g** *gesprochen;* **h** *nützlich*

〰️ **CD 2, track 30   Seite 108, Aktivität 2**

Ich heiße Fatima. Ich wohne in Österreich und ich war letztes Jahr beim Jugendparlament in Wien. Wien ist die Hauptstadt von Österreich. Das Jugendparlament dauert immer zwei Tage. Das Jugendparlament ist für Schüler und Schülerinnen in der neunten Klasse. Man kann über Themen wie zum Beispiel Naturschutz sprechen und ich finde das sehr wichtig. Am ersten Tag trifft man Politiker und andere Jugendliche. Am zweiten Tag spricht man im Parlament über ein Thema. Ich hatte Angst, aber ein Politiker hat mir geholfen. Ich denke, es waren zwei nützliche Tage.

3 📖 [GCSE] **Lies die Fakten über die *Lindenstraße*, eine deutsche Seifenoper (*soap opera*). Richtig (R), falsch (F) oder nicht im Text (NT)?**

Students read the text and decide whether each statement is true, false or not in the text. They may need extra help to distinguish between 'false' and 'not in the text': a statement is 'false' is if there's contradictory information in the text to make the statement obviously incorrect; a statement is 'not in the text' if we have no idea, as the text doesn't include any information about this.

Answers: **a** F; **b** NT; **c** R; **d** F; **e** NT; **f** R

➕ Students correct the false sentences.

Answers:
a Lindenstraße *war eine* <u>Seifenoper</u>.
d *Es gab in der Serie ein* <u>griechisches</u> *Restaurant*.

4 📖 **Was passt zusammen? Verbinde die Fragen (1–6) mit den Antworten (a–f).**

Students match the questions and answers. Remind them to check carefully the question words and tenses used in the questions, as this will help them work out which answer they are looking for.

Answers: **1** b; **2** d; **3** f; **4** c; **5** e; **6** a

5 💬 **Macht Dialoge. Benutzt die Fragen aus Aktivität 4. Verändert die <u>unterstrichenen</u> Details in euren Antworten.**

Students ask and answer the questions from activity 4, changing the underlined details to their own information. You could model the task structure and pronunciation beforehand with a confident volunteer.

5 Sprachlabor

Objectives
- Word order after *weil*, *da* and *denn*
- Time–manner–place word order
- Expressing opinions using *dass*
- The imperfect tense
- Pronunciation: *z*, *ts* and *t*

Resources
- Student Book, pages 110–111
- CD 2, tracks 31–32
- Grammar, Vocabulary and Translation Workbook, pages 52–61
- Kerboodle, Unit 5

5 Virtuelle und reelle Welt

Aa Grammatik

Word order after *weil*, *da* and *denn*

Remind students that, although all of these words mean 'because', they have different word-order rules.

1 Match the beginning and ending of the sentences.

Answers: **1** b; **2** c; **3** d; **4** f; **5** a; **6** e

2 Put the words in the second half of each sentence in the correct order.

Answers: **a** da ich mitsingen kann; **b** weil er DJ ist; **c** denn es ist nützlich für Hausaufgaben; **d** weil sie es wichtig findet; **e** da er sich für Tiere interessiert; **f** denn ich liebe Französisch

Aa Grammatik

Time–manner–place word order

Students could note down some adverbs for each category (time, manner and place) to refresh their memory. They could then see if any of their words appear in activities 3 or 4. Students often find it difficult to identify adverbs of manner; remind them that they describe 'how' something is done (in contrast to 'where' and 'when').

3 Identify whether the phrases express time (T), manner (M) or place (P). Then translate the phrases into English.

Answers/Suggested translations:
a P – at home; **b** T – every day; **c** P – to the concert; **d** M – with friends; **e** M – with my parents; **f** M – on my (mobile) phone; **g** T – sometimes; **h** P – in the living room; **i** T – last weekend; **j** P – in my (bed)room; **k** T – in the evening; **l** M – alone/on my own

4 Identify the time, manner and place elements in the sentences. Then translate the sentences into English.

Answers/Suggested translations:

	Time	Manner	Place
a	am Freitag	mit meiner Schwester	ins Konzert
b	am Abend	allein	in meinem Zimmer
c	nie	–	in der Schule
d	am Wochenende	mit seinen Freunden	in den Park

a I went to the concert on Friday with my sister.
b I like listening to classical music alone in my room in the evening.
c He's never allowed to listen to music at school.
d He would like to go to the park with his friends at the weekend.

5 Write **four** sentences using all of the phrases from activity 3. Try to use different tenses and personal pronouns.

Suggested answers:
Ich sehe jeden Tag mit meinen Eltern im Wohnzimmer fern.
Du bist letztes Wochenende mit Freunden ins Konzert gegangen.
Manchmal sehe ich Filme auf meinem Handy in meinem Zimmer.
Julia hat am Abend allein zu Hause Rockmusik gehört.

⭐ Provide students with English sentences using all the adverbs from activity 3, which they can then translate into German.

Aa Grammatik

Expressing opinions using *dass*

You may wish to recap that *dass* and *das* are often confused by learners of German, but they are **not** interchangeable.

5 Virtuelle und reelle Welt

6 Match the English phrases with the German translations.

Answers: **1** b; **2** e; **3** a; **4** f; **5** c; **6** d

7 Put the words in the second half of each sentence in the correct order.

Answers: **a** dass romantische Komödien zu kindisch sind; **b** dass es viele Informationen im Internet gibt; **c** dass Tierschutz ganz wichtig ist; **d** dass wir zu viel fernsehen; **e** dass Teenager das Internet zu oft benutzen; **f** dass mein Internet manchmal langsam ist

Grammatik
The imperfect tense

You may wish to recap the difference between the perfect and imperfect tenses in meaning, formation and usage.

8 Choose the correct answer to complete each sentence.

Answers: **a** hatte; **b** spielten; **c** waren; **d** interessiertest; **e** kauften

Aussprache: z, ts and t

These tasks require lots of teacher demonstration to provide students with an excellent pronunciation model. You can also play the audio files to demonstrate correct pronunciation.

9 Listen and repeat. Then practise with your partner.

Isolate the sounds first, then move on to using the words which include the sounds.

CD 2, track 31   Seite 111, Aktivität 9

See Student Book, page 111, for audio script.

10 Practise saying the tongue twister.

Depending on the ability of the class, you could play some games with this; for example, partners saying alternate words in the sentence, whole-class repetition using different volumes or speeds, or trying to learn the tongue twister-style sentence off by heart.

CD 2, track 32   Seite 111, Aktivität 10

See Student Book, page 111, for audio script.

5 Was kann ich schon?

Resources
- Student Book, pages 112–113
- CD 2, tracks 33–34
- Kerboodle, Unit 5

Reading

1 Füll die Lücken aus.

Students fill each gap with the correct word, choosing from those provided.

Answers: **1** interessiere; **2** Abenteuerfilme; **3** Nachrichten; **4** gesehen; **5** das; **6** gefährlich; **7** Vorteil; **8** dass; **9** gehört; **10** Volksmusik

5 Virtuelle und reelle Welt

2 📖 Read Fabian's blog post. Are the statements true (T) or false (F)?

Answers: **a** T; **b** F; **c** F; **d** T; **e** F; **f** T; **g** T; **h** F; **i** T; **j** F

Listening

3 🎧 GCSE Listen to people (1–5) talking about their interests. Write the two correct letters (a–j) for each person.

Explain to students that each letter can only be used once.

Answers: **1** a, h; **2** b, f; **3** j, g; **4** i, d; **5** c, e

〰️ CD 2, track 33   Seite 112, Aktivität 3

– Ich interessiere mich für Kleidung – Röcke, Hosen, Hemden – aber auch für soziale Projekte, zum Beispiel helfe ich gern alten Menschen.

– Was mir sehr wichtig ist, ist die Umwelt, zum Beispiel Luftverschmutzung. Ich interessiere mich auch für Sport, besonders Schwimmen.

– Ich habe großes Interesse an Medien. Ja, digitale Medien, zum Beispiel Handys und Apps. Was mich auch interessiert, ist gesundes Leben, zum Beispiel gesundes Essen.

– Ich gehe gern ins Kino und sehe am liebsten die aktuellen Filme. Was mich nicht so interessiert ist die Umwelt, aber ich arbeite am Wochenende bei der Behindertenhilfe. Das finde ich wichtig.

– Tierschutz ist mir sehr wichtig. Abends, wenn ich mich entspannen will, schaue ich Videos an.

4 🎧 Listen to Daria talking about her interests. Choose the correct answer to complete each sentence.

Answers: **a** always; **b** what she is doing; **c** classical; **d** rock; **e** grandparents; **f** annoying; **g** using headphones; **h** weekend; **i** one song; **j** likes

〰️ CD 2, track 34   Seite 112, Aktivität 4

Ich bin Daria. Ich höre echt immer Musik. Ich höre klassische Musik, wenn ich meine Hausaufgaben mache. Ich mache auch viel Sport. Beim Joggen höre ich Rockmusik, denn das gibt mir viel Energie.

Volksmusik höre ich nur bei meinen Großeltern. Sie finden Volksmusik unterhaltsam, aber für mich ist diese Musik nervig. Zu Hause höre ich oft Musik mit Kopfhörern. Warum? Also, meine Eltern denken, dass meine Musik zu laut ist.

Ich war letztes Wochenende mit meinen Eltern auf einem Konzert von den *Fantastischen Vier*. Sie machen deutsche Hip-Hop-Musik. Ich habe das Konzert schrecklich gefunden – nur ein Lied hat mir gefallen. Normalerweise hören meine Eltern coole Musik. Meistens finde ich ihre Musik gut.

Writing

5 ✏️ Füll die Lücken mit den Verben in Klammern aus. Benutz die passende Form des Verbs.

Students fill the gaps with the correct form and tense of the verb in brackets.

Answers: **a** helfe; **b** habe, gearbeitet; **c** werde, lesen; **d** sind; **e** denken

6 ✏️ Bring die Wörter in die richtige Reihenfolge.

Students reorder the words and phrases to produce correct sentences. Point out to students that they should start each sentence with a word with a capital letter at the start.

Answers:
a Alex hat für sein Projekt in einem Altenheim gearbeitet.
b Wir interessieren uns sehr für Tierschutz.
c Ich höre Rapmusik, wenn ich meine Hausaufgaben mache.
d Mir gefallen Abenteuerfilme, weil ich sie spannend finde.
e Ich werde in Zukunft alten Menschen helfen.

129

5 Virtuelle und reelle Welt

7 ✏️ [GCSE] **Übersetz die Sätze ins Deutsche.**

Students translate the sentences into German. Award one mark for each part of the sentence.

> Suggested translations:
> **a** Ich interessiere mich für (1) Tierschutz (1).
> **b** Mode (1) ist mir wichtig (1).
> **c** Ich denke, dass (1) das Internet nützlich ist (1).
> **d** Ich sehe Abenteuerfilme (1) am liebsten (1)./Ich sehe (1) am liebsten Abenteuerfilme (1).
> **e** Ich höre Popmusik, (1) wenn ich zu Hause helfe (1).

5 Vorankommen!

Resources
- Student Book, pages 114–115
- CD 2, tracks 35–37
- Kerboodle, Unit 5

Bronze

1 📖 [GCSE] **Read Karla's message and answer the questions in English.**

Point out to students that two details are required for the answer to question d.

> Answers: **a** four hours per day; **b** They think it's too long because she doesn't do her homework. **c** more than eight hours per day; **d** They are fun(ny) and relaxing. **e** Which (TV) programmes do you like (watching) best/most (of all)?

2 🎧 **Listen and choose the correct answer to complete each sentence.**

> Answers: **a** German pop; **b** sing along; **c** terrible; **d** in his room; **e** liked

〜〰️ **CD 2, track 35   Seite 114, Aktivität 2**

Ich heiße Jakob. Meine Lieblingsmusik ist Schlagermusik. Ich höre Schlager gern, weil ich mitsingen kann. Meine Schwester denkt, dass meine Musik schrecklich ist. Deshalb höre ich meine Musik meistens in meinem Zimmer. Ich benutze mein Handy, aber ich benutze keine Kopfhörer. Meine Kopfhörer sind kaputt. Letzte Woche am Mittwoch bin ich ins Konzert meiner Lieblingsband gegangen. Es hat mir gut gefallen.

3 ✏️ **Answer the questions in German.**

Students answer the questions for themselves.

Silber

4 📖 **Read Stefanie's description. Are the statements true (T) or false (F)?**

Check that students are familiar with the term 'influencer': someone with an online presence on social media, often advertising a lifestyle or products (different from an online celebrity).

> Answers: **a** T; **b** F; **c** T; **d** F; **e** T; **f** F

130

5 Virtuelle und reelle Welt

5 🎧 GCSE Listen to Elias talking about his use of the internet and complete the sentences in English.

> Answers: **a** every day; **b** family abroad/in Australia; **c** useful, dangerous; **d** sleep; **e** midnight; **f** so late in the evening/at night

〰️ **CD 2, track 36   Seite 114, Aktivität 5**

Ich bin Elias. Ich benutze das Internet jeden Tag. Ich benutze gern das Internet, weil man mit der Familie im Ausland sprechen kann. Ich habe zum Beispiel eine Tante in Australien und da finde ich das Internet praktisch. Meine Eltern denken, dass das Internet nützlich aber auch gefährlich sein kann. Meine Mutter findet zum Beispiel, dass ich nicht genug schlafe, weil ich bis Mitternacht am Computer oder Handy sitze. In Zukunft werde ich nicht so spät am Abend das Internet benutzen.

6 ✏️ GCSE Übersetz den Text ins Deutsche.
Translate the text into German.

> Suggested translation:
> Früher/In der Vergangenheit gab es nicht so viel Technologie. Es gab nicht so viele Fernsehsendungen/Sendungen und man hörte auch mehr Radio, da/weil es kein Internet gab/denn es gab kein Internet. Heute ist die Technologie sehr nützlich/praktisch, aber das Leben ist nicht so ruhig.

Gold

7 📖 GCSE Lies den Artikel über die App *Ich bin wählerisch!* Beantworte die Fragen auf Englisch.

Students read the article and answer the questions in English. You may wish to explain that *wählerisch* means 'picky' but it's also linked to *wählen*, which means 'to vote'.

> Answers: **a** elderly people/seniors; **b** read (stories or newspapers) with them; **c** climate change or racism; **d** children and young people; **e** say 'No' and swipe left; **f** you can watch an explanatory video

8 ✏️ GCSE Übersetz den Text im Kästchen, ‚Wie benutzt man die App?' ins Englische.

Students translate the text in the green box into English.

> Suggested translation:
> How do you use the app?
> There's a quiz and questions. You answer the questions with 'Yes' or 'No'. When/If you don't know the answer to a question, you say 'No' and swipe left. You can then see an explanatory video. When/If you know the answer, you say 'Yes' and swipe right.

9 🎧 GCSE Hör zu. Eine Expertin, Frau Doktor Steeger, spricht über die Nutzung des Internets. Wähl die <u>vier</u> richtigen Sätze.

Students listen and choose the four correct statements.

> Answers (in any order): b, e, f, g

〰️ **CD 2, track 37   Seite 115, Aktivität 9**

– Frau Doktor Steeger. Wie lange sind Jugendliche im Internet?
– Also, Jugendliche benutzen zwei bis drei Stunden pro Tag das Internet. Manche Kinder haben das Handy fast immer in der Hand.
– Und was machen die meisten Jugendlichen im Internet?
– Natürlich spielen viele junge Menschen Spiele online aber nicht alle. Mehr als 80 Prozent sehen Filme im Internet.
– Was denken die Eltern?
– Mehr als die Hälfte der Eltern checken nie, welche Internetseiten ihre Kinder besuchen. Die Kinder besuchen Internetseiten, aber mehr als fünfzig Prozent der Eltern wissen nicht, was für Webseiten ihre Kinder im Internet besucht haben! Ich denke, es ist wichtig, dass Eltern etwas Kontrolle haben, denn Kinder verstehen nicht, dass das Internet Nachteile hat. Sie sehen nur die Vorteile.

5 Virtuelle und reelle Welt

10 GCSE Übersetz die Sätze ins Deutsche.

Students translate the sentences into German.

Suggested translations:
a Ich höre nicht gern Rockmusik, wenn ich mich entspanne.
b Ich interessiere mich für die Umwelt, denn es ist wichtig./da es wichtig ist./weil es wichtig ist.
c Ich werde in Zukunft mit Tieren arbeiten./ In Zukunft werde ich mit Tieren arbeiten.
d Ich benutze das Internet am Abend./Ich benutze am Abend das Internet./Am Abend benutze ich das Internet.
e Meine Eltern denken, dass das Internet gefährlich sein kann.

11 GCSE Wie benutzt du Technologie? Schreib einen Text (zirka 80 Wörter).

Guided by the bullet points, students write in German about their experiences with technology.

🎁 Extra

You could provide students with a checklist of all of the topics covered in the unit; for example, cinema, music, social media.

6 Willkommen in Berlin!

Unit overview			
Page reference	**Vocabulary**	**Grammar**	**Strategy**
120–121 6.1 Wollen wir nach Berlin fahren?	Planning a trip to Berlin	Revising the future tense with *werden*	Carrying out online research
122–123 6.2 So leben wir in Berlin!	Learning about life in Berlin	Using a range of tenses	Dealing with unfamiliar vocabulary

6 Los geht's!

Resources
- CD 2, track 38

Starter
- Students note any facts they know about Berlin.

Plenary
- Ask students to summarise some new things that they have learnt from the lesson in a 3–2–1 activity: three famous landmarks, two key words and one interesting fact. They can share these with the class or with a partner.

1 Verbinde die Titel (1–5) mit den Bildern (a–e).

Students match the Berlin landmark names with the correct photos.

Answers: **1** b; **2** c; **3** a; **4** e; **5** d

2 Berlin in Zahlen! Rate mal! Füll die Lücken mit den passenden Zahlen aus.

Students choose the correct number to complete each sentence.

Answers: **a** 3,7 Millionen; **b** 1989; **c** 1700; **d** 80; **e** 1000; **f** 70 Millionen; **g** 13; **h** 3

➕ Students write the numbers in full in German and/or translate the sentences into English.

🎭 Kultur

Students could try to pronounce other words in the dialect (for example, from the texts in activities 3 and 4), and their partner tries to guess the words.

🎵 **CD 2, track 38   Seite 118, Kultur**

See Student Book, page 118, for audio script.

3 What did they do in Berlin? Read the tweets and make notes in English for each person.

Answers:

@Reisefieber: did a city tour, went for a walk, saw the Brandenburg Gate and the Reichstag building, went on a boat trip

@theworldismyteacher: went to the cinema, ate Currywurst

@Tanzfee: went dancing in clubs/discos

@Weltenbummler: went to the Checkpoint Charlie museum, took part in a tour round a nuclear bunker at the city museum

⭐ Provide students with the correct information, which they then assign to the correct person; for example, did a city tour – @Reisefieber.

4 Lies den Text zum Foto. Finde die vier Fehler im Text.

Students read the description of the photo and identify the four mistakes in the text.

Answers:
Auf dem Foto gibt es eine kleine Straße mit vielen Autos. Es gibt auch viele Leute. Sie sitzen in Cafés oder gehen spazieren. Unter den Tischen stehen kleine orange Kerzenlichter. Die Wände der Häuser sind weiß. Rechts sind zwei Straßenmusiker: Sie spielen Trompete und Gitarre.

➕ Students correct the mistakes.

Answers: mit **keinen** Autos; **Auf** den Tischen; Die Wände der Häuser **sind grau/bunt/haben buntes Graffiti**; Sie spielen Trompete und **Kontrabass**

🎭 Kultur

There are some printable activities for children on the buddy-baer.com website.

6.1 Wollen wir nach Berlin fahren?

Objectives

- Vocabulary: Planning a trip to Berlin
- Grammar: Revising the future tense with *werden*
- Strategy: Carrying out online research

Resources

- Student Book, pages 120–121
- CD 2, tracks 39–41
- Grammar, Vocabulary and Translation Workbook, pages 62–63
- Kerboodle, Unit 6

Homework and self-study

- Student Book, page 121, activity 8
- Grammar, Vocabulary and Translation Workbook, pages 62–63

Starter

- Students note down as much as they can remember about the German words *wollen*, *will*, *werden*, *weil* and *wenn*. These words are easily confused and appear frequently in this lesson. Students could recall their meaning, their effect on word order, how *wollen* and *will* are linked, or how the verbs are used with other verbs. You could discuss the false friend *will* ('want', not 'will').

Plenary

- Students return to the key words from the Starter activity above and, in pairs, write a sentence including as many of them as they can; for example, *Ich **will** nach Berlin fahren, **weil** es toll ist und ich **werde**...* Can anyone write a sentence including every word?

1 **Lies Toms Pläne. Bring die Pläne (a–f) in die richtige Reihenfolge.**

Students read about Tom's plans in Berlin and work out the correct order for the texts.

Answer: d, a, c, f, b, e

> **Tipp**
>
> If students require further help, elicit or remind them of the German translations of the time phrases and sequencers listed in the *Tipp* box.

2 **Hör zu. Ist alles richtig?**

Students listen to Tom's plans in the correct order and check their answers from activity 1. Ensure that they correct any mistakes.

> **CD 2, track 39   Seite 120, Aktivität 2**
>
> d – Am Freitag werde ich mit meinem Freund Sven nach Berlin fahren. Wir werden um acht Uhr morgens mit dem Zug fahren. Wenn wir in Berlin ankommen, werden wir mit der U-Bahn zu unserem Hotel fahren.

a – Zuerst werden wir auf den Fernsehturm gehen, weil wir tolle Fotos von oben machen wollen.

c – Am Freitagabend werden wir an einer Imbissbude Currywurst essen, weil das sehr typisch für Berlin ist und weil es nicht so teuer ist.

f – Ich interessiere mich für moderne Architektur und will am Samstagmorgen den Glasdom auf dem Reichstagsgebäude sehen. Wenn es nicht zu viele Besucher gibt, werden wir in das Gebäude gehen. Die Architektur ist so beeindruckend.

b – Wir werden dann vom Reichstag nach Kreuzberg fahren. Sven interessiert sich für Kunst und will berühmte Graffiti sehen. Wir werden in Kreuzberg den Astronauten von Victor Ash sehen.

e – In Kreuzberg werden wir am Abend Döner Kebab essen und dann zum Hotel zurückfahren.

> **Grammatik**
>
> Check that students understand what an infinitive is and remind them that the second verb goes to the end of the clause.

135

6 Willkommen in Berlin!

3 📖 GCSE **Lies Toms Pläne noch einmal und beantworte die Fragen in ganzen Sätzen auf Deutsch.**

Students answer the questions about Tom's plans in full sentences in German. Remind them to use the future tense and *wollen* in their answers.

> *Answers:*
> a *Tom und Sven werden in einem Hotel übernachten.*
> b *Sie werden Currywurst und Döner Kebab essen.*
> c *Tom will den Glasdom auf dem Reichstagsgebäude sehen.*
> d *Sven will berühmte Graffiti sehen.*
> e *Sie werden am Samstagnachmittag nach Kreuzberg fahren.*

⭐ Provide students with sentence starters (the subject and the correct form of *wollen* or *werden*) for each answer.

Sprachmuster

You could give or elicit further examples of adverbs of time, manner and place.

⚠ Achtung!

Remind students of this important point before they start their translations for activity 4.

4 🔄 GCSE **Übersetz die Sätze ins Deutsche.**

Students translate the sentences into German.

> *Suggested translations:*
> a *Wir werden nach Berlin fahren.*
> b *Ich werde mehr über die Geschichte lernen.*
> c *Ich werde die Berliner Mauer sehen.*
> d *Tom möchte im See schwimmen.*
> e *Anna wird Second-Hand-Kleidung auf dem Markt kaufen.*

5 🎧 **Hör zu und lies die Informationen. Verbinde die Touren (1–4) mit den Personen.**

Students look at the four profiles and listen to the descriptions of each tour. They match each person to the most suitable tour, based on the information in his/her profile. Before students listen, ensure that they understand the vocabulary and the reference to Banksy. You may also wish to point out that the *sportlich* profile (Aysa) will match with a water-sports activity (*Kanutour*).

> *Answers:* **1** *Aysa;* **2** *Kai;* **3** *Annika;* **4** *Herr Kohl*

〰 CD 2, track 40   Seite 121, Aktivität 5

1 Sind Sie fit und aktiv? Auf unserer Kanutour werden Sie wichtige Gebäude in Berlin aus erster Nähe sehen und können die besten Fotos machen. Sie werden das Reichstagsgebäude und die Museumsinsel sehen und wir werden am Schloss Charlottenburg vorbeifahren. Die Tour beginnt jeden Tag um 11 Uhr.

2 Auf unserer alternativen Tour werden Sie Berlin ganz anders sehen. Wir werden Ihnen keine Touristenattraktionen, sondern Straßen mit den besten Graffiti zeigen. Sie werden viele moderne Kunstwerke sehen. Die Tour gibt es auf Deutsch oder auf Englisch.

3 Auf der historischen Tour werden Sie Nazi-Gebäude und die Berliner Mauer sehen. Sie werden mehr über die letzten Tage Hitlers lernen. Wir werden Ihnen den Bunker mitten in der Stadt zeigen. Wir werden etwa zwei Stunden zu Fuß gehen.

4 Wenn Sie viel sehen wollen, aber nicht gern viel zu Fuß gehen, ist unsere Bustour genau richtig für Sie! Für nur 15 Euro können Sie so oft Sie wollen ein- und aussteigen. Sie werden alle wichtigen Museen in Berlin sehen. Sie werden bequem zu allen Sehenswürdigkeiten kommen.

6 Willkommen in Berlin!

6 🎧 **Hör noch einmal zu. Mach Notizen zu jeder Tour (1–4) auf Deutsch.**

Students listen again to the descriptions of the four tours and make notes in German. Explain that they are not expected to identify every detail or to write in full sentences.

> *Answers:*
> **1** *Kanutour; die wichtigen Gebäude in Berlin: das Reichstagsgebäude, die Museumsinsel, das Schloss Charlottenburg; Sie können Fotos machen, beginnt jeden Tag um 11 Uhr*
> **2** *alternative Tour; Straßen mit den besten Graffiti, moderne Kunstwerke; auf Deutsch oder auf Englisch*
> **3** *historische Tour; Nazi-Gebäude, die Berliner Mauer, Bunker; lernen mehr über die letzten Tage Hitlers, zwei Stunden zu Fuß*
> **4** *Bustour; alle wichtigen Museen, Sehenswürdigkeiten; kostet 15 Euro*

> 〰️ **CD 2, track 41   Seite 121, Aktivität 6**
> See activity 5 for audio script.

7 💬 **Macht Dialoge. Stellt und beantwortet die Fragen.**

Using the bulleted questions and answers as support, students create a dialogue, asking for and giving information about a trip to Berlin. You could model the task structure and pronunciation beforehand with a confident volunteer. You may wish to give students time to make notes and prepare before they begin.

> ✱ **Strategie**
> Remind students that they should try to access information in German too, even though they may not understand everything. If they add *für Kinder* after their search terms, this will bring up sites designed especially for young people and the language will be easier to understand.

8 ✏️ **Finde im Internet Informationen über Sehenswürdigkeiten in Berlin und mach ein Poster für eine Touristentour.**

Guided by the bullet points, students create a poster for a tourist trip in Berlin.

➕ Students plan a trip to Berlin on a certain budget, including flight, accommodation, entertainment and food.

6.2 So leben wir in Berlin!

Objectives
- Vocabulary: Learning about life in Berlin
- Grammar: Using a range of tenses
- Strategy: Dealing with unfamiliar vocabulary

Resources
- Student Book, pages 122–123
- CD 2, track 42
- Grammar, Vocabulary and Translation Workbook, pages 64–65
- Kerboodle, Unit 6

Homework and self-study
- Student Book, page 123, activity 5
- Grammar, Vocabulary and Translation Workbook, pages 64–65

Starter
- Provide students with a list of words that make up compound nouns used in the names of the Berlin attractions they have met in previous lessons; for example, *Fernseh, Reichstags, Strand, -turm, -gebäude, -bad*. They match the words to create the correct names.

Plenary
- Prepare in advance a 'trapdoor' speaking activity. Write a short paragraph about a trip to Berlin, including key vocabulary from this and previous lessons, with three different options for key words; for example, *Ich bin letzte Woche/letztes Jahr/letzten Monat nach Berlin gefahren. Es war interessant/toll/schön*. Students choose an option for each sentence, then take turns to read the whole text aloud, trying to guess their partner's choices. If they choose correctly, they continue; if they're incorrect, they swap over and have to start again at the beginning next time.

---

1 📖 **GCSE** A city with many faces! Read the texts about Berlin districts. Who says each statement: Elif (E), Hansjörg (H), Otto (O) or Christiane (C)?

Encourage students to identify key words in the statements and to look for similar terms in the texts to help them work out who would be likely to say each statement.

Answers: **a** C; **b** O; **c** E; **d** E; **e** H; **f** C; **g** H; **h** O

Sprachmuster
Remind students that these constructions are different in German and English: in English we don't say 'since four years', and in German *für vier Jahre* is incorrect.

Strategie
Use some examples from the texts in activity 1 to demonstrate how these strategies can help students work out meaning; for example, for question e, they might not know the word *Gegend* but they do know *schön* and *Parks*.

2 🎧 **GCSE** Hör zu. Was sagt Hanna über ihr Leben in Berlin? Beantworte die Fragen (1–3) auf Deutsch.

Students listen and answer the questions in German.

Answers: **1 a** sehr cool; **b** Kanu gefahren; **2 a** Joggen, entspannend; **b** auf den Secondhandmarkt gegangen; **3 a** auf ein Konzert gehen; **b** Berlin ist manchmal gefährlich

➕ Students write their answers in full sentences.

Suggested answers:
1 a Sie findet ihre Gegend sehr cool.
b Sie ist früher oft Kanu gefahren.
2 a Sie geht oft joggen, weil das entspannend ist.
b Sie ist am Sonntag auf den Secondhandmarkt gegangen.
3 a Sie wird nächste Woche auf ein Konzert gehen.
b Er muss mitkommen, weil Berlin manchmal (ein bisschen) gefährlich ist.

6 Willkommen in Berlin!

CD 2, track 42   Seite 123, Aktivität 2

1. Ich wohne in Berlin, Prenzlauer Berg und ich denke, dass mein Stadtteil sehr cool ist. Es gibt hier viele Familien und nette Cafés und Parks. Berlin ist eine Großstadt, aber Berlin ist auch sehr grün, denn es gibt hier eine Million Bäume. Es gibt auch einen Fluss: die Spree. Als ich klein war, bin ich oft mit meinen Eltern auf der Spree Kanu gefahren, weil mein Vater Wassersport liebt.

2. Letzten Samstag war ich im Park joggen. Am Wochenende gehe ich oft joggen, weil das entspannend ist. Außerdem bin ich am Sonntag mit meiner Freundin auf den Secondhandmarkt am Mauerpark gegangen. Da kann man immer tolle Sachen finden. Ich habe eine coole Lederjacke gekauft.

3. Nächste Woche werden wir auf ein Konzert gehen. Wir werden die Berliner Sängerin Joy Denalane sehen. Ich bin totaler Fan! Ich darf nur auf das Konzert gehen, weil mein Bruder mitkommen wird, aber das ist okay, weil Berlin manchmal schon ein bisschen gefährlich ist.

Grammatik

Recap the difference between the perfect and the imperfect tenses if necessary, including the fact that there are two possible auxiliary verbs in the perfect tense and how to decide which one to use. This is useful revision and preparation for activity 5.

3 Copy and complete the table with the time markers.

This could also be a useful opportunity to revise the time–manner–place rule (as these are all adverbs of time).

Answers:

Past	Present	Future
gestern	normalerweise	nächste Woche
letzte Woche	heute	morgen
vor drei Jahren	jetzt	

➕ Students write sentences using these time markers.

Extra

You could collate class responses so that students can add them to their own table.

Suggested answers:
Past: *letztes Wochenende, letzten Sonntag, als ich zehn Jahre alt war, letzten Monat*
Present: *oft, täglich, jeden Montag, einmal pro Woche, jeden Abend, meistens*
Future: *in der Zukunft, in zwei Jahren, nächstes Wochenende, übermorgen, in zwei Tagen, später*

4 Stellt euch vor, ihr wart letztes Jahr in Berlin. Lest den Berliner Eventkalender und macht Dialoge. Stellt und beantwortet die Fragen.

Students create a dialogue about a trip to Berlin, using the event calendar as an information source and the example as support. You could model the task structure and pronunciation beforehand with a confident volunteer. You may wish to give students time to make notes and prepare before they begin.

5 Schreib eine Postkarte aus Berlin.

Guided by the bullet points, students write a postcard from Berlin.

⭐ Provide sentence starters for each bullet point.

139

6 Kultur

Resources
- Student Book, pages 124–125
- CD 2, tracks 43–44

1 📖 **Read the text about East Berlin and write a list of the verbs in the imperfect tense. Then translate the verbs into English.**

To aid students' understanding of the text, refer them to the words in the glossary box and point out that *prägten* is an imperfect tense form of the verb *prägen* ('to shape/characterise/influence/leave its mark on').

Answers/Suggested translations:
kontrollierten – controlled, hatten/hatte – had, prägten – shaped/left their mark on, war – was, waren – were, konnten – could, lernte – learnt, (es) gab – there was, durften – were allowed

⭐ Provide students with the English translations so that they only need to find the German verbs in the text.

🧩 Sprachmuster

You could remind students of the difference between the perfect and imperfect tenses.

2 📖 **Lies den Text noch einmal. Finde die passenden Wörter (a–h) auf Deutsch.**

Students find in the text the German equivalents of the English vocabulary. Encourage students to use their language detective skills to find the words; for example, by looking for (near-) cognates and using context to help them.

Answers: **a** *die Allierten;* **b** *unterschiedlich;* **c** *geteilt;* **d** *getrennt;* **e** *politische Partei;* **f** *Automarke;* **g** *sozialistisch;* **h** *schwieriger*

3 📖 GCSE **Lies den Text noch einmal. Richtig (R), falsch (F) oder nicht im Text (NT)?**

Students read the text again and decide whether each statement is true, false or not in the text. They may need extra help to distinguish between 'false' and 'not in the text': a statement is 'false' is if there's contradictory information in the text to make the statement obviously incorrect; a statement is 'not in the text' if we have no idea, as the text doesn't include any information about this.

Answers: **a** F; **b** F; **c** R; **d** R; **e** NT; **f** R; **g** F; **h** NT

4 ✏️ **Schreib die Sätze im Imperfekt auf.**

Students rewrite the sentences in the imperfect tense. After students have completed activity 4, ask them to read the information box at the top of page 125. You could then show students a basic map depicting East and West Germany, East and West Berlin, and the occupation zones (such as the map in activity 1 on page 24). You could also show further images linked to life in East Germany, such as Trabants or the *Ampelmännchen*, to enrich students' cultural knowledge of Berlin.

Answers:
a *Ich lebte in Westberlin.*
b *Ich hatte einen Volkswagen.*
c *Ich arbeitete für die SED.*
d *Wir wohnten in einer Villa in Charlottenburg.*
e *Es gab keine Coca-Cola im Supermarkt.*

➕ Students translate their imperfect tense sentences into English.

Suggested translations:
a *I lived in West Berlin.*
b *I had a Volkswagen.*
c *I worked for the SED.*
d *We lived in a villa in Charlottenburg.*
e *There was no Coca-Cola in the supermarket.*

6 Willkommen in Berlin!

5 🎧 **Hör zu. Wohnten die Personen (1–8) in Ostberlin (O) oder Westberlin (W)?**

Students note down whether each speaker lived in East or West Berlin. They will need to use their cultural knowledge of what life was like in East and West Berlin to help them.

Answers: **1** O; **2** O; **3** W; **4** W; **5** W; **6** O; **7** W; **8** O

CD 2, track 43   Seite 125, Aktivität 5

1. Bei uns zu Hause gab es nie Coca-Cola.
2. Wir hatten einen blauen Trabant. Unser Trabi war ein tolles Auto!
3. In den Sommerferien sind wir nach Italien gefahren.
4. Mein Vater hatte einen Mercedes.
5. Mein Vater war ein Jahr arbeitslos.
6. Meine Mutter arbeitete für die SED.
7. Als Kind war mein Lieblingsessen Bananen mit Joghurt.
8. Mein Lieblingsfach in der Schule war Russisch.

6 ⟳ **GCSE Translate the text into English.**

Remind students that they can work out the meaning of unfamiliar words using the context. For example, what might *kletterten* mean in the context of a wall?

Suggested translation:
The wall between East and West Berlin fell on 9th November 1989. That was a very emotional and important moment for Germany. Many young people climbed over the wall and you could watch it on TV in the whole of Germany. After many years, the people from East Berlin could travel to West Berlin again.

7 🎧 **GCSE Listen to the people (1–5) describing what they did on 9th November 1989. Copy and complete the table in English.**

Answers:

	Age	Activity	Emotion/Opinion
1	12	watched TV with parents	(very) exciting
2	20	party with friends	(really) cool
3	48	called/phoned cousin (in East Berlin)	(very) happy
4	23	packed rucksack and went to West Berlin	free (at last)
5	50	with friends in restaurant	(a bit) scared, (very) difficult

⭐ For each speaker, provide students with one or two answers already filled in in the table, so they can concentrate on the remaining information.

CD 2, track 44   Seite 125, Aktivität 7

1. Ich war 12 Jahre alt und ich habe mit meinen Eltern den Mauerfall im Fernsehen gesehen. Ich fand das sehr spannend.
2. Ich war 20 Jahre alt und habe mit meinen Freunden eine Party gefeiert. Wir fanden das total cool.
3. Ich war 48 Jahre alt und ich war sehr glücklich. Ich habe mit meiner Cousine in Ostberlin telefoniert und sie hat uns eine Woche später besucht.
4. Ich war 23 Jahre alt und fand das Leben in Ostberlin gar nicht gut. Ich habe sofort einen Rucksack gepackt und bin nach Westberlin gegangen. Ich war endlich frei!
5. Ich war 50 Jahre alt und hatte ein bisschen Angst. Ich war mit meinen Freunden in einem Restaurant. Ich hatte eine gute Position in der SED und fand den Mauerfall sehr schwierig.

8 💬 **Macht ein Rollenspiel. Stellt und beantwortet die Fragen mit den Informationen unten.**

Using the bulleted questions and the prompts provided below, students ask and answer questions, taking on the role of a German person who experienced the fall of the Berlin Wall, as detailed in the profiles. You could model the task structure and pronunciation beforehand with a confident volunteer. You may wish to give students time to make notes and prepare before they begin.

141

6 Willkommen in Berlin!

➕ For freer practice, students create their own dialogues, making up their own responses rather than basing them on the profiles given.

9 ✏️ [GCSE] **Schreib deinen Tagebucheintrag über den Tag des Mauerfalls.**

Guided by the bullet points, students create a diary entry about the day the Berlin Wall fell. Remind them to write in the correct tense for each bullet point.

➕ Students could find out what their parents or older relatives did on 9th November 1989 and try to write about it in German; for example, *Meine Mutter war in Manchester. Sie hat ferngesehen. Sie hat das interessant gefunden.*

6 Sprachlabor

Objectives
- Revising the future tense with *werden*
- Using a range of tenses
- Pronunciation: *z*, *w* and *zw*

Resources
- Student Book, page 126
- CD 2, tracks 45–46
- Grammar, Vocabulary and Translation Workbook, pages 62–65
- Kerboodle, Unit 6

Aa Grammatik

Revising the future tense with *werden*

Remind students that the future tense in English can be 'I will' or 'I'm going to', but this is expressed with just one verb in German. Discuss the false friend *ich will* ('I want'), if appropriate.

1 **Put the letters in the correct order to write the present tense forms of *werden*.**

Answers: **a** werde; **b** wirst; **c** wird; **d** werden; **e** werdet; **f** werden

2 **Find and correct the mistake in each sentence.**

The mistakes are all grammatical rather than logical errors. If more guidance is needed, remind students to check for the correct form of *werden*, the use of an infinitive and correct word order.

Answers:
a Meine Mutter **wird** auf den Flohmarkt gehen.
b Wir werden Currywurst **essen**.
c Wir **werden** zur Berlinale gehen.
d Ich werde mehr über die Geschichte **lernen**.
e **Wirst** du in Berlin Kreuzberg wohnen?

⭐ Tell students what the mistake is in each sentence so they can focus on the correction.

3 **Write about these future plans using the *ich* form. Write full sentences.**

Suggested answers:
a Ich werde in einer Villa wohnen.
b Ich werde einen Mercedes haben.
c Ich werde viel reisen.
d Ich werde berühmt sein.
e Ich werde Flüchtlingen helfen.

⭐ Provide students with a list of the key German vocabulary needed so they can focus on the grammatical construction of the sentences.

➕ Students write predictions about what family members will do in the future, using the third person singular.

4 **Translate the sentences into German.**

Suggested translations:
a Ich werde in Berlin wohnen.
b Ich werde viele Fotos machen.
c Meine Mutter wird ins Museum gehen.
d Mein Vater wird zum Brandenburger Tor gehen.
e Tom und Hussain werden einen Film sehen.
f Wann wirst du Berlin besuchen?

142

6 Willkommen in Berlin!

> **Aa Grammatik**
> **Using a range of tenses**
>
> Before starting this section, ask students to split a piece of paper into four sections and, in pairs, to note down everything they can remember about each of the four tenses (present, perfect, imperfect and future): this could be information about usage and formation, or examples in either or both languages. They may be pleasantly surprised by how much they know and it will help you to identify any misconceptions or gaps in their knowledge.

Aussprache: z, w and zw
These tasks require lots of teacher demonstration to provide students with an excellent pronunciation model. You can also play the audio files to demonstrate correct pronunciation.

5 What is the tense in each sentence: present, perfect, imperfect or future?

> Answers: **a** future; **b** perfect; **c** imperfect;
> **d** present; **e** imperfect

7 Listen and repeat. Then practise with your partner.

Isolate the sounds first, then move on to using the words that include the sounds.

> CD 2, track 45   Seite 126, Aktivität 7
> See Student Book, page 126, for audio script.

6 GCSE Translate the text into German.

8 Practise saying the tongue twister.

Depending on the ability of the class, you could play some games with this; for example, partners saying alternate words in the sentence, whole-class repetition using different volumes or speeds, or trying to learn the tongue twister-style sentence off by heart.

> Suggested translation:
> Letzten Sommer bin ich mit meiner Familie nach Konstanz gefahren/gegangen. Ich habe viel Wassersport gemacht. Es war super/fantastisch/ wunderbar/toll, weil ich sportlich bin und Wasser liebe. Nächstes Jahr werden wir nach Freiburg fahren. Meine Schwester wird auf die Uni in Freiburg gehen, aber zuerst wollen/möchten wir die Stadt zusammen besuchen.

> CD 2, track 46   Seite 126, Aktivität 8
> See Student Book, page 126, for audio script.

6 Was kann ich schon?

> **Resources**
> - Student Book, page 127
> - CD 2, track 47
> - Kerboodle, Unit 6

Reading

1 📖 Lies den Text und finde die passenden Wörter (a–e) auf Deutsch.

Students read the text and find the corresponding German words for the English vocabulary.

> Answers: **a** chaotisch und dreckig; **b** aufregend;
> **c** Parks, Seen und Wälder; **d** Büro;
> **e** billiger als

143

6 Willkommen in Berlin!

2 📖 Read the text again and choose the correct answer to complete each sentence.

Answers: **a** *beautiful, exciting;* **b** *tolerant;* **c** *people of different nationalities;* **d** *a concert;* **e** *natural areas;* **f** *music scene*

Listening

3 🎧 Hör zu. Sprechen die Personen (1–5) über <u>letztes</u> (L) oder <u>nächstes</u> (N) Wochenende? Schreib auch die Aktivität auf. Schreib die Tabelle ab und füll sie aus.

Students listen, decide whether each speaker is describing last weekend or next weekend, and note down the activity. The speakers do not explicitly state if they are describing last weekend or next weekend, so students have to infer this information from the tense(s) used. Remind them to write in German; their answers do not need to be in full sentences.

Answers:

	L/N	Aktivität
1	L	im See geschwommen
2	L	ins Stadtmuseum gegangen
3	N	einkaufen gehen
4	N	Fotos von (coolen) Graffiti machen, nach Kreuzberg fahren
5	L	spazieren gegangen, Currywurst gegessen

〜 CD 2, track 47   Seite 127, Aktivität 3

1 Hey, ich bin im See geschwommen, weil es so heiß war. Es war sehr entspannend, aber es gab zu viele Leute.

2 Ich bin mit meiner Schulklasse ins Stadtmuseum gegangen und habe viel über die Stadt gelernt. Es war wirklich interessant.

3 Wir werden einkaufen gehen. Normalerweise gehe ich lieber auf Märkte, aber meine Mutter will in Designergeschäfte gehen.

4 Ich werde mit meinem Freund Fotos von coolen Graffiti machen, denn wir machen gerade ein Kunstprojekt in der Schule. Wir werden nach Kreuzberg fahren, weil es da ein paar sehr coole Bilder gibt.

5 Wir haben nicht viel gemacht. Wir sind ein bisschen spazieren gegangen und haben an einer Imbissbude Currywurst gegessen.

Writing

4 ✏️ [GCSE] Übersetz den Text ins Deutsche.

Students translate the text into German.

Suggested translation:
In der Zukunft werde ich in Berlin wohnen, weil die Stadt interessant und spannend ist. Ich habe viel über Berlin gelesen und ich denke, dass die Stadt fantastisch ist. Ich interessiere mich auch für die Geschichte.

5 ✏️ Schreib einen Blogeintrag über Berlin (zirka 60 Wörter).

Guided by the bullet points, students write a blog entry about Berlin. Award one mark for each of the following: correct use of the perfect tense, correct word order, correct use of a modal verb, correct use of *weil*, correct use of *dass*, topic-specific vocabulary, and accurate spelling. There are seven marks in total.

1 Sprungbrett

1 In Urlaub

> **Resources**
> - Student Book, pages 128–129
> - Kerboodle, Unit 1

1 📖 **Read the article and answer the questions in English.**

Pre-teach *Mond*, to give students a good understanding of the context of the article.

> Answers: **a** fly to the moon; **b** 28; **c** one week; **d** 4.3 billion euros; **e** USA and Russia

2 📖 **Lies Erikas SMS und beantworte die Fragen.**

Students read Erika's message and answer the questions. Explain that they do not need to answer questions 3–5 in full sentences.

> Answers: **1** a; **2** a; **3** in Rom; **4** schön/sonnig und heiß; **5** gut/wunderschön/richtig cool

3 📖 **Translate your Swiss friend's email into English for your parents.**

> Suggested translation:
> Every year, I visit/go to the Christmas market in Basel with my friends.
> Last weekend I was at the Christmas market again. It was great!
> First I drank hot cocoa and after that ate a waffle. It was fun!

> 💡 **Tipp**
> You could elicit or discuss some other examples of previously learnt time markers and sequences which would give a clue to the tense; for example, *immer* or *danach*.

4 ✏️ **Du hast einen Tagesausflug mit deiner Familie gemacht. Du schickst dieses Foto an deinen Freund/deine Freundin in Österreich. Schreib vier Sätze auf Deutsch über das Foto.**

Students write four sentences about the photo, using the bullet points for guidance.

> 💡 **Tipp**
> Encourage students to apply the strategies to their writing in activity 4; for example, they could give their opinion in the present tense in their response to the final bullet point.

5 ✏️ **Translate the sentences into German.**

> Suggested translations:
> **a** *Letztes Jahr habe ich meine Sommerferien in Frankreich verbracht.*
> **b** *Ich bin mit dem Auto gefahren/gereist.*
> **c** *Ich habe eine (Fahr)radtour gemacht und ich habe die Sehenswürdigkeiten besichtigt.*
> **d** *Man kann auch eine Bootsfahrt machen.*

6 ✏️ **Du schreibst an deinen deutschen Freund/deine deutsche Freundin über deine Ferien. Du musst ungefähr 40 Wörter auf Deutsch schreiben.**

Students write approximately 40 words about a past holiday, guided by the bullet points: the first day, the weather, activities and travel/transport. Remind them that this information/experience doesn't need to be true.

2 Sprungbrett

> **Resources**
> - Student Book, pages 130–131
> - CD 2, tracks 48–50
> - Kerboodle, Unit 2

1 🎧 **Listen to a pedestrian asking for directions to the train station. Choose the correct answers.**

This task is typical of multiple-choice questions in the GCSE exam. Recap or share with students the strategy of eliminating any incorrect answers to narrow down the options.

> Answers: **1** b; **2** a; **3** c

CD 2, track 48   Seite 130, Aktivität 1

– Entschuldigen Sie, wie komme ich zum Bahnhof bitte?

– Zum Bahnhof, mal sehen. Ähm… Nehmen Sie die erste Straße links… Äh… Dann gehen Sie geradeaus und der Bahnhof ist auf der rechten Seite.

– Können Sie das bitte wiederholen?

– Nehmen Sie die erste Straße links. Dann gehen Sie geradeaus und der Bahnhof ist auf der rechten Seite.

💡 Tipp

It would be helpful to go over the *Tipp* box before students start activity 2. Remind them that the more they write, the more chance there is of making a mistake: giving additional, incorrect information could mean a right answer becomes wrong.

2 🎧 **Alex spricht über sein Zuhause und seine Großeltern. Hör zu und beantworte die Fragen auf Deutsch.**

Students listen and answer the questions in German. Remind them to pay attention to the number of details required for each answer to avoid losing marks.

> Answers: **a** in einem Einfamilienhaus (1) in der Schweiz (1); **b** weil es interessant ist; **c** das Wetter; **d** in München; **e** Man kann viel machen (1), aber es ist sehr laut (2). **f** in Stuttgart

⭐ Provide students with the first word or two of each answer. Sometimes simply not knowing how to begin their answer can be the barrier to students being able to answer in German.

CD 2, track 49   Seite 130, Aktivität 2

Teil 1

Ich wohne in einem Einfamilienhaus in der Schweiz. Ich wohne total gerne hier, weil es interessant ist, aber das Wetter ist oft kalt und windig.

Teil 2

Meine Großeltern wohnen in München. In München kann man so viel machen und ich finde das cool! Aber es ist sehr laut. Früher haben sie in Stuttgart gelebt. Das fanden sie nicht so interessant.

2 Mein Zuhause

3 🎧 **Listen to Sylvia talking about where she lives and answer the questions in English.**

Remind students to pay attention to the number of details required for each answer to avoid losing marks.

> Answers: **a** in a hotel (1) in the town/city centre (1); **b** bed, desk, wardrobe, piano; **c** She doesn't have to clean her room. **d** Her room is (a bit) small.

🎵 **CD 2, track 50   Seite 130, Aktivität 3**

Hallo, ich bin Sylvia. Ich wohne in einem Hotel in der Stadtmitte.

In meinem Zimmer habe ich alles, was ich brauche. Es gibt ein Bett, einen Schreibtisch, einen Kleiderschrank. Es gibt auch ein Klavier und ich spiele sehr gerne darauf.

Es gibt auch ein Badezimmer mit Dusche, Bad und Toiletten.

Das ist total praktisch und, weil ich in einem Hotel wohne, muss ich mein Zimmer nicht putzen. Toll, nicht? Das finde ich super.

Was mir nicht gefällt? Mein Zimmer ist ein bisschen klein. Aber sonst, perfekt!

---

4 💬 **Practise the role play.**

Using the bullet points as guidance, students prepare for a topic-based role play. They have had some practice with these tasks in *Echt 1* but will still need support to complete this task. Allow students some time to prepare individually and make notes. They should also be able to play the role of the teacher and pose the questions once they have had time to prepare.

> 💡 **Tipp**
>
> You may wish to revise question words before students start activity 4. The focus should be on forming questions accurately, rather than coming up with teacher-standard, relevant questions. A question such as *Was gibt es in deinem Zimmer?* would be perfectly acceptable, even though it's only loosely linked to the topic of the role play.

5 💬 **Practise the photo card activity.**

Using the bullet points as guidance, students prepare for the topic-based photo card. They have had some practice with these tasks in *Echt 1*, but will still need support to complete this task. Encourage them to think about possible additional questions that they might be asked, or collate a list on the board for them to choose from.

> 💡 **Tipp**
>
> Discuss with students how they can use the verb and/or tense in the given questions to help formulate their answers. For example, in relation to the third question in the *Tipp* box (*Möchtest du auf einem Hausboot wohnen?*), highlight the importance of changing the auxiliary verb, while the infinitive can be used with no change.

6 💬 **Your teacher will ask you these questions. Answer them <u>without</u> making notes, using the language you already know.**

It may be a logistical challenge to ask every student all four questions, but you can start by asking a selection of students one question each, while their peers listen to their answers. You could then develop this into a whole-class (or group/partner) speaking task, in which students ask and answer the questions with each other; you can circulate to praise where appropriate or pick up on any errors. These errors can be addressed as a whole class when the task is finished.

147

3 Sprungbrett

> **Resources**
> - Student Book, pages 132–133
> - Kerboodle, Unit 3

1 📖 **Read the posts about healthy lifestyles and answer the questions. Write J for Jens, E for Ella, C for Caspar or L for Laura.**

'Who says what' questions are common in the GCSE exam. Encourage students to develop the habit of looking for key words; for example, *Handy* for question b. However, remind them to read the text carefully, to check context and meaning fully, and not to make snap decisions just because they see a word in the text that relates to one of the questions.

> Answers: **a** L; **b** C; **c** J; **d** E

2 📖 **Lies den Artikel. Wähl die <u>drei</u> richtigen Aussagen.**

Students read the article and choose the three correct statements. Remind students to eliminate any incorrect statements if possible, to narrow down their choices.

> Answer: a, c, e

3 📖 **Translate your German penfriend's email about his weekend into English for your family.**

> *Suggested translation:*
> Hello! How are you? Normally, I eat healthily because I am very/really active. Sport is important to me. But at the weekend there was a party and I was (together) with my friends. I ate chips and drank a lot of lemonade. That wasn't a good idea!

> 💡 **Tipp**
> Help students identify the tenses in the email, if necessary. You could also recap how to form the tenses, if more support is needed.

4 ✏️ **Du schickst dieses Foto an deinen Freund in der Schweiz. Schreib <u>vier</u> Sätze auf Deutsch über das Foto.**

Students write four sentences about the photo, using the bullet points for guidance.

5 ✏️ **Translate the sentences into German.**

> *Suggested translations:*
> **a** Nach dem Abendessen entspanne ich mich.
> **b** Man soll Yoga oder Tai-Chi machen.
> **c** Willst du ins Café gehen?
> **d** Es tut mir leid, aber ich habe kein Geld.

> 💡 **Tipp**
> Ensure that students understand the terms 'infinitive', 'modal verb', 'reflexive verb' and 'reflexive pronoun', giving examples if necessary. You may also wish to elicit or reiterate that the verb is always the second idea, not necessarily the second word.

6 ✏️ **Du schreibst an einen Freund/eine Freundin über deine Alltagsroutine. Du musst ungefähr 40 Wörter auf Deutsch schreiben.**

Students write approximately 40 words about their daily routine, guided by the bullet points: when they get up, when they go to bed, how they help at home and what they did last weekend. Remind them that this information/experience doesn't need to be true.

> # 4 Sprungbrett

4 Meine Klamotten

> **Resources**
> - Student Book, pages 134–135
> - CD 2, tracks 51–53
> - Kerboodle, Unit 4

1 🎧 **Listen to two Austrian teenagers talking about clothes. Choose the correct item of clothing (a, b or c) for each person.**

As a preparation task, students could note down the items of clothing in German to help them when listening.

> Answers: **Arno** c; **Lola** a

➕ Students note down any additional details each speaker gives.

> Answers: **Arno**: relaxed style; **Lola**: also likes wearing a T-shirt

> 〰️ **CD 2, track 51**   Seite 134, Aktivität 1
>
> – Was trägst du gern, Arno?
> – Naja, mein Stil ist ziemlich lässig. Ich trage gern ein schwarzes T-Shirt. Und du, Lola? Was trägst du gern?
> – Ja, ich trage auch gern ein T-Shirt, aber mein Lieblingskleidungsstück ist meine Jeansjacke.

2 🎧 **Hedda spricht über ihre Geburtstagsparty. Hör zu und schreib den richtigen Buchstaben.**

Students choose the correct multiple-choice options. Encourage them to note the answer options in German before starting, so they know what to listen out for.

> Answers: **1** b; **2** b

> 〰️ **CD 2, track 52**   Seite 134, Aktivität 2
>
> Meine Geburtstagsparty letzten Samstag hat viel Spaß gemacht. Die Party hat um halb neun begonnen und alle meine Freunde sind gekommen. Ich habe viele Geschenke bekommen. Mein Vater hat mir eine Kette gegeben, von meiner Mutter habe ich Ohrringe bekommen und meine Freundin Birgit hat mir eine schöne Sonnenbrille geschenkt.

3 🎧 **Listen to three friends discussing what they wear for different occasions. Answer the questions.**

Encourage students to note down the answer options in German before starting, so they know what to listen out for.

> Answers (in any order): **1** a, c, e; **2** a, b, f

> 〰️ **CD 2, track 53**   Seite 134, Aktivität 3
>
> – Meistens trage ich Jeans, eine Jacke, ein Cap und Turnschuhe. Aber dieses Wochenende werde ich ein Kleid tragen. Ich werde meinen Geburtstag feiern: PARTY! Und du, Marco?
> – Ich trage lieber einen Kapuzenpullover, eine Hose und Sneaker. Dieses Wochenende werde ich nach Innsbruck fahren und dort Ski fahren. Kai, was trägst du?
> – In der Woche trage ich ein Hemd, eine Hose, Schuhe und eine Jacke. Am Wochenende werde ich aber Dirt-Jump-Rad fahren…

4 Meine Klamotten

4 💬 **Practise the role play.**

Using the bullet points as guidance, students prepare for a topic-based role play. They have had some practice with this type of task, but will still need support to complete it. Allow students some time to prepare individually and make notes. They should also be able to play the role of the teacher and pose the questions once they have had time to prepare.

> 💡 **Tipp**
>
> You may wish to revise question words before this task and collate some ideas for the unprepared questions and possible answers.

5 💬 **Practise the photo card activity.**

Using the bullet points as guidance, students prepare for a topic-based photo card. They have had some practice with this type of task, but will still need support to complete it. Encourage them to think about possible additional questions that they might be asked, or collate a list on the board for them to choose from.

6 💬 **Your teacher will ask you these questions. Answer them <u>without</u> making notes, using the language you already know.**

It may be a logistical challenge to ask every student all four questions, but you can start by asking a selection of students one question each, while their peers listen to their answers. You could then develop this into a whole-class (or group/partner) speaking task, in which students ask and answer the questions with each other; you can circulate to praise where appropriate or pick up on any errors. These errors can be addressed as a whole class when the task is finished.

> 💡 **Tipp**
>
> Encourage students to refer to the suggestions in the *Tipp* box when they are preparing their answers.

5 Sprungbrett

5 Virtuelle und reelle Welt

Resources
- Student Book, pages 136–137
- Kerboodle, Unit 5

1 Read the posts about young people's interests and answer the questions. Write A for Anja, C for Cem or L for Ludwig.

Answers: **a** A; **b** L; **c** C; **d** A; **e** C; **f** L

2 Lies Janinas Blogeintrag. Wähl die <u>vier</u> richtigen Aussagen.

Students read the blog and choose the four correct statements.

Answer (in any order): b, c, e, g

3 Translate your Austrian exchange partner's message into English for your friend.

Suggested translation:
At the moment we're doing a project at school about environmental protection. I think (that) there's too much rubbish/litter on the street and I would like to help. Yesterday, I collected rubbish/litter with my class. It was strenuous/tiring/hard work, but I found it useful. Next year I will do/be involved in a project again. Perhaps I will/Maybe I will/I might work with refugees. Will you also do a project?

4 Du schickst dieses Foto an einen deutschen Freund/eine deutsche Freundin. Schreib <u>vier</u> Sätze auf Deutsch über das Foto.

Students write four sentences about the photo, using the bullet points for guidance.

⭐ Before students start the task, collate some key vocabulary as a class, such as nouns, verbs and adjectives to describe the picture; for example, *Mutter, Kinder, glücklich*.

💡 Tipp
Remind students they could also use *Ich denke,...* to say what they think is happening.

5 Translate the sentences into German.

Suggested translations:
a Ich sehe gern Zeichentrickfilme./Ich mag Zeichentrickfilme.
b Ich mag Sportsendungen/Mir gefallen Sportsendungen nicht, weil ich sie langweilig finde.
c Gestern habe ich klassische Musik gehört./Ich habe gestern klassische Musik gehört.
d Ich denke, dass das Internet viele Vorteile hat.
e Ich interessiere mich für Mode.
f In der Zukunft werde ich Menschen helfen./Ich werde in der Zukunft Menschen helfen.

6 Du schreibst an deinen Freund/deine Freundin in der Schweiz über digitale Medien.
Du musst ungefähr 40 Wörter auf Deutsch schreiben.

Students write approximately 40 words about technology, guided by the bullet points: how and how often they use digital media, the advantages and disadvantages of digital media, their parents' opinion about digital technology and how they used their phone yesterday. Remind students that this information/experience doesn't need to be true.

💡 Tipp
Before students declare their written work for activity 6 'finished', tell them to read the notes in this *Tipp* box. They could also swap with a partner and peer-assess each other's work. Alternatively, while you are circulating, you could point out errors.

151

Workbook answers

1 In Urlaub

1.1 Ferienaktivitäten (page 4)

1 1 b; 2 c; 3 a

2 a you can go window shopping / walking around the town
b to the Schluchsee
c canoeing or bike riding
d great mountains and fantastic / super weather
e to Switzerland and to France

3 Students' own answers

Suggested answers:

Activities should match location! F g

Stadt: einen Stadtbummel machen / Sehenswürdigkeiten besichtigen / Ausflüge machen / eine Radtour machen / eine Bootsfahrt machen

Berge: klettern / wandern / zelten / Kanu fahren / Wildwasser-Rafting machen

Meer: schwimmen / tauchen / schnorcheln / windsurfen

Extra

Students' own answers

Using the infinitive (page 5)

1 a klettern; b sehen; c essen; d machen; e zelten

2 a Am Meer kann man schnorcheln.
b In London kann man Sehenswürdigkeiten besichtigen.
c Man kann das Museum besuchen.
d In München kann man einen Stadtbummel machen.
e An der Nordsee kann man zelten.

3 a Man kann hier Tennis spielen. / Hier kann man Tennis spielen.
b Man kann ein Konzert sehen.
c In Basel kann man einen Stadtbummel machen.
d In den Bergen kann man zelten.
e Man kann Wildwasser-Rafting machen.

1.2 Wo hast du deine Ferien verbracht? (page 6)

1 1 f; 2 d; 3 b; 4 a; 5 e; 6 c

2 a Ägypten – gesehen
b New York – gemacht
c Italien – gegessen

3 1 habe; 2 Frankreich; 3 gespielt; 4 haben; 5 gemacht; 6 Ausflug; 7 gemacht; 8 gesehen; 9 war

Using the perfect tense with *haben* (page 7)

1 Students' own answers

Suggested answers:

1 Ich habe Tennis / Fußball / Basketball / Rugby / Tischtennis / Hockey / Volleyball, etc. gespielt.
2 Ich habe Pommes / Kuchen / Pizza / Eis / Kebab / Hähnchen, etc. gegessen.
3 Ich habe einen Film / ein Konzert / Sehenswürdigkeiten / den Eiffelturm, etc. gesehen.

2 a habe – gemacht
b hat – gespielt
c hat – besucht
d habe – verbracht
e haben – gesehen

3 Suggested answers:
a Am Montag habe ich eine Radtour gemacht.
b Am Dienstag habe ich Tennis gespielt.
c Am Mittwoch habe ich eine Bootsfahrt gemacht.
d Am Donnerstag habe ich ein Konzert gesehen.
e Am Freitag habe ich ein Museum besucht.

1.3 #Wanderlust! (page 8)

1 1 d; 2 f; 3 a; 4 h; 5 b; 6 g; 7 c; 8 e

2 a 1 Fahrrad
b 2 Auto – 3 gefahren
c 4 Zug – 5 gefahren
d 6 ist – 7 Flugzeug
e 8 sind – 9 Bus – 10 gefahren
f 11 ist – 12 Motorrad – 13 gefahren
g 14 Schneemobil – 15 gefahren
h 16 sind – 17 Schiff – 18 gefahren

153

Workbook answers

3 Suggested answer:

Last year, I travelled across Asia. First, I went to China by plane, then I went to India by train. From India I went to Thailand by ship. And then I went to Malaysia by motorbike. Afterwards, I went / flew home. It was terrific!

Using the perfect tense with *sein* (page 9)

1 a bin; b ist; c sind; d sind; e Seid; f Bist

2
a Ich bin nach Paris gefahren.
b Ich bin nach Manchester gefahren.
c Ich bin nach Stuttgart gefahren.
d David ist nach Leipzig gefahren.
e Ich bin nach Amsterdam geflogen.
f Wir sind nach Barcelona gefahren.

3
a Ich bin mit dem Auto gefahren.
b Ich bin nach Japan geflogen.
c Dann bin ich zu Hause geblieben.
d Meine Mutter ist ins Museum gegangen.
e Zuerst sind wir mit dem Zug nach Dresden gefahren.

1.4 Wie war das Wetter? (page 10)

1 a T; b T; c F; d T; e F; f F; g T; h T

2

Weather – Rhine Valley	very warm and sunny
Weather – Lake Maggiore	hot
Maximum temperature	39 degrees
Water temperature	22 degrees
Weather – summer	very nice, often rainy
Weather – winter	lots of snow, very cold

3 Suggested answers:
a Morgens war es sonnig.
b Mittags war es warm / heiß..
c Abends gab es Regen und es war kalt.

Using the imperfect tense (page 11)

1 a war; b war; c gab; d gab; e war; f war; g war

2 1 es war; 2 Es war heiß; 3 Es gab; 4 war nicht toll; 5 gab es; 6 es war

3
a Das Wetter war gut.
b Es war oft sonnig.
c Morgens gab es manchmal Regen.

d Nachts war es immer warm.
e Es war toll!

1.5 Ich reise gern (page 12)

1
1 gar nicht, ein bisschen
2 ziemlich, ein bisschen
3 total, voll, sehr, echt, richtig

2 a T; b Y; c T; d T; e Y; f Y; g T

Using different personal pronouns (page 13)

1 1 hast; 2 hat; 3 haben; 4 haben; 5 bin; 6 ist; 7 sind; 8 seid

2 Correct answers include:

Ich habe eine Woche in Berlin verbracht.

Er hat seine Tante besucht.

Wir sind mit dem Flugzeug geflogen. / Wir haben ein Museum besucht.

Meine Eltern haben ein Museum besucht. / Meine Eltern sind mit dem Flugzeug geflogen.

Du bist allein nach Spanien gefahren?

3 Letztes Jahr sind wir mit dem Auto nach Wales gefahren. Wir haben in einer Ferienwohnung übernachtet und wir haben viel Sport gemacht. Ich habe Tennis gespielt und meine Schwester ist geklettert. Was hast du gemacht?

2 Mein Zuhause

2.1 Wie ist deine Alltagsroutine? (page 14)

1
1 b Ich putze.
2 f Ich stehe auf.
3 d Ich wasche ab.
4 c Ich bereite vor.
5 a Ich trockne ab.
6 e Ich bügle.

2
a six o'clock
b washes clothes
c lays the table
d washing up and drying up
e nothing

154

Workbook answers

3 Ich sauge jeden Tag Staub.
Zweimal pro Tag wasche ich ab und trockne ab.
Zuerst putze ich das Badezimmer.
Ich decke immer den Tisch.
Ich mache alles!

Separable verbs in the present tense (page 15)

Grammatik

ab; vor; an

1 aufwachen; abwaschen; vorbereiten; abtrocknen; anrufen

2
a Ich stehe um sieben Uhr auf.
b Meine Mutter wäscht zweimal pro Tag ab.
c Wir bereiten die Party vor.
d Mein Bruder trocknet nie ab.
e Mein Vater sieht den ganzen Tag lang fern.

3
a Clara räumt auf.
b Clio wäscht ab.
c Lara sieht fern.
d Ali geht aus.
e Lexie ruft Freunde an.
f Max trocknet ab.

2.2 Wie komme ich zu…? (page 16)

1 a Bahnhof; b Bushaltestelle; c Flughafen; d Fluss; e Hochhaus; f Kino; g Kirche; h Moschee; i Museum; j Park; k Restaurant

2 Our office is on Beethoven Street. Take bus number 122 from the train station to the Olympia Museum. Then go left and take the third street. Our office is in a high-rise building, number 80. It is on the right hand side.

Using es gibt with the accusative case (page 17)

1

Es gibt einen	Es gibt eine	Es gibt ein	Es gibt keine
Bahnhof Flughafen Fluss	Kirche Moschee	Museum Café	Parks Restaurants Hochhäuser

2 1 keinen; 2 keinen; 3 kein; 4 kein; 5 keine; 6 eine; 7 ein; 8 kein

3 Suggested answer:

In meinem Dorf gibt es zwei Kirchen, einen Park, ein Museum, fünf Restaurants und einen Fluss, aber es gibt keinen Flughafen und keinen Bahnhof.

2.3 Bei uns (page 18)

1 1 d; 2 h; 3 a; 4 c; 5 e; 6 f; 7 b; 8 g

2
a very good
b flat, in the city, 10th floor
c terraced house, on the outskirts of town
d quite boring

Students' own answers

Suggested answers:

Nasrin: Früher habe ich in einer Wohnung in der Stadt gewohnt, aber ich fand das zu klein. Jetzt wohne ich in einem Doppelhaus in einem Dorf und das ist toll!

Sven: Früher habe ich in einem Wohnmobil in den Bergen gewohnt, das war ziemlich schön. Jetzt wohne ich in einem Einfamilienhaus am Stadtrand und das ist besser.

Using the present, perfect and imperfect tenses together (page 19)

1 a Pr; b P; c I; d I; e Pr; f P; g I; h Pr

2 1 hat; 2 gewohnt; 3 war; 4 fand; 5 wohnt; 6 findet; 7 gefällt; 8 wohne; 9 finde; 10 waren; 11 haben; 12 gewohnt; 13 fand; 14 gab

155

Workbook answers

3

Present	Past
Mein Vater <u>wohnt</u> in einem Wohnmobil, es <u>ist</u> zu klein für eine Familie!	Meine Vater hat in einem Wohnmobil gewohnt, es war zu klein für eine Familie!
In unserer Straße <u>gibt</u> es nur Einfamilienhäuser.	In unserer Straße gab es nur Einfamilienhäuser.
Ich wohne in einer Wohnung, das ist super!	Ich <u>habe</u> in einer Wohnung <u>gewohnt</u>, das <u>war</u> super!
Es gibt viele Hochhäuser in Frankfurt.	Es <u>gab</u> viele Hochhäuser in Frankfurt.
Ich finde mein Haus total schön.	Ich <u>fand</u> mein Haus total schön.

2.4 Mein Schlafzimmer (page 20)

1 **1** das Fenster; **2** die Lampe; **3** die Wand; **4** die Tür; **5** der Kleiderschrank; **6** der Teppich; **7** das Bett; **8** die Kommode; **9** der Stuhl; **10** der Schreibtisch

2 **a** F; **b** F; **c** T; **d** T; **e** T; **f** F; **g** F; **h** T

3 Students' own answers in the form of a drawing of the layout of the tree house in Finn's blog. The drawing should show a desk and chair next to the door, a dog's bed under the window, a carpeted floor (or rug) and a poster on the wall.

Extra

Students' own answers about their own dream tree house.

Using prepositions with the dative case (page 21)

1 **a** dem; **b** der; **c** der; **d** dem; **e** dem; **f** dem

2 **a** auf dem; **b** neben dem; **c** über der; **d** in dem; **e** hinter der; **f** vor dem

3 **a** Die Maus ist hinter dem Kleiderschrank.
b Die Maus ist in dem Bett.
c Die Maus ist auf dem Schreibtisch.
d Die Maus ist neben dem Computer.
e Die Maus ist vor der Tür.

2.5 Mein zukünftiges Zuhause (page 22)

1 **1** c; **2** d; **3** f; **4** b; **5** a; **6** e

2

Name	Used to live…	Now lives… + opinion	Will live… + opinion
Hannah	high-rise building, city centre	semi-detached house, village; quite boring	campervan; super
Alex	houseboat, river	detached house, mountains; very idyllic	flat, coast; fun

Suggested answer:

Früher habe ich in einem Reihenhaus in einem Dorf gewohnt. Jetzt wohne ich in einem Wohnblock in der Stadtmitte, das ist bequem. In der Zukunft werde ich auf einem Hausboot an der Küste wohnen, das wird cool sein!

3 Students' own answers

Suggested answers:

a Ich werde in einem Haus an der Küste wohnen / leben, weil ich surfen liebe / weil ich gern surfe.

b Ich werde auf einem Hausboot auf dem Fluss wohnen / leben, weil das entspannend ist.

Using the future tense with werden (page 23)

1 **1** c: ich werde sein
2 d: du wirst leben
3 e: es wird geben
4 f / 4 a: wir werden fahren / werden haben
5 b: ihr werdet wohnen
6 f / 6 a: sie/Sie werden fahren / werden haben

2 **a** Ich werde in einem Einfamilienhaus am Stadtrand wohnen.
b Mein Vater wird in einem Wohnmobil wohnen.
c Der Prinz und die Prinzessin werden in einem schönen Schloss wohnen.
d In der Zukunft werden wir in einem Reihenhaus wohnen.
e Nächstes Jahr wird Thomas in der Stadtmitte wohnen.

Workbook answers

3
- **a** Ich werde in einer Stadt wohnen und es wird spannend / aufregend sein.
- **b** Mein Bruder wird in den Bergen wohnen und er wird klettern.
- **c** Meine Eltern werden in einem Haus an der Küste wohnen und es wird schön sein.
- **d** Nächstes Jahr werden wir auf einem Hausboot wohnen und es wird Spaß machen!

Units 1–2 Wiederholung

Bronze/Silber (pages 24–25)

1

In den Ferien	Zu Hause
schnorcheln	putzen
Bootsfahrt machen	abwaschen
wandern	aufräumen

2 **a** Hans: Konstanz; **b** Maria: St Moritz; **c** Robert: Berlin; **d** Daniela: St Moritz; **e** Martin: Konstanz; **f** Larissa: Berlin

3 Award one mark for each translated sentence/ part of a sentence with the correct information.

I travelled by bus to Rome (1). It was very sunny (1). I stayed in a youth hostel (1). The youth hostel was in the city centre (1) and there were eight beds in the room (1)! I walked around the city (1) and I saw a concert (1). It was really great (1)!

4 Down: **1** kalt; **2** Regen; **3** windig

Across: **4** wolkig; **5** sonnig; **6** neblig

5 **a** detached; **b** on the outskirts of town; **c** cold; **d** tidies up; **e** foggy; **f** snow

6 Award one mark for each translated sentence/ part of a sentence with the correct information.

Ich wohne in einem Reihenhaus in Salzburg (1). Ich habe in einer Wohnung gewohnt / Früher habe ich in einer Wohnung gewohnt (1). Wir haben drei Schlafzimmer (1) und einen Garten (1). Die Stadt ist sehr schön (1). Im Sommer ist es warm (1) und im Winter gibt es Schnee (1). Man kann Ausflüge machen (1).

Silber/Gold (pages 26–27)

1 **1** c; **2** b; **3** d; **4** f; **5** e; **6** a

2 Award 1/2 mark for each correct detail in **a** and **c** (one mark in total) and one mark for the other parts (**b**, **d**, **e** and **f**).

- **a** washes up and dries up
- **b** tidies the house
- **c** nothing, watches TV and listens to music
- **d** There was a problem / Henry did everything wrong.
- **e** vacuum cleaned it
- **f** cleaned it with ketchup

3 Award one mark for each translated sentence/ part of a sentence with the correct information.

Usually I clean every day (1). I do the vacuum cleaning and iron (1), but it is really exhausting (1)! Last week, I went on holiday (1). I spent four days in a small hotel (1), it was wonderful (1). I did a bicycle tour (1), I found it relaxing (1).

4 Award one mark for each correctly ordered phrase.

Answer sequence: c; d; a; f; e; b

5 **1** d; **2** c; **3** a; **4** f; **5** e; **6** b

6 Award one mark for each translated sentence/ part of a sentence with the correct information.

Ich habe / Früher habe ich in einem Doppelhaus in einem Dorf gewohnt (1), aber es war zu ruhig (1). Jetzt wohne ich in einer Wohnung in der Stadt (1). Es gibt ein Badezimmer und eine kleine Küche (1). In meinem Schlafzimmer (1) gibt es einen Schreibtisch und einen Computer (1). In der Zukunft werde ich in einem Einfamilienhaus wohnen (1) und ich werde jeden Tag putzen (1).

3 Das Alltagsleben

3.1 Meine Alltagsroutine (page 28)

1 **1** e h; **2** d g; **3** a j; **4** b i; **5** c f

2 **a** F; **b** T; **c** T; **d** F; **e** F; **f** T

3 Students' own answers

Suggested answers:
- **a** Ich stehe um … Uhr auf.
- **b** Ich ziehe mich um … Uhr an.
- **c** Ich entspanne mich um … Uhr / nach dem Abendessen.
- **d** Ich gehe um … Uhr ins Bett.

157

Workbook answers

Using reflexive verbs in the present tense (page 29)

1
a   ich rasiere mich
b   du ziehst dich an
c   er/sie/es duscht sich
d   wir waschen uns
e   ihr amüsiert euch
f   sie/Sie entspannen sich

2
a   Ich wasch**e** mich um neun Uhr.
b   Wir duschen <u>uns</u> jeden Tag.
c   Mein Vater rasiert <u>sich</u> jeden Sonntag.
d   Wir entspann**en** uns im Wohnzimmer.
e   Mein Bruder interessiert <u>sich</u> für Rockmusik.

3 1 dusche mich; 2 entspannt sich; 3 sehen fern; 4 Amüsierst dich; 5 rasieren uns; 6 wasche mich

3.2 Willst du woanders zur Schule gehen? (page 30)

1 a 5; b 2; c 1; d 4; e 3

2 1 Morgen; 2 mich; 3 Schule; 4 weil; 5 dann; 6 Ende; 7 zu Hause

3 a F; b F; c T; d F; e T; f T; g F; h NM

Using sequencers with reflexive and separable verbs (page 31)

1 a dusche; b mich an; c sich; d ab; e ein

2
a   Um sechs Uhr wache ich auf.
b   Zuerst wasche ich mich.
c   Dann rasiere ich mich.
d   Danach entspanne ich mich.
e   Abends räume ich mein Zimmer auf.

3
a   Zuerst stehe ich auf.
b   Um acht Uhr dusche ich mich.
c   Danach ziehe ich mich an.
d   Nach der Schule entspanne ich mich.
e   Später wasche ich ab.
f   Um neun Uhr schlafe ich ein.

3.3 Wollen wir uns treffen? (page 32)

1 1 f; 2 e; 3 c; 4 a; 5 d; 6 b

2 1 this evening / tonight; 2 later; 3 on Saturday; 4 tomorrow; 5 after school; 6 in the afternoon

3 Students' own answers for **c** and **d**, suggested answers given below:
a   Ich kann nicht, ich muss meine Oma besuchen.
b   Ich kann nicht, ich muss meine Hausaufgaben machen.
c   Ich kann nicht, ich muss mein Bett machen.
d   Ich kann nicht, ich habe kein Geld.

Using wollen + the infinitive (page 33)

1

ich	will	
du	willst	
er/sie/es	will	+ infinitive
wir	wollen	
ihr	wollt	
sie/Sie	wollen	

2
a   <u>Willst</u> du ins Kino <u>gehen</u>?
b   Ich <u>will</u> nach der Schule Tennis <u>spielen</u>.
c   Mein Bruder <u>will</u> immer nur Netflix <u>sehen</u> / <u>gucken</u>.
d   Wir <u>wollen</u> keine Hausaufgaben <u>machen</u>.
e   <u>Wollt</u> ihr in die Stadt <u>gehen</u>?
f   Anja und Ben <u>wollen</u> Skateboard <u>fahren</u>.

3A Ich will ins Kino gehen, aber ich muss meine Hausaufgaben machen.

3B
1   Ich will in den Park gehen, aber ich muss meinen Opa besuchen.
2   Ich will Netflix sehen / gucken, aber ich muss mein Zimmer sauber machen / putzen.
3   Er will in die Stadt gehen, aber er hat kein Geld.

3.4 Projekt: Gesund leben (page 34)

1 Any six:
You should be active.
You should do sports.
You must always drink a lot of water.
You must take a break.
You should think positively.
You must sleep enough.
You should not look at your Smartphone at night.

158

Workbook answers

2 Correct answers include:
Man soll positiv denken.
Man muss Zeit mit Freunden verbringen.
Man soll nicht bis Mitternacht fernsehen.
Man soll viel Wasser trinken.
Man muss pro Tag fünf Portionen Obst und Gemüse essen.

Extra
Students' own opinions

3 Students' own answers
Suggested answers:
a Man soll / muss genug schlafen.
b Man soll / muss genug / drei Liter Wasser pro Tag trinken.
c Man soll / muss positiv denken / eine Pause machen.
d Man soll / muss Obst und Gemüse / gesund essen.

Revising *man soll* and *man muss* (page 35)

1 a essen; b schlafen; c machen; d treiben; e verbringen; f gucken

2 a Man soll nicht frühstücken. = *You should not eat breakfast.*
b Man soll in der Nacht fernsehen. = *You should watch TV at night.*
c Man soll kein Wasser trinken. = *You should not drink water.*
d Man muss jeden Tag Pizza essen. = *You must eat pizza every day.*
e Man muss sehr faul sein. = *You must be very lazy.*
f Man soll sehr gestresst sein. = *You should be very stressed.*

3 Students' own answers
Suggested answers:
a Man soll / muss gesund / Obst und Gemüse essen.
b Man soll Fahrrad fahren.
c Man soll / muss viel / genug Wasser trinken.
d Man soll abends lesen.
e Man soll / muss Zeit mit Freunden verbringen.

3.5 Wer macht was bei euch? (page 36)

1 1 b c; 2 e h; 3 a d; 4 f g

2 a His mother isn't well and he likes helping.
b cooks
c his sister
d cleans the bath(room)
e bakes them cakes

3 Students' own answers
Suggested answers:
a Ich bekomme _____ Pfund / kein Geld, wenn ich zu Hause helfe.
b Ich putze das Bad / Ich sauge Staub / Ich koche / Ich decke den Tisch / Ich räume auf / Ich wasche ab / Ich gehe einkaufen.
c Ich helfe, weil meine Eltern arbeiten / weil ich gern helfe / weil ich das wichtig finde / weil ich Geld bekomme.
Ich helfe nicht, weil meine Mutter / mein Vater alles macht / weil ich das langweilig finde / weil ich keine Zeit habe.
d Ich gehe in die Schule / Ich sehe fern / Ich koche, wenn meine Eltern arbeiten.

Revising subordinate clauses with *weil* and *wenn* (page 37)

1 Circle: 1 arbeiten; 2 ist; 3 ist; 4 macht
Word order rule: The verb is at the end of the *weil/wenn* clause.
Translation – suggested answers:
1a I help at home when my parents work.
2b My brother never helps because he is lazy.
3c My dad works in the garden when it is sunny.
4d I cook often because it is fun.

2 a Ich helfe zu Hause, wenn ich keine Hausaufgaben habe.
b Ich wasche das Auto heute nicht, weil es stürmisch ist.
c Mein Vater kocht am Wochenende, weil meine Mutter jeden Samstag arbeitet.

Workbook answers

d Ich putze das Bad, weil ich Geld dafür bekomme.

e Mein Vater saugt Staub, wenn er Zeit hat.

f Wir helfen alle im Haushalt, weil es wichtig ist.

3 a sie faul ist

b es sonnig ist

c er Geld dafür bekommt

d ich Zeit habe

4 Meine Klamotten

4.1 Was trägst du gern? (page 38)

1 **a** Hemd; **b** Hose; **c** Jacke; **d** Kleid; **e** Mantel; **f** Stiefel; **g** T-Shirt; **h** Turnschuhe; **i** Rock

2 a Hannah trägt ein <u>Kleid</u>, einen <u>Mantel</u>, <u>Turnschuhe</u> und ein <u>Cap</u>.

b Boris trägt <u>Jeans</u>, ein <u>T-Shirt</u>, <u>Stiefel</u> und einen <u>Kapuzenpullover</u>.

c Yusuf trägt eine <u>Jacke</u>, ein <u>Hemd</u>, eine <u>Hose</u> und <u>Schuhe</u>.

3 Students' own answers

Suggested answers:

Am Wochenende trage ich gern	einen Mantel, einen Kapuzenpullover, einen Rock
	eine Hose, eine Jacke
Mein Bruder (etc.) trägt gern	ein T-Shirt, ein Hemd, ein Kleid, ein Cap
	Schuhe, Turnschuhe, Stiefel, Jeans

Using verbs with the vowel change 'a' to 'ä' (page 39)

1 waschen / schlafen

a ich wasche   **g** ich schlafe

b du wäschst   **h** du schläfst

c er/sie/es wäscht   **i** er/sie/es schläft

d wir waschen   **j** wir schlafen

e ihr wascht   **k** ihr schlaft

f sie/Sie waschen   **l** sie/Sie schlafen

2 **1** essen; **2** trage; **3** gehen; **4** trägt; **5** wäscht; **6** schläft

3 **a** trägst; **b** schläfst; **c** fährst; **d** wäschst

4.2 Wie ist dein Stil? (page 40)

1 **1** a; **2** d; **3** e; **4** c; **5** b

2 **a** gestreift = striped

b schwarz = black

c bunt = colourful

d kariert = checked

e golden = gold

f blau = blue

3 Students' own answers

Suggested answers:

Ali trägt schwarze Jeans und einen langen / großen Kapuzenpullover. Er trägt eine goldene Kette und ein Cap und er trägt auch Turnschuhe.

Maya trägt lange gestreifte Socken und Stiefel. Sie trägt auch einen grauen Rock und eine karierte Jacke.

Using accusative adjective endings (page 41)

1 **a** blauen – m; **b** schwarze – pl; **c** weißes – n; **d** langen – m; **e** gestreifte – f; **f** coole – pl

2 **a** schwarze; **b** teure; **c** langes; **d** rotes; **e** gelben; **f** gestreiftes

3 **a** Ich trage schwarze Turnschuhe.

b Ich habe eine weiße Tasche.

c Er trägt ein gelbes T-Shirt.

d Sie trägt immer einen gestreiften Rock.

e Am Wochenende trage ich ein kariertes Hemd.

4.3 Wo kaufst du lieber deine Klamotten? (page 42)

1 **a** Internet; **b** Einkaufszentrum; **c** Secondhandläden; **d** Flohmarkt; **e** Klamotten; **f** Shoppen

Workbook answers

2 1 d; 2 c; 3 b; 4 e; 5 a

3 Students' own answers

Suggested answers:

a Normalerweise kaufe ich meine Kleidung...

im Einkaufszentrum / im Internet / auf dem Flohmarkt / in einem Outlet /

in Secondhandläden / in Designerläden / …

„…weil das praktisch / umweltfreundlicher ist / ich gern in viele Läden gehe / …

b Ich gehe (sehr) oft / manchmal / selten / nie / jeden Monat / jede Woche shoppen.

c Wenn ich viel Geld habe, kaufe ich...

d Ich habe mein(en/e) ... gekauft.

Using possessive adjectives in the accusative case (page 43)

1 Matching pairs: meinen Mantel; meine Kette; mein Kleid; meine Turnschuhe

2 a meine; b meine; c mein; d meinen; e meine

3 Suggested answers:

a Ich habe meine Schuhe letztes Jahr gekauft.

b Ich habe meine Sonnenbrille letzte Woche gekauft.

c Ich habe meinen Kapuzenpullover gestern gekauft.

d Ich habe mein Kleid am Montag gekauft.

4.4 #Shoppen (page 44)

1 1 f; 2 d; 3 e; 4 a; 5 c; 6 b

2 a Geld; b zu teuer; c ausgeben; d kaufen; e einkaufen; f ich möchte

3 On Sunday (Saturday), I will go shopping. I want to (will) go to the shopping centre because the shops there are super. First, I will buy shoes, I would like black (white) trainers, but I would not like to spend a lot of money. Afterwards, I will buy (expensive) sunglasses. My father (mother) will look for brown boots. It will be difficult (fun)!

The future tense with werden and ich möchte (page 45)

1

ich	werde / möchte	
du	wirst / möchtest	
er/sie/es	wird / möchte	+ infinitive
wir	werden / möchten	
ihr	werdet / möchtet	
sie/Sie	werden / möchten	

2 a werde; b werden; c wird; d Wirst; e werden; f Werdet

3 a werde – I will go shopping on Saturday.

b Möchtest – Would you like to go to the shopping centre?

c aussuchen – Sana would like to look for cool sunglasses.

d möchten – We would like to wear earrings to school.

e ausgeben – My parents will spend a lot of money on classic clothes.

4.5 Party! (page 46)

1 1 d; 2 a; 3 c; 4 e; 5 b

2 b; c; e; g

3 Students' own answers

Suggested answer:

Letzte Woche bin ich auf eine Party gegangen und ich habe ein rotes Kleid getragen. Nächstes Jahr werde ich zu einem Rugbyspiel gehen und ich werde einen schwarzen Kapuzenpullover tragen.

Revising the perfect tense with haben and sein (page 47)

1 gefahren; gegangen; geblieben; geflogen; gelaufen

2 a bin; b habe; c habe; d ist; e sind; f hat

3 a Letztes Jahr bin ich nach Spanien geflogen.

b In Spanien habe ich meine Tante besucht.

c Wir sind auf ein Festival gegangen.

d Ich habe ein schönes Flamenco Kleid getragen.

161

Workbook answers

e Mein Bruder hat viele Fotos gemacht und er hat viel getanzt.

f Wir sind um Mitternacht nach Hause gegangen.

Units 3–4 Wiederholung

Bronze/Silber (pages 48–49)

1. Award one mark for **a**, **b** and **e**. Award 1/2 mark for each correct detail in **c** (one mark in total) and one mark for each correct detail in **d** (two marks in total).

   a because he never has any stress
   b 7:00 am
   c shower, get dressed
   d plays or goes jogging
   e sleeps (for 3 hours)

2. Award two marks for each part.
   1 Fußballer(in): b; e
   2 Busfahrer(in): a; c
   3 Nanny: d; f

3. Award one mark for each translated sentence/ part of a sentence with the correct information.

   a I shower (1) when I have time (1).
   b My brother goes jogging (1) when the weather is good/nice (1).
   c I lay the table (1) because I like to help (1).
   d My brother never cleans the bathroom (1) because he is very lazy (1).

4. Award 1/2 mark for each correct odd one out and 1/2 mark for each reason why.

   a Apfel – not an item of clothing
   b Schrank – not an item of clothing
   c Kino – not an item of clothing
   d Cap – not footwear / not plural
   e Hose – not accessories
   f Hemd – not solely for females

5. **a** Stil; **b** lässige; **c** muss; **d** Kleid, Ohrringe; **e** kauft

6. Award one mark for each translated sentence/ part of a sentence with the correct information.

   Mein Modestil ist cool (1). Ich trage oft Jeans (1) und ein schwarzes Cap (1) und ich trage immer meine Sonnenbrille (1). Ich shoppe gern (1) und ich kaufe meine Klamotten/Kleidung im Einkaufszentrum (1). Letzte Woche habe ich eine Jacke gekauft (1) und mein Freund/meine Freundin hat ein blaues Hemd gekauft (1).

Silber/Gold (pages 50–51)

1. **a** 7:30; **b** healthy; **c** looks after the children; **d** cleans; **e** skirts; **f** always

2. Award one mark for each part in the weekly planner (**b** and **c**) and one mark for each sentence with the correct information (**a**, **d**, **e** and **f**).

   Weekly planner: **b** Wednesday: clean the bathroom; **c** Thursday: look after sister

   Sentences:

   a Am Dienstag muss ich das Abendessen kochen.
   d Am Freitag muss ich das Auto waschen.
   e Am Samstag muss ich meine Oma besuchen.
   f Am Sonntag muss ich schlafen!

3. Award one mark for each translated sentence/ part of a sentence with the correct information.

   This week was/has been so stressful (1)! On Monday, I cleaned the bathroom (1), on Tuesday, I helped my dad in the garden (1), on Wednesday, I cooked the dinner (1). Now, I want to relax (1). Would you like to go to the cinema on Friday (1)? Do you have time (1)? Shall we meet at 8pm at the train station (1)?

4. Award three marks for part A and three marks for part B of this activity (one mark for each correct answer/information/order)

   A: a = 2; **b** = 3; **c** = 1

   B: a last week; **b** because she visited her grandmother; **c** he had a shower

5. **a** F; **b** T; **c** F; **d** F; **e** T; **f** F

6. Award one mark for each translated sentence/ part of a sentence with the correct information.

   Mode ist mir wichtig (1). Ich werde ganz/ziemlich viel Geld (1) für Turnschuhe/Sneakers ausgeben (1), weil ich Turnschuhe/Sneakers liebe (1)! Normalerweise kaufe ich Klamotten/Kleidung lieber im Einkaufszentrum (1). Letzte Woche habe ich eine rote Jacke gekauft (1). Am Wochenende möchte meine Freundin (1) ein blaues Kleid aussuchen (1).

Workbook answers

5 Virtuelle und reelle Welt

5.1 Kino, Kino (page 52)

1
- a Zeichentrickfilm – *cartoon*
- b Dokumentarsendung – *documentary*
- c Krimi – *crime series*
- d Nachrichten – *news*
- e Abenteuerfilm – *adventure film*
- f Kino – *cinema*
- g Horrorfilm – *horror film*
- h Sportsendung – *sports programme*

2 1 b; 2 d; 3 f; 4 c; 5 a; 6 e

3 Hi! Ich bin totaler Kino Fan. Am liebsten sehe ich Actionfilme, weil <u>sie sind spannend</u>. Manchmal <u>ich sehe</u> Komödien, aber Zeichentrickfilme gefallen mir nicht. Ich sehe Zeichentrickfilme nicht gern, da <u>sie sind so kindisch</u>. Was siehst du gern?

Extra

Suggested answers:

1 The verb goes to the end of the clause after *weil* (*weil sie spannend sind*).

2 The verb is in second position (*Manchmal sehe ich*).

3 The verb goes to the end of the clause after *da* (*da sie so kindisch sind*).

Using subordinate clauses with *weil* and *da* (page 53)

1
- a Ich sehe nicht gern Sportsendungen, weil ich Sport langweilig finde.
- b Am liebsten sehe ich Komödien, da sie lustig sind.
- c Mein Vater sieht jeden Tag Nachrichten, weil er das wichtig findet.
- d Meine Lieblingssendung ist eine Dokumentarsendung, weil sie wirklich faszinierend ist.
- e Ich muss um acht Uhr zu Hause sein, da dann meine Lieblingssendung kommt.

2 Suggested answers:
- a weil/da sie wichtig sind. / weil/da das wichtig ist.
- b weil/da sie dumm sind.
- c weil/da sie interessant sind.
- d weil/da es entspannend ist. / weil/da ich das entspannend finde.
- e weil/da sie zu gruselig sind.

3 Students' own answers

Suggested answers:

- a Ich mag Sportsendungen, weil/da sie interessant / spannend sind / weil/da ich Sportfan bin.
  Ich mag Sportsendungen nicht, weil/da sie langweilig sind.
- b Am liebsten sehe ich …, weil/da sie … sind.
- c Ich sehe … nicht gern, weil/da sie … sind.
- d Ich gehe oft ins Kino, weil/da ich Filmfan bin / weil/da es entspannend / lustig / toll ist / weil/da ich Filme liebe.
  Ich gehe nicht oft ins Kino, weil/da es zu teuer ist / weil/da ich lieber fernsehe / weil/da ich nicht viel Geld habe.

5.2 Musik liegt in der Luft (page 54)

1 a Was für; b Wer; c Wie; d Wo; e Wann; f Warum

2

	favourite music	favourite musician	when	instrument	concert
Sonja	classical	Harry Styles	on the way to school	cello	last Friday – classical concert
Mo	rap	Sammy Deluxe	every day	none / –	last year – Eminem

3 Students' own answers

Suggested answer:

Ich heiße Lilly. Am liebsten höre ich Schlager. Meine Lieblingssängerin ist / heißt Helene Fischer. Ich höre jeden Abend / abends Musik. Ich spiele Gitarre. Letzte Woche bin ich auf ein Konzert von Yvonne Catterfeld gegangen.

Using time–manner–place word order (page 55)

1 **Manner: 2:** mit meinen Freunden, allein, zusammen, mit meiner Mutter

Time: 1: letzte Woche, am Wochenende, gestern, abends

Place: 3: in der Schule, in Hamburg, auf dem Konzert, in meinem Zimmer

2
- a Sie singt manchmal leidenschaftlich in der Dusche. = *Sometimes she sings passionately in the shower.*

163

Workbook answers

b Ich höre am Abend mit meiner Schwester in meinem Zimmer Musik. = *In the evenings, I listen to music in my room with my sister.*

c Ich habe gestern mit meiner Band im Park gespielt. = *I played with my band in the park yesterday.*

d Wir sind oft zusammen in Berlin auf Raves gegangen. = *We often went together to raves in Berlin.*

e Mein Bruder möchte jeden Tag allein im Wohnzimmer MTV sehen. = *Every day, my brother would like to watch MTV alone in the living room.*

3 a Meine Schwester hört jeden Tag mit Freunden im Wohnzimmer Popmusik.

b Ich möchte nächste Woche mit meinem Bruder auf ein Konzert gehen.

c Ich habe letzten Samstag allein im Park Gitarre gespielt.

5.3 Sicher im Internet (page 56)

1 Wie oft benutzt du das Internet?

Ich spiele Computerspiele.

Mein Bruder chattet mit seinen Freunden.

Meine Eltern kaufen viel bei Amazon.

Ladet ihr Musik runter?

2 a P; **b** N; **c** P; **d** N; **e** N; **f** N; **g** N; **h** P

3 Students' own answers

Suggested answers:

a Ich spiele Computerspiele.

Ich lade Musik runter.

Ich chatte mit Freunden / Familie.

Ich kaufe Kleidung / Geschenke / etc.

Ich benutze soziale Medien.

Ich gucke / sehe Netflix / YouTube-Videos.

b Ein Vorteil ist, dass man viele Informationen findet.

..., dass man mit Freunden im Ausland in Kontakt bleiben kann.

..., dass man alles von zu Hause kaufen kann.

..., dass man den Weg findet.

..., dass man unabhängig sein kann.

c Ein Nachteil ist, dass es Cyber-Mobbing gibt.

..., dass man mit Fremden sprechen kann.

..., dass man nicht sehr aktiv ist.

..., dass man nicht genug schläft.

..., dass nicht alle Informationen richtig sind.

Extra

Students' own answers

Expressing opinions using *dass* (page 57)

1 a Ich denke, dass das Internet gefährlich ist.

b Ich denke, dass mein Bruder nicht aktiv genug ist.

c Ich denke, dass das Internet mehr Vorteile als Nachteile hat.

d Ich denke, dass soziale Netzwerke sehr cool sind.

e Ich denke, dass ich das Internet für meine Hausaufgaben brauche.

f Ich denke, dass man im Internet billig einkaufen kann.

2 a Ich denke, dass das Internet sehr nützlich ist.

b Meine Mutter denkt, dass ich nicht genug schlafe.

c Mein Vater denkt, dass soziale Netzwerke dumm sind.

d Ich glaube, dass meine Schwester das Internet zu viel benutzt.

e Es ist wichtig, dass ich nicht mit Fremden sprechen darf.

5.4 Technologie heute und damals (page 58)

1 1 c; 2 e; 3 b; 4 a; 5 d

2A Meine Mutter denkt, dass das Internet gefährlich ist, weil sie als Kind kein Internet <u>hatte</u>. Es <u>gab</u> keine sozialen Netzwerke und es <u>gab</u> kein Cyber-Mobbing. Sie denkt, dass alles besser <u>war</u>, aber ich glaube das nicht. Sie <u>ging</u> in die Bibliothek, um Information zu finden, aber ich frage ‚Siri', das ist schneller und praktischer. Meine Mutter <u>hatte</u> mit 18 Jahren ein Handy, einen Discman und eine digitale Kamera, aber mein Handy kann alles!

2B a because she did not have internet as a child

b social networks and cyber bullying

c that everything used to be better

164

Workbook answers

   d asks 'Siri'

   e 3 (mobile, Discman, digital camera)

3 1 waren; 2 hatten; 3 konnte; 4 spielten; 5 gab; 6 hörte; 7 hatten; 8 kaufte; 9 war

Recognising and using the imperfect tense (page 59)

1
ich habe	ich hatte
ich lese	ich las
ich gehe	ich ging
ich bin	ich war
ich sehe	ich sah
ich kaufe	ich kaufte

2 a P; b P; c I; d P; e I; f P; g I; h I

3 a Ich machte meine Hausaufgaben ohne Computer.

   b Ich telefonierte nur selten, weil das teuer war.

   c Ich las gern Zeitschriften.

   d Ich spielte Brettspiele.

   e Ich ging jedes Wochenende in die Bibliothek.

5.5 Ich engagiere mich (page 60)

1 a Umweltschutz – *environmental protection*

   b Tierschutz – *animal protection*

   c Altenhilfe – *helping the elderly*

   d Flüchtlingshilfe – *helping refugees*

   e Obdachlosenhilfe – *helping homeless people*

   f Behindertenhilfe – *helping people with disabilities*

2
	charitable cause	does…	has done… / will do…
Arne	help for the homeless	collects money and works in soup kitchen	sold cakes (last Saturday)
Sana	nature and animal protection	works in animal shelter (on Saturdays)	will collect rubbish in park (in future)
Kezia	help for the elderly	goes shopping with grandmother	sang in old people's home (yesterday)
Yusuf	help for refugees	donates pocket money and books	will teach German to Syrian children (in future)

3 Students' own answers

   Suggested answer:

   Ich interessiere mich für… Flüchtlingshilfe / Umweltschutz / Tierschutz / Altenhilfe / Obdachlosenhilfe / Behindertenhilfe.

   Ich helfe gern Flüchtlingen / Tieren / Obdachlosen, etc.

   Ich finde das wichtig, weil…
   ich mich für die Umwelt / Tiere / Natur interessiere.
   meine Oma alt ist.
   mein Bruder behindert ist.
   meine Eltern Flüchtlinge waren.

   Present: Ich verkaufe / arbeite / spende / helfe / unterrichte / gehe…

   Past: Ich habe … verkauft / gearbeitet / gespendet / geholfen / unterrichtet.
   Ich bin … gegangen.

   Future: Ich werde … verkaufen / arbeiten / spenden / helfen / unterrichten / gehen.

   Extra

   Students' own answers

Revising the use of different tenses (page 61)

1
Present tense	Perfect tense	Future tense
ich **arbeite**	ich habe **gearbeitet**	*ich werde arbeiten*
ich **spende**	ich habe **gespendet**	ich werde **spenden**
ich sammle	ich habe **gesammelt**	ich werde **sammeln**
ich **gehe**	ich bin **gegangen**	ich werde **gehen**
ich **helfe**	*ich habe geholfen*	ich werde **helfen**

2 a hat, gegessen; b wohnen; c finde; d habe, gespendet; e bringt; f werde, arbeiten

3 a Animal protection is very important to me. I love animals and I donate money to the animal shelter.

   b Last year, I watched a documentary about refugees. It was very sad. I collected 100 euros with my school.

   c In the future, I will work in an old people's home. I will help many people, but it will not be easy.

6 Willkommen in Berlin!

6.1 Wollen wir nach Berlin fahren? (page 62)

1 1 f; 2 a; 3 c; 4 e; 5 b; 6 d

2 **Arrival:** Monday – 12 o'clock

   Accommodation: Motel One, Potsdamer Platz

   Monday: relaxing / swimming at Wannsee Lake

   Tuesday: visit Checkpoint Charlie Museum

165

Workbook answers

Wednesday: learn more about art and culture; go to Museum Island / Museumsinsel

Thursday: go to Television Tower / Fernsehturm

3 Students' own answers

Suggested answer:

Ich werde zum / auf den Fernsehturm gehen, weil man dort gute Fotos machen kann. / weil man von oben Fotos machen kann.

…, weil das interessant / schön ist.

Ich werde den Reichstag besuchen, weil ich mich für Architektur interessiere.

…, weil ich das wichtig / interessant finde.

…, weil ich über die deutsche Geschichte lerne.

Ich werde zur Imbissbude gehen, weil ich gern esse. / weil ich Currywurst liebe.

…, weil das entspannend ist.

Revising the future tense with *werden* (page 63)

1 ich werde   wir werden

du wirst   ihr werdet

er/sie/es wird   sie/Sie werden

2
a Am Montag werden wir das Brandenburger Tor sehen.
b Am Dienstag werde ich eine Bootsfahrt auf der Spree machen.
c Am Mittwoch wird meine Freundin an einer Imbissbude Currywurst essen.
d Am Donnerstag werden wir in das Reichstagsgebäude gehen.
e Am Freitag werde ich mit dem Bus nach Charlottenburg fahren.

3 Students' own answers

Suggested answers:

a Ich werde nächste Woche / am Sonntag / im August nach Berlin fahren.
b Ich werde in einem Hotel / in einer Pension / in der Stadtmitte übernachten.
c Ich werde das Brandenburger Tor / die Berliner Mauer / den Reichstag / den Fernsehturm sehen.
d Ich werde Currywurst / Kebab essen.
e Ich werde eine Bootsfahrt machen / ein Museum besuchen / auf ein Konzert gehen / einkaufen gehen.

Extra

Students' own answers

6.2 So leben wir in Berlin! (page 64)

1 a N; b N; c P; d P; e P; f N

2
a Ich denke, dass mein Stadtteil cool ist.
b Es gibt hier viele Touristen und nette Märkte und Bars, aber es gibt Probleme mit der Kriminalität.
c Am Wochenende gehe ich sehr gern auf Konzerte.

3
a I love Berlin because the city is so international and historic.
b At the weekend, I often go jogging in the park with my brother.
c I learnt a lot about the history in the city museum.
d I will see the Berlin marathon with my family next September.

Using a range of tenses (page 65)

1 **wohnen:** ich wohne, ich habe gewohnt, ich werde wohnen

sehen: ich sehe, ich habe gesehen, ich werde sehen

besuchen: ich besuche, ich habe besucht, ich werde besuchen

kaufen: ich kaufe, ich habe gekauft, ich werde kaufen

gehen: ich gehe, ich bin gegangen, ich werde gehen

2 Meine Großmutter hat als Kind in der Türkei gewohnt [perfect], aber jetzt wohnt [present] sie in Berlin. Manchmal vermisst [present] sie die Türkei, vor allem das Wetter. Wir haben [present] viele türkische Freunde in unserem Stadtteil und es gibt [present] tolle türkische Restaurants. Letzte Woche hatten [imperfect] wir eine große Familienparty, wir haben laute Musik gehört [perfect] und getanzt [perfect]. Es war [imperfect] toll! Morgen werden wir ein Picknick im Park machen [future] und nächsten Monat werden wir zusammen in die Türkei fliegen [future].

3
a Gestern bin ich zum Karneval der Kulturen gegangen.
b Nächste Woche werde ich meine Freunde im Café treffen.
c Morgen werde ich eine Jacke auf dem Flohmarkt kaufen.
d Normalerweise mache ich eine Radtour am Wannsee.
e Letztes Jahr habe ich coole Graffiti gesehen.

Units 5–6 Wiederholung

Bronze/Silber (pages 66–67)

1 news = die Nachrichten

cartoons = Zeichentrickfilme

crime series = Krimis

important = wichtig

relaxing = entspannend

exciting = spannend

2 Award one mark for each sentence.

Students' own answers

Suggested answers:

a Ich sehe gern… Zeichentrickfilme / Krimis / Sportsendungen / Nachrichten / Dokumentarsendungen / Reality-TV-Serien.

b Ich sehe nicht gern… Zeichentrickfilme / Krimis / Sportsendungen / Nachrichten / Dokumentarsendungen / Reality-TV-Serien / Kindersendungen.

c Ich finde Krimis / Dokumentarsendungen / Nachrichten / Reality-TV-Serien interessant.

d Ja, ich sehe viel fern. / Ich sehe fünf Stunden pro Tag fern.

Nein, ich sehe nicht viel fern.

e Mein Vater / Meine Mutter / Mein Bruder / Meine Schwester sieht gern Krimis / Sportsendungen / Nachrichten / Dokumentarsendungen / Reality-TV-Serien.

f Ich finde Horrorfilme super / interessant / schrecklich / furchtbar / (zu) gruselig / dumm.

3 Award one mark for each translated part of a sentence with the correct information.

a I like watching cartoons (1) because they are funny (1).

b I don't like watching documentaries (1) as/because they are boring (1).

c I go to the cinema quite often (1) because it is fun (1).

d I can't go to the cinema on Saturday (1) because I have to/must help my mother (1).

4 1 a; 2 b; 3 b; 4 a; 5 b; 6 a

5 a Ich denke, dass das Internet praktisch ist.

b Meine Mutter denkt, dass soziale Netzwerke gefährlich sind.

c Mein Lehrer denkt, dass Cyber-Mobbing ein Problem ist.

d Mein Vater denkt, dass das Internet früher sehr langsam war.

e Ich denke, dass das Internet viele Vorteile hat.

f Meine Eltern denken, dass ich zu oft Computerspiele spiele.

6 Award one mark for each translated sentence/part of a sentence with the correct information.

Ich benutze das Internet jeden Tag (1). Ich spiele Computerspiele (1) und ich benutze soziale Netzwerke (1). Ich finde das Internet sehr praktisch (1), aber meine Mutter denkt (1), dass Cyber-Mobbing ein Problem ist (1). Nächstes Jahr werde ich mit meinem Freund/meiner Freundin nach Berlin fahren (1) und wir werden viel Information im Internet lesen (1).

Silber/Gold (pages 68–69)

1 Award one mark for each correctly matched pair.

Sportsendung – Fernsehen

klassische Musik – Mozart

Schlager – deutsche Musik

Filme – Kino

Vorteil – mit Freunden sprechen

Nachteil – Cyber-Mobbing

2 Award one mark for one correct answer for each part.

cinema	too expensive and doesn't like films
comedies	dumb / stupid
cartoons	childish
pop music	too loud and too fast
rap music	annoying
social media	far too dangerous and not interesting

3 Award one mark for each translated sentence/part of a sentence with the correct information.

My uncle used to be / was a rock star (1). He played the guitar in a band (1) and had concerts in Berlin, London and New York (1). I think that that/this is super cool (1). There were no social networks (1) but his photo / picture was in lots of / many magazines (1). Fans listened to the music on the radio (1) because there were no mobile phones (1).

4 1 e; 2 a; 3 d; 4 f; 5 b; 6 c

Workbook answers

5 **a** F; **b** F; **c** T; **d** F; **e** F; **f** T

6 Award one mark for each translated sentence/part of a sentence with the correct information.

Berlin ist eine tolle Stadt (1). Ein Vorteil ist (1), dass die Stadt sehr grün ist (1) und man kann viel über (die) Geschichte und Kultur lernen (1). Ein Nachteil ist (1), dass es manchmal gefährlich ist (1). Es gibt auch viele Obdachlose (1). In Zukunft möchte ich in einer Suppenküche arbeiten (1).